JEAN RACINE:
MYTHOS AND RENEWAL
IN MODERN THEATER

Other books by Bettina L. Knapp:

Louis Jouvet   (1956)
That was Yvette   (coauthor, 1964)
Louise Labé   (1964)
Cymbalum Mundi   (1965)
Aristide Bruant   (1968)
Jean Genet   (1969)
Antonin Artaud   (1969)
Jean Cocteau   (1970)

Jean Racine:
Mythos and Renewal
in Modern Theater

Bettina L. Knapp

The University of Alabama Press
University, Alabama

TO
Alba and Estelle

SPECIAL ACKNOWLEDGMENT
Passages from Racine's writings as quoted in the
present work are from THE COMPLETE PLAYS OF
JEAN RACINE, translated by Samuel Solomon.
Copyright © 1967 by Samuel Solomon. Reprinted
by permission of Random House, Inc.

Preface

GONE is the age when the drama of Racine could be considered as the private preserve of native French scholars, sole possessors of urbane politeness and accustomed in their salons to discussing elaborate etiquettes of courting, of loving and hating simultaneously, and challenging their rivals to innocuous duels. The warmest admirers of Racine's tragedies in the second half of this century are found in the schools and colleges of America and of Britain. The very difficulty, amounting to a near-impossibility, of finding a medium and a rhythm which will not betray Racine in English, challenges translator after translator. A good many of the most incisive critical studies of Racine, in the last three or four decades, have appeared in English in this country or in the British isles.

The present one, by one of the finest scholar-teachers of literature in American universities, should for a long time be regarded as the most sensitive, most judicious, and most comprehensive general presentation of the Racinian theater in English. It is more than a labor of love and devoted care; it is a work of passion, of the kind of passion which, far from blinding the writer possessed by it, sharpens his judgment and deepens his insight. Dr. Knapp is at home in several arts. She has devoted works of unusual acumen to such "relevant" and influential contemporaries as Antonin Artaud and Jean Genet. Returning to Racine after a prolonged sojourn with such theorists or practitioners of the "theater of cruelty," she received a profound shock from the one dramatist who, three centuries ago, had already resorted to all the devices of cruelty.

Naive Englishmen had once, with Macaulay, called the French classical dramatist "the graceful, the tender, the melodious Racine." Those are the very last adjectives which modern commentators would

affix to the creator of Nero and of Phèdre. Jean-Louis Barrault is fond
of likening the Racinian characters to bears or to tigers in a cage, madly
pursuing the one whom they would devour. We find his criminals more
refined in their perverseness, or in their lust for sexual power over the
unfortunate beings whom they love and hate, than Richard III or Lady
Macbeth. Bettina Knapp quotes approvingly in her introduction the
words of Antonin Artaud: "A true theatrical work disturbs the senses
in repose, liberates the repressed unconscious, foments a virtual revolt."

It is her overpowering emotional shock at a rediscovery of Racine
which she succeeds in communicating to us in this learned and sensitive
study. As an expert critic should do, she then analyzes the elements
in those tragedies which the poet used and fused in order to "please"
and electrify his audiences. The plots are tersely summarized, in a
fashion which skillfully sets off Racine's originality as a builder of
structured dramas, doubtless the most impeccably structured since
Sophocles. The delineation of the characters is appraised. In a realm
already invaded by hosts of former commentators, the critic brings
freshness and vividness. She never lapses into banalities.

What is even more praiseworthy, she does not strive for paradox-
ical originality and for the display of dazzling subtlety, a temptation
which several recent French writers on Racine could not resist. It
is too facile to coin a new terminology and to pin new-fangled labels
onto old motives or devices. Dr. Knapp does not address herself pri-
marily to other scholars with a vain desire to outshine them by her
smartness. She looks for judiciousness, common sense and insight, and
she scorns pretentious obscurity. Her quotations from Racine are mostly given in the recent and remarkable translation of Racine's tragedies
by Samuel Solomon.

Yet this is not the book of a traditional literary critic who ven-
erates so-called classical literature so superstitiously that he would
refuse all recourse to other branches of knowledge. Bettina Knapp
makes use of modern theories on psychoanalysis, on archetypes and
myths. She depicts several of Racine's formidable women as oppressive
embodiments of the Mother Principle, stresses the obsession of the
dramatist with pairs of enemy brothers and generally with an incestuous atmosphere, if not with outright incest such as fascinated several
Elizabethan dramatists. She shows Racine as a poet of the night, both
the physical darkness haunted by frightened waiting for the light of
day which will reveal their criminal thoughts, and of the tenebrous
jungle of their subconscious and their desires. She needed no recourse
to Hegelian terminology and to philosophical jargon to underline the
monstrous nature of much of Racinian love. It is a destructive sensual

force, more primitive and amoral than any love portrayed by the Greek tragic poets and by Shakespeare. The men in love, and more often the women who are the imperious and the brutal ones in Racine, attempt to dominate and to possess, as masters would slaves, the meeker creatures whom they desire: Junie, Monime, Andromaque, Bajazet, Hippolyte. The loved one recoils, aghast, and flees or perishes, ensnared and resigned. Mauriac had rightly remarked that, behind the veneer of formal language and the magnificent flow of alexandrine verses, under their sumptuous and queenly veils and jewels, Racine's women (Hermione, Agrippine, Roxane) are, through their instincts and their lust, much closer to fishwives than to court ladies.

Indeed, despite superficial appearances, the refined imagery, and the impeccable construction of the plays, Racine's tragedies stand at the opposite pole from the Greeks, much further away from the Hellenic spirit than the tragedies of Shakespeare, who probably knew no Greek. They do not allow the lyrical element or the epic narrative to serve as a respite from fierce anguish; they banish the comic relief just as they banish music and lyrics; they do not indulge in the luxuriance of images of which Shakespeare is fond. Resignation to the laws of fate, as even Lear, Othello, or Antony evince as they die, admission of their guilt and of their progress in seeing and understanding such as Sophocles' Oedipus expresses at the end, are alien to Racinian heroes. Behind the magnificent order of acts and scenes following progressively upon each other, behind the organization of their elaborate speeches, the characters are doomed to inner chaos and to rebellion against the external order and against themselves. They desperately strive to see clearly into themselves, yet they all fall victims to their profound, incurable anarchy and as dupes of their own miscalculations. Strindberg, O'Neill himself, and Sartre, though he would not acknowledge it, are in that sense Racine's true successors.

Each play of Racine is carefully studied in Bettina Knapp's volume. The originality of each is brought out, with deftness and with rare penetration. Each is discreetly replaced in Racine's life and amid the events of the era. But Racine's inner life and the secret of his workmanship are hardly better known to us than those of an ancient Greek or of Shakespeare. One is thus brought back to the text and, led by this learned and artistic critic, to a more zestful enjoyment of the tragedies through the perceptive commentaries made upon them. It is a pleasant surprise for the reader to discover that those tragedies, composed for a Parisian audience as different from ours as could be, taking place among mythological or mythical characters, strike us, thousands of miles and three hundred years away, as true, vibrantly alive, and meaningful for us. A rich critical study like this one, coming after several others on tragic writers and after much speculation on the essence of tragedy, is a sign of the audacity with which Americans, once intent upon dismissing or forgetting the tragic, now maturely face art and life. "Dare to be tragic and ye will be redeemed," proclaimed the prophet of *Also sprach Zarathustra*. We may well be ready for an aesthetic redemption as we enter upon the last third of our century, understanding the literary and artistic achievement of other cultures and the tragic vision of bygone ages as we never had before.

Henri Peyre
The City University, New York

Contents

Introduction

To write one more volume on Jean Racine when a vast bibliography on this seventeenth-century dramatist already exists might seem surprising at first, yet I felt compelled to do so for the following reason: in preparing a graduate course at Hunter College I reread all of Racine's tragedies and was *seared* by this new exposure. Inexplicably, I thought. As a result I sought to understand, then articulate, the reasons for these new and deep-seated reactions.

Just as modern historians avail themselves of the finest scientific methods in their studies of past civilizations, I have to this end adopted a psychological approach (of the Jungian school) in order to sound out the creatures of Racine's fantasy, and an aesthetic and theatrical point of view to attempt to understand the reasons for the extreme modernity and eternally appealing quality of his works.

I

With the help of this "double" focus I have tried to illuminate the chiaroscuro in which Racine's dramas are enshrouded and into which they plunged me. Partial answers to puzzling questions can be gleaned by analyzing Racine's dramas themselves—the characters, for example. Who exactly were these mythical presences moving about in a circumscribed orbit, standing forth finely incised against a mysterious, impalpable backdrop? What were these beings, these emanations, really like? What did each know and feel about the other? What were their ideational patterns, their ontological concepts? What did Racine project upon them? How could such creatures as Iphigenia and Phaedra, for example, succeed in *branding* me—and today? What was Racine's attitude toward religion? How did a man, imbued since childhood with

feelings of sin, salvation, and guilt, react to the godhead? What conflicts did life in the theatre, considered sinful by the orthodox, arouse in
Racine's psyche? As my study of the plays progressed, patterns became
evident in terms of the characters themselves, the symbolic language
in which they spoke, and the themes which they brought to life.

Certain protagonists (or antagonists, as the case may be) might
be regarded as archetypal figures who have sprung almost bodily from
Racine's unconscious. They blaze their way through his dramas in various forms and usually in a whirlwind. If female characters such as
Agrippina, Roxana, and Hermione are seen only in their specifically
personal or social aspects as mothers, mistresses, or sisters, their import is limited because they remain circumscribed by their families,
their ties, their times, and their situations. However, considered as collective figures, another dimension is added: they become timeless, eternal symbols, common to humanity in general.

To a great extent Agrippina, Hermione, Roxana, and other protagonists symbolize the destructive mother principle in nature, flourishing
in certain ancient matriarchal societies (Phoenicia, Canaan, Babylonia).
As such, these negative mother images become remarkably potent, capable of inflicting damage on young and old, of altering concepts, of
destroying the *status quo*. Agrippina, for example, a *vagina dentata*
type, struggles viciously with her son Nero in her power struggle; Hermione crushes Pyrrhus and Orestes; Roxana wants total domination
over her lover and, in exercising her formidable will, has him killed. In
juxtaposition to these virulent female figures are the positive Mother
types: Andromache and Jehoshebath, for example, who typify the
sturdy, well-meaning, and affirmative aspect of the mother archetype.
Relatively passive women likewise emerge: Antigone, Junie, and Athalida, who wish all were well but do nothing overtly to change matters.

Father figures are also present in Racine's tragedies in both their
negative and positive aspects. Less flamboyant usually than the female
of the species, they are generally involved in the possessing of kingship
or love. Mithridates, Agamemnon, and Nero are all kings or emperors.
Each views life from his own darkened room. The first sees the world
as a battleground whereupon he and his archenemies, the Romans, are
forever struggling. A positive force at the beginning, his continually
bellicose acts have led to a negative way of life. Agamemnon experiences extreme conflict because he has not yet been able to separate his
personal life (as represented by his daughter Iphigenia) from his collective existence as king and supreme ruler (which requires the sacrificing of his personal existence to a great extent). Nero is the adolescent
who seeks to fulfill a ruler's function—both pragmatically and stoically

—but is unfit for the task and, therefore, fails in his endeavor. Jehoiada, a patriarchal figure, stands out as extraordinarily positive in Racine's panoply of gods and monsters. In him the *coniunctio* has been realized: the necessary unification between the personal father (husband and father of two children) and the collective father figure (high priest of the Temple in Jerusalem and, therefore, spiritual and guiding force of a people).

Lesser beings also figure in Racine's group of constellations—pairs; for example, the warring brothers (Eteocles and Polynices) who are so incompatible that they destroy each other; good friends (Iphigenia and Eriphile), one of whom must be sacrificed if the positive aspect is to survive. Weakly structured youths insinuate their ways into Racine's tragedies as do maidens: Orestes, who goes insane; Hippolytus, who is destroyed; Antigone, who kills herself; Junie, who ends her life as a vestal virgin. Each protagonist is meaningful in his own right and also vis-à-vis the other characters in the dramas.

Racine deals with the eternal in man. Upon the *prima materia* of the myth or the historical event in question, he builds his drama, an edifice of intertwining and coagulating forces. The myths Racine dramatizes (Phaedra, Iphigenia, etc.) are not to be envisaged as euhemeristic allegories because such an attitude might limit their scope. They should be looked upon as a means of revealing unknown contents, as an unquenchable source of extraordinary secrets which seem to cascade forth in rich and bold imagery, as a whole arcane world upon which Racine projects and into which he withdraws whenever sufficiently stirred.

Themes burgeon forth from Racine's imagination—a perpetually fertile land. Indeed, he seems merely to have to pluck one or two or more topics from this prolific realm to furnish us with a dream. Political themes are adumbrated: the King, for example, as he functions in society, in such a figure as Pyrrhus; as military leader, as witnessed by Agamemnon and Mithridates. Problems concerning personal relationships are also treated by Racine: Mother–Son or Mother–Lover situations such as in *Phaedra*, for example, where the heroine struggles to win Hippolytus' love and, in so doing, unwittingly causes his destruction; the power lust as enacted by Agrippina, who seeks to emasculate her son and is, to a great extent, successful. Studies in the growth and makings of heroes are drawn in depth; the hero's struggle to emerge victorious from parent identification or *participation mystique,* as portrayed in Eteocles and Polynices; the fight Pharnaces knew when trying to break a patriarchate; the hero par excellence, Alexander the Great, who achieved judgment and objectivity in his outlook. The immense question of evil predominates in Racine's work and is manifested in such creatures as Eriphyle, Haman, Athaliah. Represented symbolically, these "evil" creatures can be looked upon as instigators or perpetrators of action, necessary forces which add to the dynamism of the work. The enactment of the entire religious ritual also assumes an important role in Racine's drama: sin (Phaedra), guilt (Orestes), sacrifice (Iphigenia), and redemption (Phaedra).

II

Aesthetically, Racine succeeds in scorching his readers or viewers by the effulgent charge he shoots through his poetry. Calamitous moments burst forth with torrential force only to be superseded by periods of extreme calm and silence. These seconds of repose are then followed by precipitous activity, sharpening the intensity of the already ebullient emotions, underscoring by this febrile activity the aggressiveness and cruelty of the characters themselves in terms of their thoughts and their comportment. In such an atmosphere of extremes, which pervades every corner and crevice of Racinian drama, viewers find their nerves worked upon, their serenity traumatized. Their senses are aroused to unparalleled peaks by the imagery overflowing in each portentous line.

The visual sense, for example, is irritated by such images as fire and flame, and calmed by a vision of a blue expanse of water; the auditory sense is deafened by sounds of thunder, marching men, armaments, and battles, and alarmed when confronted by such epithets as "whispering walls"; the sense of smell is affected by smoke, incense, dankness; the sense of touch is incited by flesh tones; taste buds are energized by descriptions of feasts and banquets. All these images affect the spectator or reader viscerally: shocking him, blistering him, enfeebling him—ushering forth an atmosphere of extreme pathos as well as of enormous thrills.

The vigor of Racine's imagery, which causes empathetic situations to arise, propels the reader or spectator into another dimension, a world where the intellectual notion of linear time is nonexistent. The figures Racine conjures forth wander about in a realm consisting of a type of "fluid time." The past, for example, surges forth into the present, disorienting the status quo as well as the emotional stability of the characters in question and introducing, because of this varied optic, a whole new series of associations into the conflicting attitudes of the moment, creating, thereby, other dynamisms which alleviate or increase existing antagonisms. When, for example, Andromache prays at the tomb of her dead husband, her past not only overflows into her present, but in so doing imbues her with the strength necessary to charter her course.

The corrosive effect of Racine's plays (both psychologically and aesthetically) bring Antonin Artaud's statement to mind: "A true theatrical work disturbs the senses in repose, liberates the repressed unconscious, foments a virtual revolt . . . and imposes both a heroic and difficult attitude on the assembled collectivity."[1]

That an analogy should exist between what Antonin Artaud advocated in his "Theatre of Cruelty" and Jean Racine's works is indeed strange in view of the fact that the twentieth-century innovator despised French classical theatre, which laid so much stress on the spoken word and so little on the visual experience. Yet, astoundingly, Racine's tragedies follow certain Artaudesque credos: the theatre, for example, considered as a ritual able to arouse a *numinous* experience within the spectator, and the theatre based on *myths, symbols,* the *unconscious,* and *gestures.* These dynamic entities, used by Antonin Artaud to arouse man's irrational forces so that a collective theatrical event could be turned into a personal and living experience, are also typical of Racine's dramas.

Let us take Racine's *Iphigenia* as an example. The various themes, personality traits, situations, and conflicts contained in this work can be transformed by an imaginative and sensitive director into vitally important concrete realities on stage. He can achieve such a goal by altering the theatre's acting area, by encouraging actors to become living symbols, by using words, images, lights, rhythms, sounds, and time as instrumentalities designed to work on the audience's nerves.

To arouse audiences to a peak of excitement, Artaud suggested that no separation should exist between stage and orchestra. During the production of *Iphigenia,* audiences would sit in the middle of the stage on mobile chairs. Galleries would be built all about the theatre, allowing the action to unfold on all levels and dimensions—in height and in depth. This diffused action in space would grip and assault the spectator, as though a world were forcing itself in upon him. Symbolically speaking, the outside world would be acting upon man's inner being.

Actors and their gestures, looked upon as *hieroglyphics* or *symbols,* would become transforming agents by means of which mysterious contents could be revealed to the spectator: Clytemnestra's rage and tears, Achilles' strength and audacity, Ulysses' cerebral and pondered outlook, Eriphyle's bestiality, Agamemnon's indecisiveness—all these abstract notions would become part of a concrete stage language made viable by means of the actor's individual movements and motions as

well as by a series of meaningful choreographed patterns. When Agamemnon, for example, describes his anguish, he does so in terms of
his physical world:

> Stunned, as you may well suppose,
> I felt my blood run cold through all my limbs.
> I was struck dumb, and no word could I say
> Until a thousand sobs had cleared the way.
> I blamed the Gods, and, without hearing more
> To disobey, upon their altars swore.[2]

The emotions as revealed in Agamemnon's monologue can be expressed by the actor concretely on stage by means of half-gestures,
stifled body movements, controlled and rhythmic sobs, contracted gait
—all giving the impression of iced-over feelings, paralysis.

Words, heretofore spoken only on the stage area, would burst
forth from various parts of the theatre, lending a disquieting feeling to
the events portrayed. Dialogues would be spoken in a stylized manner
or manipulated like solid objects, as in such phrases as: "The Gods are
lately cruel, deaf to me."[3] "Is he, my lover, all aflame to see me?"[4]
"I see you redden at this outrage."[5] "But sword, fire, blindfold, all are
ready now."[6] The primitive function of words might be restored to
them by clever vocal techniques. In this way, they would again be
possessed of their incantatory nature, their supernatural aura, their
mesmerizing and magical effects (as in hymns, prayers, onomatopeia,
repetitions, etc.)—all uttered in such a way as to bring out their double
nature, their spirituality and sensuality. Certain stanzas are capable of
being enunciated with metered vocal effects, with rhythmic interchang-
es, with awe-inspiring crescendoes and diminuendoes underscoring the
metaphysical implications (employing such words as oracle, altar,
fatal, heaven, wind, incense); operatic tonal effects could even be
achieved as, for example, in Clytemnestra's speech:

> What streams of blood have you made gush for her?
> What heaps of ruins here proclaim your fights?
> What corpse-strewn fields condemn me hold my tongue? . . .
> To me your love has tried to save her, brute!
> A fatal oracle commands she die.
> Do oracles in fact say what they seem?
> Can Heaven, high Heaven, be honoured by a murder.
> With a thirst that craves the flow of innocent blood?[7]

Emotions clothed in colorful images would express the most violent and tender feelings: burned suns, smouldering embers, glowing

coals, torches flaming against the night's blackness, blues, whites, icy tones of the purest hues standing bleakly against an expanse of light. If these colors were extracted from Racine's verse and expressed visually by flashing them on screens throughout the acting areas, their impact would make for striking results. When, for example, Agamemnon vacillates, Racine has recourse to the extraordinary interplay of hues ranging from brilliant oranges and reds to the harshest of blacks, thereby underscoring the extreme play of emotions. Eriphyle, on the other hand, as representative of evil, walks in darkness, in the shades of her dismal realm. To usher forth antithetical moods, however, harsh colors are brought into sharp focus: vibrant and flashing reds crash forth like blood gushing from a gaping wound.

Lighting effects can be used as a dramatic instrumentality, creating an atmosphere capable of moving the spectator to frenzies of terror, eroticism, or love. Flashed forth in sheets, waves, drops, torrents, or in any other manner, brilliance, clarity, fire, glaciers, scalding irons, smoke, etc. (all indicated in Racine's verse), surrounding and symbolically holding the spectators in a tightening vise, would effectively provoke extreme reactions in them.

Lighting effects would also create a series of rhythmic patterns to accompany or lend emphasis to the words themselves. Together or separately, they would be able to lull the spectator into a natural state of receptivity or plunge him forcefully, by their choppiness, into a nervous and frenzied state. Indeed, Racine is forever accelerating or slackening the rhythms of his tirades. In this manner he builds up suspense until a peak of anguish is reached and then suddenly, without forewarning, all motion stops, halting the spectator's profound involvement only to thrust him speedily forward moments later into a gaping abyss. When, for example, at the end of the play, Calchas prepares for the ritual murder, the atmosphere becomes sharpened to electric intensity. His hand rises slowly; then, a pause, after which Eriphyle shrieks "Stop." Motion has come to a virtual standstill. With unforeseen alacrity, Eriphyle rushes toward the altar and stabs herself, after which she seems to be engulfed in flames. The entire picture, as described by Racine, has suddenly turned into a grandiose spectacle, a three-dimensional apocalyptic vision:

> Frenzied she flies and on the nearby altar
> Seizes the sacred knife and stabs herself.
> Her blood has hardly flowed, reddening the earth,
> When Heaven's thunder bursts upon the altar;
> The winds in happy shudders tease the air

And the sea responds with all her mighty moaning,
While groans the farther shore flecked with foam
And of itself the pyre's flame sudden flares.
The sky flashes with lightning and gapes open,
Wrapping us in a chaste, assuring awe. . . .[8]

Racine's rhythmic technique, which is basic to his poetry, can be used with pedal effect to flood audiences with sensations of the most virulent types.

Sound effects also play an important part in adding to the force of the production. Emanating from all areas of the theatre, screams, studied breathing sounds, noises of all types would bombard the spectator at appropriate moments, breaking down his inhibitions and rational attitudes, tearing at his nerves. Indeed, Racine's entire work elicits aural emanations of every type: a shrieking voice in the ear, sounds echoing from the air, stillness of tears, silence of the winds, honor speaking forth, groaning shores, foaming waves, thundering skies, harsh flames sounding out their furor, nerve-shattering sparks, angry cries swelling intensity, hortatory winds, etc. . . .

To further stimulate the spectator's unconscious, past events as related in Racine's lengthy tirades would be projected on screens placed in various areas of the theatrical arena. By means of a system of flashbacks, the Racinian monologue, part of a dead past, would burst forth into the present, lending it renewed vitality and intensity. Time sequences, no longer experienced as consecutive entities, would be looked upon as disparate moments in space to be lived and experienced poignantly and a multitude of times. Such intrusions from past to present and vice versa would cause the spectator to feel a loss of equilibrium followed by an inability to discern differences between illusion and reality, the unconscious and the conscious, the individual and the collective. Each being, thereby, would watch the spectacle, participating fully in the undifferentiated collective turmoil about him.

It is no wonder that Racine's tragedies viewed from within and without, as a psychological search and as a theatrical spectacle, can make for a thrilling and breathtaking experience——today!

III

My deepest appreciation goes to Dr. Edward Edinger in the preparation of this volume on Racine for his profound analytical insights; to Vernon Brooks for his fine editorial help; to Professor Alba della

Fazia Amoia for reading the manuscript and for her wise counsel; to Estelle Weinrib for her encouragement and kindness; and, finally, to Random House, Inc., for graciously granting permission to quote from *The Complete Plays of Jean Racine*, translated by Samuel Solomon.

To my husband Russell S. Knapp, to my mother, Emily Gresser Liebowitz, and to my children, Albert and Charles, my gratitude and appreciation for their patience and understanding.

PART I—STORM

There is no escape from yesterday because yesterday has deformed us, or been deformed by us. . . . Yesterday is not a milestone that has been passed, but a daystone on the beaten track of the years, and irremediably part of us, within us, heavy and dangerous.
(SAMUEL BECKETT, *Proust.*)

Storm

"I find two men within me . . ."[1]

IN the seventeenth century it took a day or two by post to travel the seventy-six kilometers from Ferté-Milon to Paris—or two or three days by horse. Ferté-Milon, a quiet and rather majestic town, was part of the Duchy of Valois. A strong military province at one time, it could still boast of a magnificent castle built by Louis d'Orléans in the fifteenth century. Though partially in ruins, its beautiful bas-relief depicting the crowning of the Virgin was still intact. Two extraordinarily impressive Gothic cathedrals stood out sharply from a distance, breaking up, as it were, the relatively even panoramic view of the village. These religious edifices, one devoted to the cult of Notre Dame, the other to that of Saint Nicolas, were known particularly for their remarkably colorful stained glass windows.

Jean Racine was baptized on December 22, 1639 in Ferté-Milon.[2] His reception into the world did not augur anything out of the ordinary. His mother, Jeanne Sconin, and his father, after whom he had been named, were hard-working people who belonged to the upper bourgeoisie. It had even been said that the Racines had been technically ennobled several generations earlier: the "Rat" and the "Cygne" painted on their home could easily attest to this fact.[3]

Certain members of both the Racine and Sconin families had and still worked for the administrative body of their home town, known as the "grenier à sel," in charge of indirect tax collection. Other members had been connected in some official capacity with the Kings of France or had been artisans, business people, priests, merchants. . . . Certainly, Jean Racine's heritage represented a cross-section of French life.

The first two years of Jean's life were spent seemingly uneventfully, but the soothing pattern of normalcy was to be sharply altered with his mother's death on January 29, 1641, shortly after the birth of his sister Marie. Certainly, the boy was too young to realize the vast implications of such a loss. As for Marie, she was never to know the comfort of a mother's love. Perhaps to insure a certain degree of continuity in his home, at least for the children's sake, Jean's father married Madeleine Vol, the daughter of a notary, on November, 4, 1642.

Tragedy was to incise itself still more severely into the family picture. Three months after his marriage, on February 6th, Jean Racine senior died, leaving a large legacy of debts. Suitable homes now had to be found for both Jean and Marie because Madeleine was either unwilling or unable to care for them. She herself remarried in 1664, leaving Ferté-Milon permanently after that event.

ʃ   ʃ   ʃ

Orphaned and penniless, the young child was taken in by his paternal grandparents, the Desmoulins, who were righteous, kind, and highly moral people. It must have been a sacrifice for them to feed still another mouth. They were so poor in fact that when their daughter (the future Sister Agnès de Sainte-Thècle) wanted to enter a convent, they were unable to pay the customary dowry. Life was arduous for Jean at the Desmoulins and, as he grew older, he felt the stigma of poverty even more keenly. His sister, more fortunate, economically speaking at least, was brought up by her maternal grandparents, the Sconins, who were rather well-to-do.

Despite such paucity of material possessions, Jean must have responded to the warmth of his grandparents' personalities and to the equity of their ways. Differences in attitudes were apparent between the Desmoulins and the Sconin households. These were felt most keenly on certain occasions which one customarily considers as festive, but which, in Jean's eyes, were looked upon as painful. When, for example, he was invited to the Sconin home for family reunions, he was treated like a poor relative. Humiliated, disheartened, he returned home heavy in heart. Rancor and feelings of bitterness may have been aroused in him at this time over the utter injustices of "God's creatures." A trench was being dug within Racine, separating the Sconin family and what they represented—a world of material wealth and spiritual neglect—from the Desmoulins—with little financial security but great riches of the soul.

Misfortune was further heaped upon the young Racine, now barely ten years old. In 1649 his grandfather, whom he had grown to love, died. His grandmother, perhaps financially unable to keep up the expense required in running a private home, retired to the Jansenist convent-monastery at Port-Royal des Champs. Her grandson followed. It was here, befriended by the deeply religious Jansenists, that Jean Racine was to live and to be educated.

Marie Desmoulins' move to Port-Royal was not surprising in the least to those familiar with her ways and her family ties. She had always maintained close relations with the Jansenists. Her two sisters lived at Port-Royal, one had even become a nun, Sister Julienne de Saint-Paul. Nephews too, Nicolas Vitart, for example, had been sent to Port-Royal to be educated at the famous "Petites Ecoles." The Jansenists enjoyed a wide reputation for the excellence of their schools.

Marie Desmoulins, it has been surmised, was first introduced to the Jansenist sect in 1638. On July 14th of that year, the French government had ordered the disbandment of this profoundly religious order. As a result, three of its outstanding proponents, Claude Lancelot, Antoine Le Maître, and his brother, Le Maître de Séricourt, left Port-Royal, their home, and went to live at Ferté-Milon, in Marie Desmoulins' town. There, these brilliant men exerted not only an enormous influence on the Racine family, but on the entire town as well.[4]

✶ ✶ ✶

Port-Royal had once been a Cistercian Abbey, founded in 1204 by Mathilde de Garlande and Eudes de Sully. It was situated on a low and marshy site, in a thickly wooded area of the Chevreuse valley, about eight miles south-west of Versailles. In the early days only twelve nuns made up the order. Soon, however, the religious community developed rapidly and with it, a laxity of morals. Dances were held, and merrymaking, rather than religious zeal, became the note of the day. The situation grew so awkward that the Abbess of the convent was excommunicated in 1574.[5]

An eleven-year-old girl, Mother Angélique, of the famous Arnauld family, became Abbess of Port-Royal in 1603. Endowed with a will of iron, a heart of gold, and remarkable insight, she reformed the Abbey very nearly single-handedly. Her devotion to her religion was so fervent as to drive her sometimes to extremes. On one occasion which stands out as noteworthy in this respect—on September 25, 1609— labeled the "journée du guichet," she denied her own father entry into the convent because it was a particularly religious day.

Though the nuns at Port-Royal, under Mother Angélique's eagle eye and kindly disposition, worked with fervor and speed, the climate in the Crevreuse Valley was damp, the conditions unsanitary, and typhoid was forever breaking out. So many members of the religious community had suffered so incredibly from illness of one nature and another that Mother Angélique decided to move her group to Paris. In 1625, in buildings situated on what is now called the Boulevard de Port-Royal, she, together with the nuns of her order, pursued their good works and devoted their lives to humanity and to God.

The male members of this religious group lived in solitude in Paris, in buildings adjacent to those occupied by the nuns. In 1638, however, they decided to renounce the world and live in the abandoned buildings of Port-Royal des Champs. The "Solitaires," as they were now called, worked long and arduously trying to clear the land, drain the marshes, and renovate the buildings, making the general area fit to live in. Mother Angélique and her religious community decided to return to Port-Royal des Champs once the work had been completed. The Solitaires, therefore, had to vacate the convent and move to a nearby farm also owned by the Abbey—les Granges, as it was called. Les Granges was situated on a plateau with an extraordinarily beautiful view of all surrounding areas—certainly an atmosphere conducive to spiritual meditation.

Jansenism was introduced into Port-Royal in 1636 by the priest Saint-Cyran. Officially, the doctrine of Jansenism was created in 1640 with the publication of the *Augustinus* by Cornelius Jansen, called Jansenius, Bishop of Ypres. In this religious work he declared that the ideas of Saint Augustine concerning grace had been misinterpreted and that he was now explicating them correctly. Since Adam's fall, he explained, man has never possessed free will: he is subject either to *grace* or to *concupiscentia*. If God were to grant him eternal grace then he would never veer toward sin. Since this is not the case, man is drawn to evil. On the other hand, God endows certain people with what is called "efficacious grace"—when they cannot help but do good. Salvation comes to pass when God grants this special grace. Man's future, under this concept, is *predetermined* and depends wholly upon God and not upon man's deeds or any human intermediary.

According to both Jesuit thinking and Papal decree, man is given *free will*. It is he who choses to do good or evil. Neither grace nor *concupiscentia* determine his action or his situation.

The Jansenist doctrine which preached the "all-powerful" nature of grace, ran contrary to the Catholic Church, to Jesuit *dicta*, and was, consequently, considered heretical. Louis XIV, his ministers, and most particularly the Sorbonne theologians, made up of a majority of Jesuits, were unfavorably disposed toward the Jansenists. Indeed, the Jesuits had good cause to frown upon their rigorous point of view. The Jesuits had been accused of laxity of morals, of casuistry, of having transformed the holiest of sacraments, communion, into a hypocritical ritual and confession into a parody because of its frequency and the lack of sincerity brought to it. Sins, the Jansenists felt, could not be adjusted with facility, nor could they be remedied through senseless verbiage. Penitence, prayer, pain must be part of pardon and purification. The relations between the Jansenists and the "all-powerful" Jesuits grew stormy. Several dates mark extremes of such antagonism: 1638, when the Solitaires were forced to disperse and leave Port-Royal; 1642, when the *Augustinus* was condemned by Pope Urban VIII; 1653, when Pope Innocent X condemned the Five Propositions extracted from the *Augustinus* which had been appealed by the Jansenists in the ecclesiastical courts; 1656, when Blaise Pascal, the Jansenist mathematician and philosopher, launched his attack against the Jesuits in the form of sardonic epistles entitled *The Provincial Letters*; 1661, when the "Petites Ecoles" were closed. By 1668, on the surface at least, the struggle between the Jansenists and the Jesuits seemed to have subsided. On that date the "Paix de l'Eglise" (or of Clement IX) as it was called, was proclaimed, when the Jansenists signed the act of faith given them by Pope Alexander VII. The battle, however, raged again a year later, after it was decreed that one third of the revenue accruing to the Jansenists was to be placed under Jesuit management. The situation grew steadily more serious. By 1706 no more novices were permitted to enter Port-Royal. A year later, the Jansenists were forbidden the sacraments. In 1709 the Solitaires were dispersed. In 1710 the buildings at Port-Royal were leveled. In 1711 the three thousand buried at Port-Royal were disinterred and removed to other areas so that never more would another "heretical" sect arise on that ground.

✦   ✦   ✦

When the Solitaires did live at Port-Royal des Champs, Jansenism had not only become a religious doctrine but a way of life. Indeed, the Jansenists were unique in their way: austere, honorable, extraordinarily fervent. Among them too were many brilliant minds: specialists in letters, philosophy, logic, law, language, science, mathematics.

Antoine Le Maître (1608–1658), for one, had enjoyed a fine career as a lawyer in Paris when he left that city in 1638 for Port-Royal. The popular writer Guez de Balzac had said of him that if Cicero and Demosthenes had known him they would have been jealous of his extraordinary rhetorical capacity. He worked in the peace and quiet of Port-Royal with his brother, Le Maître de Sacy, on a *Translation of the New Testament* and a new version of the *Life of the Saints*, among other works. Le Maître de Sacy (1613–1684) became spiritual director of the nuns at Port-Royal.[6] His brother, Simon de Séricourt (1611–1658), came to Port-Royal in 1627 after enjoying an army career.

Antoine Arnauld, known as "Le Grand Arnauld," one of the most extraordinary minds of the century, author of *The Frequency of Communion*, criticized Jesuit doctrine and, at the same time, spread Jansenist philosophy. It was this work which caused him to be censured by the Sorbonne and excluded by its Faculty of Theology in 1656. Together with Lancelot he also wrote a *General Grammar* (1660) and, with Nicole, *The Logic of Port-Royal* (1662). Dom Claude Lancelot (1615–1695) was one of the founders of the well-known "Petites Ecoles" (1645), located first in Paris at the Faubourg St. Jacques and later transferred to the "Granges" at Port-Royal des Champs.[7] Pierre Nicole (1625–1695) was one of the most distinguished teachers at the "Petites Ecoles" and perhaps the true director of Port-Royal. It was he who wrote the stinging diatribes against "evil" dramatists, the *Imaginaries* and the *Visionaries* (1667), a Latin translation of Pascal's *Provincial Letters* and, together with Arnauld, *The Logic of Port-Royal*. Arnauld d'Andilly (1658–1674), also a creative person, published a *Journal* and *Translation of the Confession of Saint Augustine*, to mention but a few of his works.

Such were only some of the volumes written by those extraordinary individuals living at Port-Royal des Champs, who fostered rigorous, clear, and penetrating thinking while also encouraging personal reflection, rectitude in all endeavors, and continual devotion to God. Racine, who had arrived at Port-Royal in 1649, remained until 1653 in this environment, which breathed God, authenticity, and asceticism as well as all those hidden and opposing forces of the flesh which exist inchoate within man and which are forever nurtured by the outside world.

ᕗ   ᕗ   ᕗ

It is believed that in 1653 Racine was sent to pursue his studies gratis at the Collège de Beauvais, a school which enjoyed a superb reputation in France at the time. After two years away from Port-Royal, with another phase of his education completed, he returned to the Jansenist community for three more years: his knowledge of the classics and religion would now be furthered in the inspired atmosphere generated by the Solitaires.

Under Jansenist tutelage Racine developed a veritable passion for study.[8] He read assiduously from Plato, Plutarch, and other Greek masters, annotating his texts as he went along. One of his teachers, Antoine Le Maître, was impressed by his "lively mind," his astonishing facility for learning. Indeed, he was so taken with Racine's aptitude for learning that he decided to train him for the law; perhaps he could eventually enjoy an exciting career in this field. He spent long hours with the young lad inculcating him with the logic, astuteness, and mental dexterity befitting one for such a life. His affection for Racine was not merely limited to the intellect, however, and was expressed in the form of great tenderness and warmth. Antoine Le Maître treated Racine as his own son and in letters even called him "mon fils." Racine must certainly have been very receptive to such displays of feeling. When away from Port-Royal on a brief trip, Antoine Le Maître wrote to Racine admonishing him to "detach himself from the world" since it stood out as piety's enemy; and he added, "Youth must always let itself be guided; it must not be emancipated."[9] Such statements must have dug deep within Racine's fiber. He would certainly return to this notion in time.

Jean Hamon (1618–1687), a very kindly doctor, guided Racine's studies after Le Maître's death in 1658. Once connected with the Medical Faculty of Paris, he had withdrawn to Port-Royal at the age of thirty-three. Racine felt so deeply toward M. Hamon, it seems, that when, years later, he made out his will, he asked to be buried at the doctor's feet.

An incident of great import which had occurred at Port-Royal in 1656 must have been deeply engraved in Racine's memory, since he mentioned it in detail in his *Abridged History of Port-Royal*, a work he wrote at the end of his life. It seems that one of the young postulants at Port-Royal had been suffering from a dangerous fistula on her eye. It had reached such proportions that it not only disfigured her face, but the doctors said she would die quite soon from the uncontrollable infection which had, as a result, permeated her entire being. A great relic had been brought to Port-Royal on March 24th of that year—one of the thorns from the "Crown of Thorns" worn by Jesus. The sick girl touched this holiest of objects with her eye. The following day her fistula disappeared and she was cured. When reputable doctors were called in to examine her and found her eye in perfect condition, without a trace of pus or infection, they could only speak in terms of a miracle: the postulant had been cured by the "holy thorn."[10]

Much time during Racine's years at Port-Royal was devoted to study, meditation, and writing. His literary endeavors were varied:

he translated Plato's *Symposium*, composed essays on Pindar and Homer, etc. He had a very special affinity for the Greek writers and for Sophocles and Euripides in particular. They must have mirrored his feelings, answered an unknown need within Racine at this juncture. So great was his passion for the ancients that it has been claimed that Racine knew many classical dramas by heart. As was to be expected, he was still a boy in many ways. He loved what was forbidden. An incident has been reported in this connection in which Racine savored an unsavory work. One day, it seems, he had been caught reading *The Loves of Theagenes and Chariclee*, a novel considered undesirable by his master at Port-Royal. Claude Lancelot demanded the book, which he burned. The irate youngster availed himself of another copy. The second met a similar fate. A third book was bought by Racine, and after memorizing the entire volume he handed it over to M. Lancelot saying, "You can burn this one as you burned the others."[11] Such an incident is an indication of Racine's strong will, his utter disregard for regulations which might restrict his desired pursuits.

Racine, however, was a many-sided individual, difficult to know and still more puzzling to assess. Just as he was an inveterate reader of Greek literature, so he was a devotee of nature in all her phases. He enjoyed wandering through the woods and fields surrounding Port-Royal to commune with nature, with those sublime forces which he could "feel" but perhaps could not yet analyze: the trees, stocky and graceful; the bushes, stumpy and delicate; the many hues orchestrating the picture—reds, browns, and golden colors of autumn and the deep greens of summer. Whatever emerged from mother earth met his eye and fixed itself there, starkly, sternly, and stormily. Racine was so deeply moved by the beauty of his surroundings that he began composing verses on prairies, on the woods, even on the monastery buildings—everything he had come to know so well. All in nature, in life, began to feed his inner world and then his pen.

The moments of solace and comfort Racine drew from nature were of short duration. A sensitive youth, he must have shared the anguish the Solitaires knew at this particular time, the dangers which they were forever facing. January 31, 1656 was a particularly difficult day for all those at Port-Royal: the enemies of Jansenism had succeeded in having "Le Grand Arnauld" expelled from the Sorbonne because of his work, *On the Frequency of Communion*. March 30th was another, even more frightening moment in the life of a community, the members of which Racine had grown to love and to admire: children, teachers, all the Solitaires were forced to leave Port-Royal.

Racine had already experienced solitude as well as financial difficulties—persecution was now to be added to the list.

Racine's reactions to such traumatic moments were certainly not
always passive. He was a fighter at heart—if not overtly at this period,
certainly unconsciously. He must, therefore, have devoured with great
relish the Jansenist Blaise Pascal's *Provincial Letters*. These eighteen
epistles by the famous mathematician-philosopher satirized unmercifully the Jesuits, their ideas concerning grace, and the fragility of their
mores and precepts. Pascal's wit, humor, and acidulous jabs certainly
must have made a profound impression upon Racine who, later on,
would himself apply similar bitter and ironic innuendoes in a seemingly
off-handed manner when dealing with his enemies.

Racine was living through monstrous and fabulous days—a time
when men fought harshly for ideas and for principles, when they expressed in moving and profound terms their belief in the divine. He
could not help but respond affectively to such traumatic moments.
Yet, he must have experienced ambivalent emotions toward both religion and life in general: an attitude of militancy which would plunge
him into the turbulent forces of the world, and contrary feelings of
detachment, inwardness, and meditation, enticing him into his own
resplendent inner realm.

The Solitaires were adept at handling dangers courageously and
astutely. During the present crisis (1656) which hovered over Port-
Royal, they acted with quiet determination. The situation had become
so precarious that they feared for their lives and because of this decided to send Racine away from their midst, to the Duc de Luynes'
Chateau de Vaumurier, not far from the Jansenist convent-monastery.

In the impressive surroundings of the adroit and affable Mon-
seigneur, Louis-Charles d'Albert, Duc de Luynes and Duc de Chevreuse, minister to Louis XIII, Racine was to be introduced to a different
type of society, that of wealth and success. It was here perhaps that he
was first exposed to the ways of the world, that a desire to ingratiate
himself became apparent, that a need to succeed in life was nurtured.

The months Racine spent at the Duc de Luynes' castle were
fruitful ones for other reasons. It was here that he renewed his acquaintance with his father's cousin, Nicholas Vitart, a former student at
Port-Royal and now a wealthy and powerful man and manager of the
Duc de Luynes' estates. The friendship which was to ensue between
them was to play an important role in Racine's future activities.

When the young poet returned to Port-Royal in 1657, broader in
his outlook upon the world and more courtly in his ways, he resumed

for a brief period his studies with Antoine Le Maître and with the other Solitaires. The time then arrived for him to be sent to one of the finest schools in Paris, the Collège d'Arcourt, to study philosophy. In October, under the eagle though distant eye of the Solitaires, he began his studies in the city which had been a source of inspiration for many and would now become a land of enchantment for Racine.

After completing his schooling at the Collège d'Arcourt, in 1659, the prospects for Racine's future could not really be considered bright. To what could a lad with no fortune and no social position look forward? Racine was now twenty years old. Though he was brilliant, handsome, and certainly poised, he was devoid of the most necessary accoutrements, those material factors which played such an important role in seventeenth century society. Choices as to a future career were open to him: the army? He was uninterested in this type of work; the law? The price to be paid for such a post was too dear; he could not possibly afford it. A government post at Ferté-Milon? That was a possibility. To return to his birthplace, however, and to slumber there in some innocuous position which not only paid little money but would submerge him in the dull routine of provincial life, had no appeal for him. Moreover, if he were to pursue this type of activity in the bourgeois-infested town of Ferté-Milon, he most certainly would be treated by those he knew as he had been years before—as a poor relative. Such prospects were tantamount to an inferno.

The well-educated and finely mannered Racine was, strangely enough, a *classless* individual, a *rootless* being—without family, fortune, or future.

Had not Nicolas Vitart, noble of heart as well as a devout Jansenist who had for a long while indulged in "secret" activities to further this sect's cause, helped Racine, he might have floundered in a sea of penury. It was he who succored the lad when he offered him a modest employ in the Duc de Luynes' establishment. Since Nicolas Vitart had become the Duc de Luynes' man of confidence, he had not only amassed a small fortune in his own right but was able, with relative ease, to have Racine taken into the Duke's household. In 1661, he had him sent to Babylone to help manage one of the Duke's estates. Such prosaic and routine activity, however, was not to Racine's liking. He complained of frightful boredom.[12] It was clear to him now. He did not enjoy what he considered an overly down-to-earth job, one which had nothing to do with the mind or the spirit. Racine also complained of the climate, of the wind in particular and the cold. Perhaps the voicing of such climatic dissatisfaction was merely an excuse. Racine had never been accustomed to any type of luxury, except most briefly at the Duc de Luynes' castle. He had always known discomfort and had lived very nearly according to Spartan ethics. The fact is that Racine wanted to return to Paris, to the city of excitement, growth, and hope.[13]

Though Racine had complained of his work, the entire incident had not been an altogether negative experience. It had reinforced his natural bent. He was now more determined than ever to follow the most precarious of careers, a literary one.

Racine was already the author of pastoral poems, of odes, songs, letters, hymns, sonnets, and elegies. Despite the fact that the influence of other writers—poets, both past and present—was clearly discernible in his verse, that he had still not developed a style he could properly call his own, there was, nevertheless, a certain glimmer, an original note which sparkled within otherwise routine lines of verse. His love for poetry in general and for the theatre in particular is certainly evidenced in a letter to a friend of his, the galant Abbé Le Vasseur.[14] In this missive he also speaks of the importance of positive criticism in a poet's formation. Because he was the recipient of such constructive suggestions, he confessed, he was able to rewrite a sonnet which he enclosed. Racine also displayed keen insight into the characters of would-be writers who practiced the art of poetry in a dishonorable manner, stepping down from the heights of Mount Parnassus to defend whatever wretched bit of scribbling they had "created" in the most vicious and insidious of ways.[15] An artist, Racine reasoned, must look at his work in an objective manner, must assume a certain distance from it and not be caught up in the swirling emotions of whatever emerges from his pen. Racine would take this view to heart and benefit from it at a later date.

A writer, however, needed much more than objectivity, perhaps even more than talent, in the seventeenth century. Soon after Racine had completed the ode he had written to celebrate the marriage of Louis XIV to the Spanish Infanta Marie-Thérèse, *The Nymph of the Seine*, he realized that he would have to ingratiate himself with those in power if he were to succeed, to win the King's favor. Only in this manner could he receive a pension, a necessity in his case.

Racine would have to approach the King in some way, through someone highly placed. Again he had recourse to his uncle Vitart, already so helpful to him in so many ways, including much needed financial aid. It was his uncle who showed Racine's poem to the man considered the patriarch of poets at this period—the pedantic writer Jean Chapelain. Fortunately for Racine, Chapelain was impressed with his literary endeavors. He suggested certain changes which the novice made at once. Indeed, Chapelain was so well disposed toward Racine that he spoke of his ode to Louis XIV's prime minister, the powerful Colbert. As a result of their meeting, Racine received one hundred louis in the name of the King. Racine's heart must have swelled with relief.

Vitart felt that such recognition was not sufficient. He therefore decided to show his nephew's poem to the distinguished Charles Perrault, future author of *The Century of Louis the Great* and famous fairy tales such as *Little Red Riding Hood, Puss in Boots*, etc. Charles Perrault also suggested certain changes to be made in the *Ode*, which Racine likewise accomplished.

Racine must have experienced the glow of satisfaction. To have one's work praised by two such highly placed individuals, Chapelain and Perrault, was by no means everybody's fortune. This kind of appreciation certainly inspired him to pursue a literary career. It seems, though there is no trace of these works, that Racine wrote a play at this time, *Amasie*, which was enacted successfully by the Marais troupe in Paris, and another one featuring Ovid as the hero. When he submitted the second work to a theatrical group, ostensibly affiliated with the Marais troupe, it was turned down. Racine gave it to a rival acting company, the Hôtel de Bourgogne, which received it unenthusiastically. Racine's sense of defeat, coming so closely upon his feelings of elation over the reception of his poem, must have been deeply disturbing to him.

Another worry came to plague Racine at this juncture. The Jansenists had expressed their concern and distaste over his choice of a literary career. They frowned upon the profane poetry he was now writing, considering such subjects as a King's marriage unworthy of a young man raised with devotion to God and honor in his heart. As long as Racine composed religious hymns, spent his hours in fruitful meditation, in the translation of spiritual documents, satisfaction was theirs; to err from this path was tantamount to sin. Yet, they were in a way to blame for Racine's extreme satisfaction with poetry of all types: had not M. de Sacy and M. d'Andilly encouraged his literary talents when he was a student at Port-Royal?

When Racine wrote his first play, *Amasie*, the Jansenists became angered. Racine's aunt, Mother Agnès de Sainte-Thècle, the daughter of the woman who had taken him in when a baby, shortly after his mother's death, who had poured out her love and affection upon him and with whom he had been so close, was utterly dismayed by his dealings in the "infamous" world of the theatre. All theatre is "sinful," she declared, anything connected with this "artificial" art is evil. Mother Agnès de Sainte-Thècle was speaking in the name of the entire religious community of Port-Royal, threatening Racine outright with excommunication if he continued his literary endeavors.

Racine must have been fired with a will to succeed, an inner frenzy which made him totally impervious to all imprecations leveled at him by the Jansenists. His desire to follow his penchant far outweighed his scruples toward those who had befriended him, who had been his parents really. Indeed, his actions and attitude at this period resembled those of a youth in the process of asserting himself, of achieving his freedom and independence, breaking the ties—even ruthlessly if need be—with the forces which, if held rigidly, could strangle him.

The Sconins also voiced their negative opinion concerning Racine's activities. In view of his precarious financial position, they suggested he go to the South of France—to Uzès—to live with his uncle, Father Antoine Sconin, Vicar-General of the diocese. It was hoped that he would be able to secure some ecclesiastical post for himself which would permit him to pay his debts and to prepare for life's way.

Racine had never been to the South of France. The gentle climate, the green-gold of the landscape, the fragrance of the lavender and jasmin fields impressed him greatly at first. In a letter to his friend, the future fabulist Pierre de La Fontaine, he described the area in which he now lived in the most poetic of terms; the magnificent fields of olive trees which clothed the landscape, their grey-green cast, their peaceful hues; also, the bitter, more painful aspects hidden behind such a facade of beauty and grandeur. When, for example, Racine tasted unripened olives, the harsh and sour taste permeated his mouth, paining every part of it.[16] The olives, looked upon as a symbol, might in Racine's case indicate an overly impulsive nature. The too hasty partaking of what is seemingly sweet can lead to great pain and future bitterness. The poet would certainly be more wary now.

During the early weeks of Racine's stay at Uzès he proved to be docile in every way, carrying out his uncle's will without remonstrance. He wore black as his uncle had suggested; he studied theology and read the works of St. Thomas. For his own edification, however, he added Aristotle's name to the list. Though he wrote commentaries on religious works, he could not let any amount of time elapse without devoting some hours to creative writing. He began the play *Theagenes and Clariclee*, which is not extant today.[17] Such imaginative outlets perhaps helped Racine face his daily tasks which, as the days passed into weeks, became more and more stultifying. What had seemed of

exquisite beauty when first he arrived in Uzès had now become dull
and routine. Moreover, his closer acquaintance with true provincial
life had made a disagreeable impression upon him. The pettiness of
the clerics he met, their daily bickering, avarice, jealousies, and desire
for personal gain in all senses of the word, ran counter to the purity of
spirit and thought that he had experienced at Port-Royal.

More and more he realized that he was definitely not fit for a
religious vocation. Though there were posts he could fill without
officially becoming a priest—despite the fact that others, like the
Abbé Claude Boyer, author of *La Porcie romaine* (1646), had combined
a religious with a literary career; and the Abbé Abeille, author of
Corialan, had done likewise—Racine rejected such a possibility outright.

Racine not only disliked the southern clergy but the southerners
in general, for their narrowmindedness, to be sure, but also for their
strange accent. He seemed unable or unwilling to understand and accept their speech, and he rejected it *in toto* along with the life he was
leading—so vehemently, in fact, that he even expressed anxiety over
the influence their southern drawl and twang would have over his
own speech. Ever since his earliest days at Port-Royal, Racine had been
very sensitive to language *per se*, to inflection and pronunciation. The
Solitaires had trained him in the art of rhetoric; they had insisted upon
purity of pronunciation and clarity of diction.[18]

More frightening than a loss of accent, however, was Racine's
growing sense of imprisonment. He not only felt inhibited in all his
actions, but exiled from everything he loved—art, literature, music.
He had reached an impasse. The longer he remained away from Paris,
the greater grew his longing to return there. Paris had now become a
city of enchantment, of light, of fervor—an image of the impossible,
an ideal.

Another, perhaps more dangerous, change had swept over Racine
at this period. He was losing his faith, and concomitant with this dim-
inution in spiritual fervor was a rejection of any type of hypocritical
attitude concerning his lack of belief. He could not, certainly, go out
of his way to hurt his aunt at Port-Royal or the Solitaires, but if a
showdown were to come he would now refuse the path of insincerity.[19]

Though Racine's close ties with Port-Royal were loosening, his
deepest hatred for the Jesuits in no way diminished. It permeated his
entire world and certainly was basic to his psychology. As a Jansenist
he had experienced first-hand the butt of Jesuit intrigue and the ruthlessness of their ways. He could not now look upon them without

experiencing a sense of rancor, bitterness, and perhaps even disgust.[20]

Feelings of growing nostalgia and melancholia permeated Racine's letters at this period. He must and would return to Paris no matter what his financial situation was at the time. Once in Paris, he had decided to seek a royal pension, large enough to provide him with the basic necessities of life. Then, he would look for a Maecenas to help him further his career.

The system of royal pensions flourished in seventeenth century France. La Fontaine, for example, was one of many poets who was the recipient of a handsome fund. The practice was to write verses to the King or to a noble for the slightest as well as the most important of occasions—the marriage of the King's brother to Henriette d'Angle-terre, the Queen's pregnancy, or the like.

Once back in Paris, Racine made a concerted effort to ingratiate himself with the King. To this end he wrote a poem to the monarch on his convalescence from the measles, which he had contracted on June 9, 1663. He sent his *Ode on the King's Convalescence* to Chapelain, who had once before admired his literary capabilities. This time too he delighted in the poet's well-turned lines and rhymes, and the elegant manner in which he expressed what could have been quite offensive. Months elapsed, however, and no money was forthcoming from either the King or his ministers, though this had been promised. Finally, in October, Racine tried again. He composed another ode, *To the Renown of the Muses*, in which he thanked the King for his graciousness and Colbert for his generosity and for facilitating a poet's way in the world. The ode must have reached the right people, because on August 22, 1664, Racine received a pension of six hundred pounds. Though this sum of money was small, it was received with gratitude, in view of Racine's lack of reputation and his inability to earn any funds whatsoever.

A few months earlier, in 1663, by dint of manipulation, intrigue, or subtle "artistry", Racine succeeded in winning a Maecenas in Monsieur le Comte de Saint-Aignan, who had not only become a member of the French Academy but was to be made Duke and peer of France.

Racine had not only acquired a benefactor but, perhaps even more important in the long run, a true friend in the person of the critic Nicolas Boileau. It was to this penetrating mind, endowed with a fine sense of humor, keen wit, extreme sensitivity, and a broad knowledge, that Racine would look for advice and encouragement for the rest of his days.

✻ ✻ ✻

The time was ready. Racine had just finished his first tragedy, *The Theban Brothers*, which he dedicated to Monsieur le Comte de Saint-Aignan, his benefactor. Molière accepted his play, which he would produce in his theatre, the Palais Royal in Paris. Excitement and perhaps visions of true success glimmered in the poet's eye. . . .

PART II—A TERRIBLE BEAUTY

. . . I want you to stop looking backward. I want you to lead me without flinching to the land of shadow and of the monster. I want you to plunge into irrevocable grief. I want you . . . to be without hope. I want you to choose evil and always evil. I want you to know only hatred and never love. I want you . . . to refuse the brilliance of darkness, the softness of flint, and the honey of thistles. I know where we're going . . . and why we're going there.
(JEAN GENET, *The Screens*.)

1

The Theban Brothers

"To detest that I may hate . . ."[1]

LA THEBAIDE or *The Enemy Brothers*, Racine's subtitle for his tragedy, and commonly known in English as *The Theban Brothers*, was presented for the first time by Molière's troupe at the Palais Royal on June 20, 1664. This work, performed only seventeen times, was considered "a failure."

Few facts can be gleaned concerning the genesis of this play. When, for example, did Racine begin working on *The Theban Brothers*? Was it before he left for Uzès in 1662 or during his stay there? Though Racine makes no mention of any such play in his correspondence with his sister Marie, he does include a paragraph concerning certain changes he was obliged to make in this tragedy in a letter to l'Abbé Le Vasseur (November, 1663). The modifications made were probably those required by Molière in his capacity as theatrical director.[2] The most plausible reason for Racine's noteworthy silence concerning his future plans for *The Theban Brothers* was his fear of further antagonizing both the Sconin family, with whom his sister Marie lived, and the Fathers at Port-Royal. Also he did not want to hurt his grandmother, Marie Desmoulins, who lived at the Jansenist convent. She who had brought him up and had always displayed so much kindness toward him was gravely ill at this period. He made frequent visits to Port-Royal to see her. When she died, on August 12, 1663, another link with the past had been broken.

There is no doubt in the mind of such scholars as René Jasinski that Racine must have received deprecating missives and even threats of excommunication from the Jansenists while he was preparing *The Theban Brothers*. Written probably at the end of 1663, a letter from

Racine's aunt, Agnès de Sainte-Thècle, who lived at Port-Royal, attests to her severe attitude concerning the dramatic arts and her nephew's partaking in such satanical works.[3]

The choice now remained with Racine: the theatre or Port-Royal,
liberation or constriction, creation or the negation of it, progress or
retrogression. Racine's decision was made the day he gave his manuscript of *The Theban Brothers* to Molière.

The Theban Brothers takes place in a room in the royal palace at
Thebes. We learn that Jocasta, Oedipus' wife and mother, bemoans the
hatred her two sons, Polynices and Eteocles, feel for each other. Their
antagonism has arisen as a result of a clause in Oedipus' will to the
effect that each son is to occupy the Theban throne during alternate
years. When Eteocles became king he banished his brother Polynices
from the land and after his own year terminated, refused to permit
him to reign. As *The Theban Brothers* opens, Polynices, who had fled
to Argos, now returns with an army to capture Thebes. Both Jocasta
and Antigone do their best to stave off the imminent combat between
the two brothers. Creon, Jocasta's brother who is determined to win
the Theban throne for himself, kindles their hatred. His own son
Menoeceus, anxious for peace, consults Tiresias the Seer, who predicts that with the voluntary death of one of the descendants of Cad-
mus, Thebes will be saved. Menoeceus, who never appears in the play,
is convinced that he is the one in question. He flings himself from the
walls of the city of Thebes in a sacrificial act. Antigone begs her beloved Haemon, Creon's other son, to stop her brothers from battling
each other. It is to no avail. Eteocles and Polynices kill each other in
hand-to-hand combat and Haemon, who has tried to separate them, is
killed inadvertently. The agonized Jocasta stabs herself. Creon, whose
way to the throne is now clear, asks Antigone, whom he covets, to share
it with him. After learning of Haemon's death, however, she takes the
very dagger used by her mother to end her own life. Creon dies.

✦ ✦ ✦

In the preface Racine wrote to *The Theban Brothers* in 1676,
twelve years after its first production, he discusses the essential differences between his own extremely simple conception of the Theban
story and that of Rotrou (1609–1650), author of the play *Antigone*.
Racine was intensely interested in expurgating all irrelevant details
from the essential conflict. Therefore he did not have Eteocles and
Polynices die at the beginning of Act III as did his contemporary because, he declared, the remainder of the play would have been like the

"beginning of another tragedy." Racine wanted the action to be simple. He therefore rejected complicated plots and, because of his keen interest in focusing all attention on one action, further departed from Rotrou's conception which, he declared, included "two different actions," one drawn from Euripides' *The Phoenician Woman* and the other from Sophocles' *Antigone*. Because Racine did not want anything to detract from the very life-blood of the incidents portrayed, he based his play almost exclusively on *The Phoenician Woman*.

Certain critics of the period had been quite shocked by what they felt was the "bloody nature" of Racine's play. Some were offended by the seemingly overt disregard of the all-important rules of "*bienséances*," which required an atmosphere of decorum on stage at all times as well as the maintenance of the dignity inherent in the art of tragedy. Dueling on stage, therefore, was forbidden. Yet, in Act IV, iii, Polynices and Eteocles draw swords in the height of passion.

Racine, somewhat on the defensive, explained that the Oedipus legend upon which his play had been based was one of the most tragic in antiquity. He could not, therefore, do otherwise than to express the utter *cruelty* of such beings. Certainly, Racine did not want to alienate his audiences by offending their sensibilities. On the contrary he sought to attract spectators, as is natural for any young writer. Yet, he himself was a man of passions and anxieties, and he had to contend with these also. Perhaps this is why he declared so outspokenly that "hatred" was the topic of his play and not "love," which was the theme of the works of so many of his contemporaries.

For Racine *The Theban Brothers* must be looked upon as "a first-born"—with tenderness and solicitude, yet as an instrument harboring its creator's characteristics and traits. *The Theban Brothers* in many respects is an aesthetic "living out" of Racine's own drama, his own rebellion. Racine was fighting two opposing forces within himself: that one inculcated in him by his Fathers at Port-Royal, consisting of self-abnegation, arduous disciplines, meditation, and solitude; the other, offered by the beguiling city of Paris and its artistic fare, encompassing creativity, joy, and a gregarious existence.

I

Considered in its broadest sense, *The Theban Brothers* is a power struggle between two opposing groups: the aggressively "heroic" and the pacifist elements within man and society. Both are destroyed, sacrificed, or swallowed up in the process, because neither, evidently, represents a viable or fecundating viewpoint.

Though the transposition and adaptation of Greek and Roman subjects were stylish in the seventeenth century[4] and Racine certainly wanted to create a reputation for himself, a still more valid reason for his returning to the Greeks for inspiration might be due to his upbringing at Port-Royal. There, he had bathed in Greek literature, committing to memory nearly entire plays of Sophocles and Euripides. He therefore felt very secure in their world which, like his, was flooded with a sense of doom, fatality, destiny . . . *hate.*

Hate, considered in a general sense, implies opposition (or duality) between two forces in the universe. Such duality or opposition in nature causes activity just as friction generates a form of energy, electricity. If opposition is nonexistent, then so is action. Motion, looked upon as perpetual combat or destruction, is a process which is implicit in the cosmic flow—in life. There arises, on the other hand, an equally strong drive for unity or synthesis from such antagonism between opposing entities in the universe. Unity predominates in the phase of preexistence known as the *void,*[5] before creation and differentiation occur. Since life as we live it daily implies a state of differentiation and activity, oneness is incompatible with it.[6]

Combat, therefore, is essential as a natural life force. It is the nature and ferocious intensity of this struggle which is of import in Racine's *The Theban Brothers.*

Eteocles and Polynices are at the threshold of life and intend to live it strongly. Hate, or the force expended in giving rise to this emotion, is the brothers' motivating urge. Each is endowed with enormous amounts of this energy (both physical and psychic) and each seeks to use it in order to accomplish his goal of self-fulfillment. The obstacle lying in his path—the other brother—must therefore be destroyed.

In that Eteocles and Polynices are endowed with dynamism, in that they are filled with gusto and the vitality of youth, they can be considered as challengers of fate, active figures fighting desperately for independence, would-be heroic types. Furthermore, they are powerful beings able to destroy or dispose of the dangers implicit in a world dictated by fate and immersed in unknown factors. Neither, however, can ever become a hero because he can never succeed in liberating himself from the other, from his origins, nor develop any kind of consciousness or self-knowledge.

Eteocles and Polynices have primitive personalities. Unlike other brother teams (Osiris=good, Set=evil; Cain=tiller of the soil. Abel= keeper of the flock, etc.), Oedipus' sons are identical twins. Neither brother has any *real* individual characteristics outside of purely political differences (Eteocles believes in popular suffrage and Polynices in divine right). Indeed, they stand only one step above the formless matter from which universal order and creation emerge. Eteocles and Polynices can be considered as potential personalities, "base" or "primitive" powers ready to erupt like volcanoes at a moment's notice. It is this factor that led them to begin fighting as far back as in their mother's womb. Eteocles asserts (Act IV,i):

> Such hate was born with us; and its dark fury
> With life itself flowed deep into our hearts.
> From tenderest infancy we stood forth foes,
> Indeed, we were so even before our birth:
> Fatal and tragic brood of incestuous blood!
> While one same womb was still enclosing both,
> In our mother's flesh intestinal war
> Engraved on her the source of our contentions.[7]

Such anthropoid psyches as they have compel them to experience their impulses intensely. Eteocles and Polynices are beings whose flesh holds together two disparate polarities: the divergencies between the goal each has set for himself and the reality of their present situation. The dynamism emerging from this inner struggle—to bring forth unity out of an essentially antagonistic situation—is externalized and becomes manifest in the violence of their actions.[8]

The personalities of Eteocles and Polynices do not evolve during the course of the drama. Their physical activity is frenetic and, therefore, cannot be used positively. Ordinarily, conflict, when channeled, implies growth. In their case, however, it is used negatively and, consequently, their inner world remains virtually static. Eteocles and Polynices are, psychologically speaking, stunted human beings. No compromise is possible between them because each is possessed and obsessed with the same desire to become King.

What does *kingship* or the *kingly* function symbolize? What magnetic qualities does such a position possess, that two brothers are willing to kill each other for it?

Power is the allurement. Neither Eteocles nor Polynices is equipped with the qualities necessary to fulfill such a position and, therefore, they will be destroyed in attempting possession of it. Symbolically, the role of King represents the ruling or the governing principle within man: supreme consciousness or self-awareness, sound judgment and self-control. As King, an individual assumes "god-like" qualities and attracts a supernatural aura about him.[9] He becomes an ideal for the masses. When clothed in this supreme ruler's function he must, of necessity, lose his personal and mortal stature and, in so doing, take on collective and eternal traits.

Neither Eteocles nor Polynices is endowed with the qualities necessary for kingship. For this reason they fail to win the title permanently. Eteocles does in fact temporarily occupy the throne, for one year. When he is obliged to defend his kingship, he proves incapable of the challenge presented by his brother. Devoid of judgment and self-control, attributes of the true King, Eteocles can only muster the extreme energy at his command; that is, frenetic dynamism which lives within the dismal depths of his unconscious and which, if properly channeled, might have brought him fulfillment. Because of the lack of relationship between the undeveloped judging function in the personalities of the two brothers and their highly activated and motivated "libido" (psychic energy), they lose all sense of proportion and, worse, all rapport with reality.

To be *King* calls for independence of personality, subjection to no inner or exterior force. In the case of Eteocles and Polynices, instincts remain their masters. They are governed or victimized by their seething power drives. Neither brother can ever develop because neither has learned the lesson that Siegfried, for example, expended his energies to experience: "fear," an attitude instilled in man when he becomes conscious of the *Self*, when he learns to differentiate between the various life activities both within and exterior to himself. Such a lesson helps separate instinctual man, who lives in an undifferentiated world, from the "reasonable" being worthy of the title of King.

Eteocles and Polynices, then, have not grown beyond the stage of the adolescent hero. Neither brother is able to cope maturely ("reasonably") with his will to power, each must behave like a child, resorting to bodily conflict. Creon declares (Act V, iii), "The Princes both, stormed out to rend each other."[10] Polynices uses brute force to obtain his object: blood. "Let blood crown me" (IV,iii). Eteocles expels his venom uncontrollably—"Flee, he must, flee, not merely beat retreat,"[11] —as he is driven by greed: "One reigns on still whenever one once reigns."[12] Neither brother has been able to use his enterprising and fighting nature fruitfully.

Since Eteocles and Polynices are both obsessed human beings, they have failed to gain autonomy over themselves and live independent lives. They are, consequently, not only chained to their unchanneled instincts, but by the same token have never succeeded in breaking away from either their origins or from the personal female figures (Jocasta and Antigone; by implication, the collective female figure), surrounding them. Symbolically speaking, this collective figure is represented by the city of Thebes, over which each brother seeks to rule.

The *city* in general can be looked upon as a mother symbol, a woman who cares for her dwellers as she does for her children. In both the Old and the New Testaments, for example, Jerusalem, Babylon, Tyre, and Rome are all treated as women with varying characteristics and personalities. In *The Theban Brothers*, when Creon tries to convince Eteocles to remain King and fight his brother, Thebes is personified as a woman with tears, fear, and trembling, horrified at the thought of losing her King. "Dreading your death, Thebes is in tears already."[13]

Both Eteocles and Polynices look upon Thebes as a "mother image." Neither has been successfully weaned. Such a close bond implies extreme dependency upon what it (she) represents. The affinity for and reliance upon Thebes felt by the brothers can be expected of a child longing for the maternal breast, but is "killing" to an adult. Indeed, it prevents him from achieving any kind of independence. Similarly, it was as a result of a quarrel over the site of a city that Romulus killed Remus. When considered from this point of view, the son who loves his mother most forcefully is the very one who is destroyed by her: he is in effect encouraging his own obsessive need for her and in turn stifles his own growth and his natural desire for independence and achievement.

Moreover, when a city is conquered by a King, such an act can be looked upon, symbolically speaking, as a marriage between male and female.[14] If Eteocles and Polynices were to become King in turn, they would in effect be continuing the incest motif begun by Jocasta and Oedipus. When, for example, Eteocles asks his mother to reign during his absence from Thebes, this is an indication of an unconscious desire to return to the security of the womb. Since incest leads to regression and finally stagnation, it is incumbent upon the city of Thebes to reject both brothers—the entire family, in fact—as unfit to rule. Interestingly enough, the final battle between the two brothers takes place before the ("her"–"its") walls of Thebes. There, the city looks on majestically and aloofly as the blood bath pursues its course.

> A spot near both the camps beneath the walls;
> And there assuming all their former fury
> Begin at last their dread and dastard duel.
> With threatening gestures and with blazing eyes,
> They seek a passage in each other's breast,
> And, rage alone inciting their strong arms,
> Both seem to hurl themselves, provoking death.[15]

Both Eteocles and Polynices sought to fulfill themselves, to assert their power over destiny and over life's antinomies. They failed in these endeavors because their efforts were unfruitful; their struggle ushered in neither growth nor development. What the two brothers stood for was no longer viable. Indeed, they carried within themselves the very seeds of their own destruction.

✓   ✓   ✓

Creon is the supreme manipulator of both people and events in *The Theban Brothers*. Insidious, hypocritical, sophisticated, suave, he wields his power cerebrally. It is he who sets brother against brother, who teaches Eteocles the art of treachery and deceit—the art of diplomacy.

> Meanwhile, hear what your brother has in plan,
> And hide, my lord, your anger, if you can;
> Pretend . . .[16]

Creon's plans seem to flow unhampered in their "ideal" course: Polynices and Eteocles kill each other in battle, Menoeceus sacrifices himself, Haemon is killed as he tries to separate the warring brothers and thereby eliminates himself not only as a contender for the throne, but for another prize—Antigone. The crown now awaits Creon. With controlled joy he asks her to become his Queen. His extreme happiness, however, is of short duration. Its termination takes place when he learns of Antigone's suicide, after which he does away with himself in order to haunt and torment her in the next world.

Creon feels no remorse, no guilt (even at the death of his two sons, Menoeceus and Haemon). Indeed, he stands "above" or "below" the strictly human level in this respect: he experiences no attachments, no bonds with other mortals save perhaps Antigone, and here too it is only for political ends. He does, however, have a "tragic flaw," to use Aristotle's words: he has eyes only for the throne, which he covets as a miser salivates after gold.

The throne, or kingship, as we have seen, symbolizes not only the governing principle within man but also unity, stability, and a synthesis of conflicting emotions. In certain respects, the throne stands for the opposite of Creon's own inner emotional situation. Creon is possessed of judgment and to a certain extent wisdom. He is not, however, a free man since he is obsessed by a lust for power. Furthermore, he experiences no unity within his own personality. The great grandson of Pentheus, who had been torn to shreds by his mother Agave in a moment of religious frenzy, the brother of the incestuous Jocasta, King of Thebes after Laius' death and forced to abandon it all when Oedipus arrived on the scene, Creon's longing for the security and spirituality symbolized by the throne grows to an extreme.

> The throne was always my most ardent aim:
> I blush to serve where once my fathers reigned;
> I burn to join the rank of my forefathers,
> I dreamt of it the moment I was born.
> For two years now this noble care consumes me;
> I take no step that leads not to the throne:
> I fan the fury of my princely nephews,
> And my ambition is the spur of theirs.[17]

Though their goals are identical, Creon, a master at scheming and deceit, is temporarily at odds with the rash and "headless" adolescents, Polynices and Eteocles. Creon fails to obtain the "crown" because he is as unfit to rule over Thebes as were Oedipus' sons. He too is obsessed with kingship; hence he overly identifies with the city of Thebes and is, therefore, victimized in his own cerebral way by the "mother image" which the city represents.

Neither Eteocles, Polynices, nor Creon are *free* individuals; they are oblivious to the judgment principle in man which would have enabled them to assume a just kingship.

Jocasta, Antigone, Haemon, and Menoeceus (though the latter is only mentioned in the play) are peace-seekers: compromisers, sacrificial and relatively passive creatures. They are not molders of destiny, but rather ineffective entities, always trying, but never succeeding in doing good. Each in turn will lose his struggle to the impulsive and instinctual aspect within man—as represented by Eteocles, Polynices, and Creon—and will take his or her own life.

Jocasta, with typical maternal ideals, pleads with her sons throughout the play to choose the course of peace:

> It rests alone on you, if moved by honour,
> To give us peace without recourse to crime,
> And triumphing today over your wrath,
> Content your brother and together reign.[18]

> I am a mother; if I love his brother,
> The king himself is no less dear to me.
> He may be hated by some cowardly courtier;
> But no true mother can betray herself.[19]

She urges her sons to learn to rule together, or, if that proves impossible, to let Eteocles reign and Polynices to carve out his own future elsewhere. So desperate is she to maintain peace and harmony between her sons that she even resorts to threats: she will kill herself, she confesses, should they fail to settle their differences amicably. No matter how hard Jocasta tries, however, war prevails. Such opposition to "mother dominion" is a natural consequence for adolescents and must be considered as part of a natural occurrence. It is the extremes to which the brothers go, however, which makes their rebellion unnatural and destructive.

Antigone also pleads with her brothers to seek peace rather than the sword. Her tactic varies from that of her mother. She tries to touch Eteocles and Polynices, to appeal to their sense of decency and goodness, to their emotions. She is as successful in her pursuits as is anyone who asks a person running a high fever to look at any situation lucidly and objectively. Though Antigone laments the loss of her brothers, she decides to remain alive for Haemon's sake. When she learns of his demise, however, Antigone is no longer interested in partaking of life's experiences. Revolted by Creon's marriage proposal, she takes her own life.

Haemon is also a self-abnegating type. He actively tries to stop the brothers from slaughtering each other. He is cut down on the battlefield, however, at the very moment that he tries to separate Eteocles and Polynices. Haemon is only a follower and not a leader, a youth devoid of sufficient dynamism to act as a counterbalancing principle to the two antagonistic forces, as represented by the brothers. As such, Haemon is ineffective and, consequently, unproductive, and must be destroyed in the course of nature's upheavals.

II

The Theban Brothers is a rather conventional play structure-wise. It begins with the usual exposition and is followed by the introduction of a parade of characters and their reactions to the given situation. Suspense throughout the drama rests on the constant vacillation of two opposing forces: hope and despair. Character delineation intrinsic in Racine's later works and in part responsible for their remarkable quality is virtually absent in *The Theban Brothers*. The creatures conjured forth in this work are like opaque masses, striking at each other blindly, perhaps senselessly, since they, paradoxically, remain in a condition of stasis.

What permits the reader to feel the glow of genius at its inception is, to be sure, the poetry of the lines, their flow, harmonies, modulations and undulations—but also the *images* embedded in them. These exist only in rudimentary form in *The Theban Brothers* since they have not yet been molded into the personalities or the situations dramatized. Yet they indicate the dramatist's future course, revealing his aesthetic approach to drama. For modern directors, Racine's stress on imagery offers enormous staging possibilities.

Racine's image-studded lines in production have heretofore remained enmeshed in the *word*; that is, part and parcel of an abstract notion. They were not endowed with a life of their own; they did not stand out from the lines; and, therefore, they played virtually no part in the drama beyond their quality as words and the appeal this could arouse within the spectator's imagination. As the centuries passed, however, the images seemed to grow hackneyed, uninspired, routinely used, perfunctorily uttered. Audiences and directors alike grew weary of what they called the static quality of Racine's dramas, its lack of action, its ultra long speeches.

Racine's brilliant images have grown tarnished from lack of polish. The grime of age may be removed by means of a visualization, a sonorization, and a stylization of this pictorial approach. The lines are to be spoken, of course, but at the same time the images which make for the dynamism of these phrases must be bodily removed from the realm of the abstract and given form. The director can avail himself of the manifold techniques which are at his disposal in a world so mechanically oriented, in order to perform his magic transmutation. He must change the amorphous into the concrete: sound effects, projections on screens, lighting, waves of heat, cold, showering of water, wind . . . all forces can come into play and are valid when creating the right climate for the drama. The director becomes the alchemist, transmuting the image-word into the material object. Once the task of clothing the immaterial has been accomplished, the image, now a viable force, can enact its own notions, spasms, or can assume any other quality. Like all theatrical entities, it now dwells in the world of matter and as such becomes a protagonist, one with which all the others will have to contend.

Images and the symbolism associated with them exist in embryonic condition in *The Theban Brothers*, ready for a director to concretize them. It is not within the scope of this book to indicate methods with which such transmutation can be accomplished, but merely to point out basic images used by Racine, their meanings and some of their ramifications.

✶ ✶ ✶

Certain images are repeated many times during the course of *The Theban Brothers*: sun, blood, abyss, thunderbolts, torches, etc. At the very outset of the drama, for example, Jocasta bemoans her fate in an apostrophe to the *Sun*. This image, interestingly enough, is going to become the very agent of her destruction.

> O thou, Sun, thou who giv'st the world its light,
> Why hast thou not left it in deepest night!
> On such dark crimes wilt thou shine dazzlingly
> And not shrink back when seeing what we see?[20]

The Sun, as a representative of the heroic principle in nature, is associated with the father-image, the masculine and active elements in the cosmos. Jocasta's personification of this force here and elsewhere attests to her longing for the stability and the power believed to reside in it. In an outburst of despair at her own inability to cope with her forceful sons, she calls for an opposing universal force: *blackness*, "black furor."[21] She questions the Sun's activities, wonders why it did not leave the world in the "deepest night" or in a state of *chaos*, in the depths of an *abyss*, that primal space known as nothingness, that region of "pure absolute Being"[22] before the world was ordered, before *light* and *enlightenment* shone through. In a complex medley of blacks and brilliant rays, Jocasta speaks forcefully of her "monstrous" (rudimentary) offsprings. Powerless, she realizes she can do nothing but try to assume the terrible guilt of incest with its resulting parricide. When, however, she can no longer face up to such a situation, see it in the *light* of reason, she destroys herself physically, but also imagistically before the act. That very Sun, or reason, to which she prayed so fervently for aid in the beginning, has been of no help. Having failed to come to terms with the thinking principle within herself, as represented by the Sun symbolism, having failed to bring forth harmony and balance out of antagonistic forces, she becomes blinded by its radiance. When the clarity of her crime burns before her, it is too potent to bear and she is consumed by it. Her entire existence then unfolds through the Sun image, from the very moment light penetrates into her situation as a radiating force until it scorches and flays her.

Other searing images are also used with extreme vigor. To underline the dangers concomitant with the throne, for example, Jocasta speaks in terms of a "dangerous abyss"[23] surrounded by "thunderbolts," shooting lightning flashing into the blackness of turbulent chaos—all these pointing up the intense activity raging within her psyche. In an apostrophe to heaven to call off its vengeful ways, she indulges in a dynamic series of antithetical images associated with height and depth, light and darkness, spirit and matter, male (heaven) and female (womb or tomb).

> Must these, my fatal cares, for ever last?
> Will the gods' vengeance never be appeased?
> Must I then suffer all these cruel deaths,
> Before they let me sink into my grave? . . .
> If thy bolt crushed the guilty ones outright!
> How infinite thy chastisements appear
> When thou let'st live those writhing in thy fear! . . .
> And must, O gods, an unintended crime
> Drawn down on us your anger for all time?
> Did I know him, alas! the son I wed?
> Yourselves, you led him to my very bed.
> Your spite it was, that brought me to the abyss:
> That vanished justice of the gods is this!
> They lead our footsteps to the edge of crimes . . .
> And, why cannot they, when their furies flare,
> Strike down such criminals as find crime fair![24]

One of the most powerful images in *The Theban Brothers* appears in Creon's speech in the last line of the play:

> . . . . My death will redeem your own death spasm;
> The bolt is falling, earth's a yawning chasm;
> I feel my thousand torments still increase
> And now sink down to hell in search of peace.[25]

Lightning now becomes visible as it falls to the earth ready to receive this destructive though illuminating principle. Creon's excruciating torments and his search for repose in the underworld is again underlined by the juxtaposition of heights ("thunderbolt") and depths ("yawning chasm"), injecting enormous visual dynamism into the picture, concretizing in this manner an abstract sense of terror. ". . . my thousand torments" is reminiscent of needles sticking into flesh and tearing it asunder—a virtual crucifixion, as Creon passes from one world to the next—into "mother earth" or the lower realms. It is interesting to note in this connection that Blaise Pascal, the Jansenist philosopher who had lived at Port-Royal, used a similar image in his *Thoughts* when describing man's precarious state in the universe.

To further increase the sense of imbalance intrinsic to *The Theban*

Brothers, Racine includes sonorous as well as scorching images which fall into the text with deafening pressure, tormenting the protagonists with excruciating force. The repetition of such images as torch, fire, sun, and flame add not only to the general turbulence of the play but to its philosophical import as well. The Sun (or any effulgent image associated with it) not only implies destruction, but purification as well. In this connection, one recalls the torch carried by Hercules to destroy the hydra Lerna—ridding the world of that horrendous beast. Similarly, each protagonist in *The Theban Brothers* is scorched by the Sun and perhaps purified also as it journeys to the lower world, there to be nourished and restored, ready for rebirth in another form.

ィ ィ ィ

The images used by Racine in *The Theban Brothers* are not only a fecund vehicle for a director's work, but a manifestation of the inner struggle Racine was experiencing at this particular time in his life. Without the conflict, the bloodshed, the destruction and concomitant purification as projected onto the events and the people in this work, Racine, the hero-artist, the genius, might never have emerged.

III

The production of *The Theban Brothers* marks Racine's first step in liberating himself from the stranglehold his spiritual fathers had upon him. The poet was breaking the bonds, seeking freedom from the stifling grip of authority. The bundle of warring factions seething within Racine were transformed in the play's *antagonists* (not protagonists), each seeking to destroy the other. His desire for literary success, emotional freedom, adulation—all fought hard against that part of him which still clung to stern authority as represented by his Jansenist Fathers. Racine had not yet been able to abstract himself sufficiently from his own turbulent situation to be able to judge it. The energy from the inner friction he was experiencing was expelled in the form of creatures such as Eteocles, Polynices, Creon, Jocasta, Antigone, and Haemon. Clothed in the flesh of human beings, these essences or sensations were in effect direct emanations from his own unconscious, acting and reacting upon each other as electric currents upon a raw nerve.

A terrible price must be paid for rebellion. To carve out one's own future independently, as every hero and creator must do, is to be strong enough to destroy what holds one in its clutches—to gain victory, thereby, over one's self and one's origins. Such a fight, however, ushers in remorse, guilt, and shame, increasing the crushing pain. As Jocasta says to Creon:

> Not always is your victory so sweet;
> She's often followed by remorse and shame.[26]

The characters in *The Theban Brothers* were destroyed because their points of view were unproductive. For Racine, however, these "antagonists" represented a stage in his development—a struggle to reject the *status quo*. Had his inner conflict perpetuated itself indefinitely, the results would have been as negative in determining Racine's future course as they were for the characters in the play. The living of this painful experience, however, ushered in a positive outcome: its projection into the play—the creation of the work of art.

2

Alexander the Great

"I came in search of glory . . ."[1]

*A*LEXANDER THE GREAT was first produced on December 4, 1665 by Molière's troupe at the Palais-Royal. Less than two weeks later, on December 18, the same play opened at the Hôtel de Bourgogne and was performed by a rival acting company. Both productions were greeted with acclaim. That Racine, however, should have permitted his play to be enacted simultaneously and by competitors was severely criticized. Such an act was considered by some as being treacherous.

The reasons which motivated this unethical state of affairs are moot. True, certain Parisian theatrical companies had for a number of years vied with one another, some going so far as to produce plays dealing with the same subject matter but written by different authors. In the middle of October 1664, for example, the Hôtel de Bourgogne had given *The Coquettish Mother* by Quinault; a week later, the Palais Royal opened with Donneau de Vizé's *Coquettish Mother*. Just before Molière's opening of *Alexander the Great*, the Hôtel de Bourgogne had produced Abbé Claude Boyer's *Alexander the Great*, which had failed miserably. Only after the unfavorable outcome did Molière accept Racine's play on the very same subject. Why Racine acted in such a strange manner and the exact role he played in this rather tenebrous affair is still unclear.[2]

Racine was young and intent upon achieving success, a *conqueror* of sorts, perhaps a pragmatist who felt that any means of achieving his goal was permissible. Success, however, requires sacrifice as well as a certain degree of ruthlessness. An adherence to the strict letter of morality and ethics in this kind of situation is frequently discarded. Racine may never have realized or may not have wanted to acknowledge his debt to Molière, the producer of his first play, *The Theban Brothers*. The outcome of this event was quite critical for Molière. He was in difficult straits financially and was still waiting to receive official permission to produce his play, *Tartuffe*, on which he was relying to ease his economic plight.

When Racine's son wrote his father's biography, *Memoirs concerning Jean Racine's Life*, he excused his father's actions by simply stating that the playwright was "dissatisfied with the actors"[3] in Molière's troupe. This may have been a factor in motivating Racine's actions, for some contemporaries considered the Hôtel de Bourgogne's troupe better suited for tragedies than Molière's company, which remained unrivaled in the field of comedy. Moreover, Pierre and Thomas Corneille, Philippe Quinault, and Gabriel Gilbert all wrote for the Hôtel de Bourgogne.

Racine's departure from the Palais-Royal troupe had other, perhaps even more painful, ramifications for Molière than the simultaneous productions of *Alexander the Great*. One of his leading actresses, Mlle du Parc, followed the miscreant to his new abode, the Hôtel de Bourgogne. Such a loss not only presented difficulties to Molière as director of a theatrical company but dealt him, seemingly, a severe emotional blow.

Mlle du Parc, charming and most beautiful, had not only been the recipient of Molière's affections, but of those of the "great" Pierre Corneille. In fact, when Corneille saw her in Rouen in 1658, he became so enamored of her that he wrote what has become celebrated verse in her honor. Thomas Corneille also succumbed to her charms but in a less flamboyant manner, as did others. Despite these amorati, Mlle du Parc was not what one would term a flighty person. On the contrary, she maintained extreme dignity in her dealings with all the gentlemen involved.

The daughter of an Italian opera singer, Mlle du Parc had married René Berthelot, called du Parc, an actor in Molière's troupe. According to the documents of the day, she was always very nearly faithful to her husband. After his demise in 1664, this attractive thirty-two-year-old widow found herself in a difficult position. Though she rejected the advances made to her by countless admirers, she succumbed to those offered by the twenty-six year old Racine. Their love was reciprocal. For the poet, a new world—the realm of passions—had just revealed itself to him.

So taken was he with fervor for Mlle du Parc and so intent was he in furthering his career, that Racine forged ahead. When breaking bonds with the past, however, when rejecting social structures that

"enchain," one must be strong enough to accept remonstrances, castigations on the part of those who feel that young men are duty-bound to
follow in the tradition of their elders. Racine was beginning to experience these rebukes in a most poignant manner. As a result, he broke
suddenly with Port-Royal.

The seeds of this quarrel with the Jansenist Fathers date back to
1664–1665, the time of the production of *The Theban Brothers*. Racine's aunt, Sister Agnès de Sainte-Thècle, who lived at Port-Royal and
for whom he felt great affection, asked him not to visit her if he
planned to continue his sinful career. In effect, she repudiated him, as
did his Jansenist Fathers. Hurt and rancor must have filled Racine's
heart at what he probably considered an unjust punishment.

Still there was no overt rift with Port-Royal. The tenor began to
alter when the Jansenist moralist, Pierre Nicole, wrote ten anonymous
letters, *Letters on Imaginary Heresy*, in which he defended Jansenist
views. That same year, the popular dramatist Desmarets de Saint-Sorlin
wrote *The Holy Ghost's Advice to the King* (1665) and shortly there-
after an *Apology to the Nuns at Port-Royal*, in which he assaulted Jansenist doctrine as well as Nicole's poor writing style. Nicole retaliated
with a second series of letters, *The Visionaries*, in which he attacked
Desmarets de Saint-Sorlin, author of the comedy *The Visionaries*
(1637), in stinging terms, labeling such novelists and dramatic poets as
"public poisoners . . ."[4]

Racine considered the above statement, intended for Desmarets
de Saint-Sorlin, as a personal attack. One wonders why he reacted in
this manner when there was no mention of his name. He must have felt
extreme guilt vis-à-vis Port-Royal and his former Fathers, who had
nurtured him during so many difficult years. To rid himself of these
unpleasant sentiments, Racine perhaps countered unconsciously with
rising feelings of hatred against his benefactors. How else can one ex-
plain Racine's riposte, the violent *Letter to the Author of the Imaginary
Heresies and the Two Visionaries* (January, 1666). In this devastating
letter Racine expressed his conviction that Jansenism is on the decline,
that Nicole's prose style is inferior and certainly pedantic.[5] Moreover,
he accused Nicole of being jealous of the worldly successes of others
and felt that, since his morality was so austere, his condemning poets
in general was understandable, but not his determination to prevent
others from "honoring them."[6]

The bitterness and pain which spread through Jansenist circles
was swift and penetrating. The Fathers of Port-Royal were seemingly
unable to understand or to accept what they felt to be a vicious and
nefarious assault on the part of one of their sons. Two anonymous and

pro-Jansenist letters were circulated at this time: *Answer to the Letter against the Imaginary Heresies and the Visionaries* (March 22, 1666) and *Answer to the Letter Addressed to the Author of the Imaginary Heresies* (April 1, 1666). These missives not only accused Racine of ridiculing humility, virtue, and penitence, the saintliest of actions and the most Christian of traits and qualities, but of speaking with the vanity of a pagan.[7]

Racine's reply, *Letter to the two Apologists of the Author of the Imaginary Heresies* (May 10), was so vitriolic that his friends, it has been surmised, prevailed upon him not to have it published. Nevertheless, though Racine's answer was never printed, copies of his letter were circulated about Paris. It seems that Racine had in the meantime acquired such a formidable reputation as a polemist that the Archbishop of Paris had offered him a canonry if he would continue his attack on Port-Royal.[8]

✦ ✦ ✦

Criticisms of Racine's iniquities were not limited to his theatrical career nor to his liaison with the beautiful and vivacious Mlle du Parc but reached powerfully into the literary field, perhaps where it hurt him most deeply. *Alexander the Great* was castigated from all directions. Indeed, the battle lines were drawn the evening of the first performance. A pro-Corneille faction had been formed as opposed to the pro-Racine group. The "great" Corneille's followers did not want any injury done the older dramatist's reputation by the emergence of Racine, who must have posed some threat even at this early date. For this reason, they sought if not to destroy Racine as an author, at least to maim him as best they could.

Saint-Evremond, one of the wittiest spokesmen in France and a man who venerated Corneille, felt that anyone who veered from the path trod by such a formidable dramatist was misguided. In a letter to Mme Bourneau (1665), he expressed his surprise at the amount of praise heaped on Racine's play. He had found *Alexander the Great* worthy of neither praise nor censure; it was simply mediocre. The characters, he maintained, were cold and lifeless, unable to involve the spectator in any way: Porus, one of the protagonists, the so-called "Indian Prince," was "purely French" judging from his speech and his demeanor; as for the play itself, it was a bundle of banalities.[9]

Other detractors came forth reprehending the young dramatist for having simplified his plot unduly, for his lack of poetic power, for having paid no attention to historical details, for his flagrant disavowal of the rules of *bienséances* which, because of such an omission, shocked audiences unduly. . . .

There were others, such as the King and Madame, Le Grand Condé, his son the Duc d'Enghien, the Queen of Sweden, and Madame de Sévigné, who lauded Racine's endeavors. The satirist Boileau, Racine's good friend, labeled critics obtuse, crude, and unimaginative in his *Satire III* (lines 185–186).

Racine was not a passive being in any sense of the word. He took up his own defense in the two prefaces he wrote to *Alexander the Great* (1666–1676). He stood up with cudgel in hand, very neatly dealing each of his detractors a blow: "One does not make such a fuss over a work when one does not admire it."[10] He went on to make short shrift of other pretentious critics who considered themselves authorities on Aristotle's *Poetics* and "who claim to subject public taste to the tastelessness of a sick mind"[11]—theirs of course. Racine defended every aspect of his play: its title, its characterizations, its simplified action, and its historical veracity. As for the later point, he declared, he had consulted such historians as Quintus Curcius and Justinian: they had written about Alexander the Great's Indian campaign, his battle on the bank of the Hydaspus River, his victory over two Indian princesses, his act of clemency. Mention had also been made of Cleophilia, an Indian Princess, who had gone to see Alexander when her kingdom was being besieged by him. He not only returned it to her, but they fell in love. From this union was born a son whom she called Alexander. The second Indian Queen who figures in Racine's play is imaginary.

✦ ✦ ✦

Racine's plot follows the very same lines.

Act I. Cleophilia, an Indian Princess, had fallen in love with Alexander and he with her when she had been his prisoner. She was returned home when the time warranted. Some years later, as the play opens, when Alexander is about to invade India, she is dismayed to learn that her brother Taxiles wants to fight Alexander's oncoming armies. Cleophilia, on the contrary, rejoices at the thought of seeing her beloved. She persuades her brother to ally himself with Alexander, affirming that such an act will not indicate cowardliness on his part but rather insight. Porus, an Indian King who considers Alexander a tyrant, will fight the would-be master of the world. He looks upon the sister-dominated Taxiles with contempt. Axiana, another Indian Queen who is loved by both Porus and Taxiles, has not yet decided to which of the two she will award her affections nor what political point of view she will adopt.

Act II. Cleophilia, who has not seen Alexander since the early days of their passion, wonders whether he still loves her. Ephestion, Alexander's envoy, assures her of the Macedonian monarch's continued love. When he asks Porus to render Alexander homage, Porus refuses to do so.

Act III. Taxiles, now on Alexander's side, takes Axiana, whom he loves, as his prisoner. Infuriated by what she considers a contemptible act of cowardliness, she openly declares her hatred for him. Alexander arrives and confesses his love for Cleophilia. As he talks, however, of further conquests in the same breath, she wonders why glory and fame seem more important to him than their love.

Act IV. Alexander wins his battle against Porus. Axiana, believing Porus dead, feels guilty toward him because she had never confessed her love for him.

Act V. Taxiles, who had wanted to be worthy of Axiana's love, provokes Porus, who kills him on the battlefield. Alexander pardons Porus and returns his kingdom to him. Axiana declares her love for him. Deeply moved by Alexander's act of clemency, Porus decides to fight alongside the conqueror.

I

The theme of Racine's *The Theban Brothers* was "hatred," conflicting forces in nature which ended destructively for the play's "antagonists" but constructively for Racine in terms of the work of art. The same dynamic quality, though muted and channeled to a great extent, is present in his *Alexander the Great*. The "Solar" force in this work is, of course, Alexander the conqueror. Like Creon in *The Theban Brothers*, he is less involved in the turbulent situation; unlike him, however, he remains the focal point of the conflict. Moreover, in *The Theban Brothers* there is only one conflicting pair of entities—the enemy brothers. In *Alexander the Great*, there are two sets of doubles: Cleophilia and her brother Taxiles, and Porus and Axiana. What determines their relationships to a great extent is the attitude they bear toward Alexander.

Alexander the conqueror, looked upon symbolically, is an aggressive and creative element in nature. A subduer of a mighty steed (Beucephalus), a military genius, a vanquisher of worlds (Greece, Syria, Egypt, Babylonia, Susa, Persepolis, parts of India),[12] he is the corporeal manifestation of youth, its irrepressible force, its brilliant and mighty energy. He is in many respects comparable to Paul Claudel's character Christopher Columbus in the play of the same name—a being capable of making or breaking worlds.

Alexander is a more complex personality type than either Eteocles or Polynices. A double rather than a single force motivates Alexander's actions: one dominant (conquest) and the other secondary (love). The Theban brothers were so obsessed with their own hatreds that they could not even begin to project upon anyone else. They lived imprisoned in their own circumscribed world. Alexander, on the contrary, is not only detached from his family, his origins, and his environment, but feels at home in the world at large. Endowed with extreme speed, restlessness, and an unlimited desire for conquest, his activities never seem to diminish. Energy, at such high voltage, cannot maintain its intensity for long periods of time and for this reason this kind of hero must of necessity die or burn out at a young age.[13]

Heroes, as stereotyped figures, whether historical or mythical (David, Arthur, Siegfried, Roland, etc.), usually pass through certain phases in their development toward maturation. Eteocles and Polynices are examples of a hero's first phase of growth. They are comparable to two young buds struggling to extract themselves from their earthbound natures, from submersion and identification with their worldly parents (in the form of mother, city, father, etc.). A struggle is required to break forth from such constricting entities into society, thereby paving the way for independence (a situation basic to the hero's personality). Such conflict is painful since it ushers in feelings of guilt and remorse at one point or another. Eteocles and Polynices, though living out their aggressive acts of war, trying their best to destroy their bridges, are unsuccessful in their attempts, which end in self-destruction. They are incapable of seeing beyond themselves, incapable of relating to others and of responding to the warmth of love or to any *feeling* but that of hate. The dynamism inherent in their struggle, however, indicates an unconscious desire to grow—the germs of liberation are there.

The second stage of a hero's development corresponds to the Alexander before the act of clemency. At this period in his growth he is still in the process of seeking out his identity. The more conscious he becomes of *self*, the greater are his powers of differentiation between his world and that of his fellow beings. While his "libido" (psychic energy) is still working full force, trying to swallow up the outside world, he is concomitantly trying to understand it, assimilate aspects of it which will be beneficial to his own growth process. He is capable of relating to others, of living with them. The world does not pose a threat to him.

Therefore, he is no longer its destroyer. His acts take on a positive turn.

The third and most noble phase in a hero's maturation process takes place when he is able to integrate the disparate forces, feelings, and passions within his own personality. In Alexander's case he becomes liberated from passionate feelings of conquest and of fear. His act of clemency is termed "sublime," as indeed it is. It shows that the "judging principle" or the "thinking element" within man can work harmoniously with his physical and sensual side. It also indicates the fact that Alexander has now become a fulfilled human being.

When Alexander first comes upon the scene, audiences do not know what to expect. He is a rather ambiguous figure. Some of the protagonists revile this conqueror for the decimation he has left in his wake. Others look upon him as the spreader of culture and enlightenment, as charming and romantic.[14] When listening to his first words one is disconcerted by the polarity existing between the gentleness of what he says and his volcanic activities as a warrior. He states emphatically his willingness to return the crowns he has conquered, his profound love for Cleophilia.

> But at the same time, do you not remember
> You promised me a place within your heart?
> Now I have come: yes, love has fought for me;
> And victory has itself redeemed my faith;
> Before you, all yields; you too must surrender;
> Your heart has promised, would it now deny?
> Ah, could your heart alone elude today
> An ardent conqueror, seeking it alone?[15]

Cleophilia, perhaps more subtle in the ways of men, declares that Alexander's true motivations are not love but rather glory, honor, and conquest. He is quick to deny this assumption and affirms vehemently that such an attitude, though true in the past, is no longer exact at present.

> I will admit at one time, while at war,
> My heart could dream of nothing else than fame;
> Peoples and kings, subjected to my rule,
> Alone were worthy objects of desire.[16]

If Alexander's assertion is really the case, then his entire frame of reference will of necessity be altered. As yet, however, one is unable to assess his contention at full value: his actions still belie his point of view. Alexander, for example, still loves to fight, as does a true warrior, and thrives on the challenges offered him. One must, however, make a distinction here between the battles waged by Eteocles and Polynices, which were provoked by hatred and a power lust, and those of Alexander, based on an intense desire to live life fully. The return of the conquered territory to the Indian Princess attests to this fact. Alexander's conquests are, in essence, immensely extraverted acts, an outward manifestation of an inner dynamism. This results in the participant's being permitted to experience that part of the world which he seeks to integrate within his own personality and which would have remained unknown to him without the performance of an overt act of great magnitude. To live violently, passionately, restlessly, to struggle, to combat—winning always, as in Alexander's case—is his way of immersing himself into life's flow. Indeed, he admits enjoying his struggle with Porus, just as the latter takes pleasure in fighting the Macedonian monarch: "We sought each other out . . ."[17] Alexander is particularly excited by this conflict because of the admiration he feels for his enemy.

> And I dare say, in losing victory,
> My foe himself has seen his glory grow;
> So fine a fall has raised his reputation.[18]

Had the Indian Prince been weak, Alexander's lust to win would not have been so fierce. Because he succeeded in subjecting him, his own power was heightened in terms of himself as well as his entourage. Certainly, he sees in Porus a double, a mirror image of himself, a proud conqueror who is able to assess his own work but whose ego has not run rampant.

Alexander is not comparable to the Prometheus hero type who has to sacrifice so much to accomplish his act of liberation, nor can he be likened to the ego-centered Don Juan figure whose lust for evildoing places him beyond the mortal sphere. Alexander is a wanderer, a restless being trying desperately to satisfy his unquenchable desire for self-fulfillment.

Furthermore, Alexander is a creative person in his own way if we consider the tension which unleashes an act and which is necessary to its accomplishment as fruitful. Psychologically speaking, the energy expended in sparking off the act has vast ramifications: it activates heretofore dormant areas within the psyche. "Psychic elements that were unused, repressed, despised, undervalued" now come into focus and take on renewed life.[19]

In Alexander's case, the actual release of energy is creative because it has ushered in a new point of view. Rather than subjugate his victims after each conquest, he learns to treat them with kindness and understanding. If conquest is looked upon symbolically as an acquisitive act, then Alexander has evolved in his struggle for independence. He has not only succeeded in assimilating external forces, but has integrated these very same entities. He has, therefore, gone beyond a mere thirst for possession; he is no longer a storage house or repository for *things*, but rather has learned to put them to use, drawing sustenance from them. Such an outlook is obvious when he tells Axiana that he seeks to conquer but not to kill, to possess but not to destroy.

> I sought out Porus, true: say what you will,
> I did not seek him out for his destruction.
> I will confess, a glutton for renown,
> I was led on by rumours of his battles;
> The mere name of a king, till then unconquered,
> Drove my heart on to tackle fresh exploits.[20]

Another dimension is added to Alexander's personality with the enactment of clemency: it reveals his ability for self-possession. The accomplishment of this altruistic act does not come easily to Alexander. When, for example, Porus loses the battle to him, the Macedonian's first impulse is an absolutely human one—he wants to destroy his enemy. Cleophilia rebukes the conqueror for his destructive outlook. Where will war lead? this thirst? this restlessness?

> What, my lord, forever wars on wars;
> Do you seek subjects even in the stars?
> Do you want as witness of your splendid show
> Regions their very peoples hardly know?
> What do you hope to fight in climes so rude?
> They will oppose to you vast solitude,
> Dim deserts never brightened by the sky,
> Where nature seems herself to droop and die.[21]

To struggle for anything (power, love, etc.) is efficacious for one's development provided it leads to self-fulfillment or gives one a modicum of satisfaction. To indulge in unchanneled conflict (Eteocles and Polynices) is to yield to an inner dynamism inherent in the personality, to become enslaved by passion's autocratic hold. Liberation cannot ensue when a complex takes hold of an individual. Mastership and conquest over self, therefore, becomes more difficult than domination over others. Racine most certainly understood this truth intellectually, but judging from his own activities at this point and his future protagonists, he had not yet assimilated its impact emotionally. Alexander is unlike any of Racine's future heroes. He was certainly modeled on Caesar Augustus in Corneille's *Cinna*,[22] a semi-god who forgave the conspirators who had tried to kill him and in this manner reached the ultimate in earthly power. Racine has attempted a similar solution in his play: the elevation of Alexander to the rank of sublime hero. Such an outcome, though perfectly fitting to Corneille's drama since his protagonists were always in the process of overcoming difficulties in their battle with destiny, sounds a false note in Racine's work. In *The Theban Brothers* the heroes were negative, powerless over the forces of destiny and most particularly over themselves. In *Alexander the Great* the outcome is quite different and actually alien to the hero's personality. There is, therefore, an artificial quality, something contrived, about Alexander. He is not a *genuine* Racinian creature. Alexander's wisdom is such that he resembles Solomon; his vigor is so enormous as to be comparable to the youthful David. Never again will this melange appear in a Racinian drama, except perhaps in splintered form, scattered throughout the disjuncted, fragmented beings peopling his world.

✟ ✟ ✟

Porus and Taxiles, though descendants of Eteocles and Polynices, live on a higher level. The Theban twins were circumscribed in their actions, subjugated by their ego, unable therefore to extract themselves from their inner dominion, incapable of assessing themselves or their acts. Moreover, they were nearly identical in points of view. The Indian princesses, on the other hand, are entities unto themselves; each is individualized. Porus, Alexander's mirror image, expresses the positive force, and Taxiles the negative.

Similarities between Alexander and Porus are reflected in certain parallel scenes and situations. When, for example, in Act I, iii, Porus tells Axiane of his intentions to fight Alexander and in so doing uses such terms as "glory" and "death," Axiane feels that his zest for battle is greater than his feelings for her. A parallel remark is made by Cleophilia when speaking with Alexander in Act III, vi. Both women object in reality to the fact that they do not occupy the center of their lovers' universe, that they do not possess complete dominion over them.

Porus knows no conflict. A man fired with hatred for Alexander, he sees him only as a destroyer of peace, a pillager of provinces, an insatiable being attracted to war, a torrent, a fury, a fire. He does not, therefore, hesitate for one moment before marching his 50,000 foot soldiers, his 200 elephants, his 300 chariots, and his archers to the banks of the Hydaspus River.

> Before his fury ravaged all the earth,
> Indus enjoyed a universal peace . . .[23]

Yet his hatred is blended with a feeling of admiration. Porus is impressed, even dazzled by Alexander's might. Such feelings inspire Porus with fear and also excitement, thereby stirring other emotions within him which serve to further incite his fighting spirit.

Taxiles, Porus' opposite, is sister-dominated. He is a weakly structured individual, still under the dominion of the world parent. In his case, his sister can be looked upon as a type of mother whose weighty control he has never succeeded in overthrowing. Cleophilia, therefore, persuades him with ease to assess his situation rationally. She convinces him that to war against a conqueror such as Alexander is to seek death. Taxiles is clever, however. In order to accept his own cowardliness without feeling degraded by his lack of fortitude, he formulates his own dialectic: appeasement, flattery, respect for the conqueror, and a sincere belief, at this particular moment at least, that peace is the best way to handle the situation. Furthermore, he looks upon the cultural benefits which would accrue from Alexander's domination, the trade routes which would be reactivated, etc. Taxiles is a collaborator type— present in all ages and in all countries—who is blind to his own inadequacies.

Taxiles, then, is a being unable to cope with the sweeping energy coming from the West in the form of Alexander. He buckles under before this invader, whom he describes variously as a "thunderbolt," a "torrent," a "noise."[24]

Porus meets force with force. He is not fearful of his enemy, but only of Taxiles because he is weak. He considers such "flabbiness" of character tantamount to treachery, and therefore evil. Strangely enough, Porus can cope with the fighting heroic type such as Alexander, but cannot enter into combat with deceit or cunning, subtleties of the type in which Taxiles indulges. Taxiles, in this respect, is a germ —in the most primitive form—of what is to become the *evil* force in Racine's future works.

Taxiles' treachery is apparent on two occasions in particular. When, after Alexander's arrival, he imprisons Axiana, whom he loves, he commits a sadistic act which binds him to his own impotence. The second instance takes place when Axiana expresses her love for Porus and her disdain for Taxiles and his fleshy, flabby self. Having dashed his artificially inflated ego to the ground, Taxiles runs to his sister (mother), demonstrating his utter inability to cope with his situation. He blames Cleophilia for his misery, as Adam had accused Eve for having encouraged him to eat of the apples: "But for your counsel sister that betrayed me . . ."[25] Having known *authentic* pain for the first time, he cannot seem to bear its cutting edges and so he rushes forth to fight, whereupon he is killed in hand-to-hand combat by his chief rival, Porus.

Porus, the creative and positive side of the double figure, survives, whereas the unproductive, negative aspect, Taxiles, is submerged through death.

✓ ✓ ✓

Cleophilia and Axiana are no longer rudimentary figures as were Jocasta and Antigone in *The Theban Brothers*, nor are they complex, in the sense of a Phaedra or a Berenice. They do not experience conflict in any profound sense, yet they are endowed with an awareness of their plight.

Cleophilia is a woman in love. Unsure of the outcome of her passion, fearful that the months of separation from Alexander might have caused his passion to diminish, she tries not only to possess the situation in which she finds herself, but to manipulate as many elements as she can to work in her favor. She accomplishes this goal by the artful handling of her brother to serve her own ends. Though her actions are allegedly motivated by her love she is not an obsessive, uncontrollable type, a being driven blind, as so many of Racine's future heroines will be. On the contrary, she is a strange combination. When it is a question of furthering the interests of her love, she is a loving woman and a lucid, cold, and calculating person at the same time. When, for example, she tries to convince her brother to adopt the course of appeasement, she stresses Alexander's positive qualities: his kindness, the fact that he is bringing the benefits of culture to their country, the foolhardiness of resistance when faced with such formidable odds—a man who "burns to see the universe subjected,"[26] a being who attracts "victory" to himself.[27]

Actually, Cleophilia plays a dual role in her brother's life, that of mother and sister. She is his family, the only one to whom he is able to turn, her victim in effect. She knows just how to provoke and persuade him, to deny and to anger him.

Cleophilia's outwardly collected attitude toward her brother undergoes subtle gradations. Under certain circumstances, for example, she resembles Taxiles. Anxious and ingenue-like particularly when it is a question of her love for Alexander, she acts in a most feminine manner—demurely, "weakly." In the beginning, she desperately wants to know whether Alexander still loves her and cannot rest until she finds out. In Alexander's presence she becomes soft and lovable, a tender and most attractive woman. Like her brother, Cleophilia is not "free" in the sense that both Porus and Alexander are. She is a "prisoner" of love. Such an idea is compatible with the role she had played vis-à-vis Alexander before the outset of the play, when she had really been his captive. Though no longer confined in her actions in the physical sense, she is still very much bound in a psychological sense. Her rapport with Alexander, therefore, has in no way been altered during the course of the years. Indeed, she thrives on this spiritual "imprisonment" or love-bondage.

Axiana, as opposed to Cleophilia, is a rather hard, selfish, demanding, and unyielding woman. She is unwilling to divulge her love to Porus though she knows such knowledge would relieve him of great anxiety. She prefers keeping both Porus and Taxiles dangling on a string for whatever "sadistic" joy she might experience. Nevertheless, her feelings can be aroused, as indeed they are when Porus begins talking of his desire to fight the conqueror. Axiana's inflated pride suddenly vanishes and she feels the hurt and resentment of neglect.

> No, jealous of his fame, I would not dream
> To stay a hero bent on victory.[28]

She now seeks revenge on the very one she loves and therefore permits him to leave for battle without confessing her passion. When, however, she fears him dead, she is filled with pangs of guilt. Axiana now knows remorse. She tries to circumvent these "new" feelings by rationalizing the motives of her action. It was Porus, she maintains, who instilled a desire for honor and glory in her and relegated love to a secondary role.

> I read my sighs as yearning but for glory;
> I thought this, all I love.[29]

Axiana's dialectics are complicated. She claims that Porus instilled a love of glory within her, that she had learned to consider power, honor, and success the *sine qua non* of love relationships. Such rationalizations are indeed true of Corneille's heroes and heroines, who are forever straining their wills to dominate situations, whose love is based on admiration and pride, who mold destiny according to their insights and subjugate their passions as they do so. For Racine, however, Axiana learns a lesson from Porus' departure for battle—that abstract notions (glory, power) do not make for happiness; that neither the "idea" nor the "ideal" is the promulgator of Axiana's love, but rather Porus the

man. To live life fully, she has now learned, one must touch, eat, enjoy
everything given one to the heights to which one's personality permits.
Life requires activity and physical relationships, not merely ideational
quiddities. This newfound attitude does not for a moment detract from
the fact that Axiana is a Queenly type and never for a moment loses the
dignity with which her title is vested.

Axiana, in many ways, resembles Porus. Neither character gives
in to feelings of tenderness except on very rare occasions, when both
have reached extremes of tension. Both display courage to the point of
heroism. Before Porus leaves for battle, for example, Axiana affirms her
intention of persuading Taxiles' army to fight against Alexander, thereby asking his army to betray their Prince. Such courage on the part of
a woman might appear extraordinary today, but was not really for
seventeenth century standards. After all, Mlle de Montpensier, la
Grande Demoiselle, daughter of Gaston d'Orléans, stood on the plat-
form in front of the Bastille at the time of the "Fronde," a parliamentary
revolution, and ordered the soldiers to fire on the royal troops.

Axiana has the courage of her convictions. She is unruffled and
unafraid to speak the truth. When Taxiles' prisoner, she belittles him
for his ignominious act, rebels against the curtailment of her power,
and provokes him to the very end of his endurance by confessing her
love for Porus.

> I worship him! and, by the end of the day,
> At once my hatred and my love will say;
> Will vow to him my firm love in your view,
> And near him swear undying hate for you.[30]

Axiana is not fearful of Cleophilia. Indeed, she harangues her,
does her best to hurt her, castigates her for dominating that fleshy
mass, Taxiles, who succumbs to the "ruses of his sister."[31] Each woman
is in fact jealous of the other; each would like to dominate the other in
particular and the situation in general.

It is Axiana who precipitates the finale and resolves the situation.
As she reviles Taxiles, she arouses something which had been slumber-
ing within his egoless depths: pride. Her words of condemnation trigger
Taxiles' self-esteem, or what is left of it. As a result, he blazes like
those horses who see flame about them—too late, however. He had
rushed forth to oppose what had already come to fruition, to overthrow what had already been solidly built. With his death, the negative
force in *Alexander the Great* slips into oblivion, whereas the more
powerful and relatively positive personalities remain, each having
found the mate of his choice.

II

Though little internal conflict or suspense is evidenced in *Alexander the Great*, there is, nevertheless, a marked development in technique and character building over *The Theban Brothers*. To increase the halo of glory surrounding Alexander, to underline the remoteness and power of this kingly being, Racine has him appear for the first time in Act II, iv. Tensions, therefore, are allowed to bubble. Audiences wonder about him. They know him only through a medley of variegated opinions: Cleophilia, who loves him, considers him the most formidable and marvelous force in the universe; Porus, whose empire he seeks to conquer, despises what he believes to be a monstrous, violent, and bloodthirsty being; because of her love for Porus, Axiana despises the Macedonian monarch; Taxiles' attitude is passive. The reactions to the conqueror are baffling at first, but are clarified as time goes on.

The scenes in *Alexander the Great* are cleverly manipulated, more closely linked. One seems to emerge directly from the other and, frequently, as a reply to it. Moreover, the characters themselves are no longer anthropoid types. They are sharply delineated, variously faceted, and they usually act and react in accordance with the characters Racine has projected onto them. Axiana, for example, is of great interest not only because of the problems which face her, but also in that she is a forerunner of certain heroines in Racine's future works. Her rapport with the other protagonists in the drama, Cleophilia in particular, experiences rather minute gradations. On the other hand, Taxiles is underdeveloped; he is weakly structured and as a result presents little interest to the reader. His fate remains unimportant. Like a dead leaf, he is the prey of the strongest forces of the moment. He is neither pathetic nor dramatic.

Racine's poetic thrust has not yet been launched. Such a condition is felt in his faltering use of symbols and images; these are less well defined than in *The Theban Brothers*, where they are used to support the conflicts of the *dramatis personae*. In Racine's first play, for example, the symbols of the city and kingship were most effectively used as vehicles to foster the tug-of-war nature of this drama. The images used most strikingly in *Alexander the Great* and the symbols associated with them are prison, chain, captive, irons, slave, enclosure, subjugation, subjection, etc. The claustrophobic atmosphere thereby created implies an enormous desire for its opposite, freedom, on the part of the protagonists. Indeed, the characters in *Alexander the Great* are enchained as were Plato's beings in his "Allegory of the Cave," either due to circumstances or because of their own personalities. They seek to break free from the bonds which constrain them, emerge from their shadow existence into light, from unconsciousness to consciousness.

Indeed, the play's central theme resides around the prison-like atmosphere into which the quaternity (Taxiles, Porus, Cleophilia, Axiana) of beings has been thrust for reasons of love or conquest, willingly or not. The manner in which each handles his or her release from bondage leads to the play's *dénouement*. The chains which bind each of the protagonists together are both real, in that Alexander is a conqueror, and also abstract, in that they are imposed upon them by their love or their family ties. Moreover, these forces serve a dual function: they permit or force communication between the protagonists which might not have been so intense had such constraining forces not existed. Chains give birth to a counterforce, and act as a vehicle toward freedom. Racine, however, has not sounded out the situation in sufficient depth to arrive at any conclusion concerning the intensity of the enchainment or the potency of the feelings for liberation to which they give rise. Only one being is really free in this drama: Alexander. He is not subjugated by love but is a true conqueror, adaptable to circumstances and environment. Cleophilia, Taxiles, Porus, and Axiana are all enchained and can only develop or evolve when external circumstances intrude to force them to take a stand.

Racine's personal brand of drama had not yet come into its own. The play's solution, the act of clemency, attests to this fact. It is not a truly Racinian note. Corneille's dialectics as manifested in *Cinna*, most specifically, influenced him in this instance. The emphasis Corneille placed on honor, power, and glory also impressed Racine, who likewise introduced these points of view in the characters of Porus and Axiana, both image-seekers. Their love, or what they considered it to be, was based on the image each had of the other: should this image falter, so might their love. A similar relationship can be found between Chimene and Rodrigue in Corneille's drama *The Cid*. Love, as dramatized in *Alexander the Great*, is not the *sine qua non* for this drama as it will become in most of Racine's later works.

*   *   *

By undergoing the influence of the most popular writer of his day, Racine was yielding to his impulse to curry favor with audiences, betraying perhaps a certain element of authenticity and originality on his part. Yet the flames of Racine's genius smolder in *Alexander the Great*, in his characters' depths one can feel the turbulence which will be implicit in his future beings. Themes are also posed (that of the hero, evil, imprisonment, love, guilt, etc.) which, though they appear in amoeba-like form in *Alexander the Great*, are nevertheless tangible and will inflate in time as the artist gains control over himself and his dramatic technique. Most of all, *Alexander the Great* fascinates because of its central theme, that of *conquest*. It mirrors Racine's own frame of mind at this period. Filled with fire, like his hero, he seeks to conquer Paris, and *nothing* will impede him in his quest.

3

Andromache

"I was then blind;
my eyes are now wide open . . ."[1]

ANDROMACHE was first performed in Madame de Maintenon's apartments on November 17th, 1667. Several days later—the date is uncertain—*Andromache* opened at the Hôtel de Bourgogne. Racine experienced his first triumph. He had conquered Paris.

Racine's success was so stunning that it has been compared to Corneille's achievement with *Le Cid* and to Molière's with *L'École des Femmes*. Praise bubbled forth. La Fontaine spoke favorably of *Andromache* in his work *The Loves of Cupid and Psyche*; L'Abbé de Pure, the reputed author of a parody of Corneille's *Cinna*, extolled it; the writer Boursault likened it in depth to *Le Cid*; Boileau, in his first *Epitre*, pointed to it as the perfect tragedy type.

Success in any form or in any milieu usually breeds hatred. Racine did not avoid such a fate. Paris was divided into two armed camps: the pro-Corneille and the pro-Racine factions. Saint-Evremond, Corneille's nephew and an intense admirer of his uncle's works, declared in a letter to M. de Lionne that if one does not delve too deeply into *Andromache* one can admire it; he further stated that the play's success really rested on the fact that great actors were there to portray the principal roles. To be sure, *Andromache* did mark Mlle du Parc's debut at the Hôtel de Bourgogne. Her performance, it was stated, was exceptionally moving and beautiful. The rest of the cast also proved both dynamic and poignant in their portrayals, though perhaps a bit too old to suit their roles. Pyrrhus, for example, was enacted by the sixty-year-old Floridor; Mlle des Oeillets, forty-six years of age, won laurels with her interpretation of Hermione; the sixty-seven-year-old and enormously fat Montfleury played a moving Orestes and put so much verve into his portrayal, in fact, that he died a little over a month after the opening (December 31, 1667), seemingly from the efforts expended in his performance.[2]

What hurt Racine's reputation as a dramatist most forcefully was Perdon de Subligny's *The Mad Quarrel.* This "slight" piece which opened on May 18, 1668 at Molière's theatre, the Palais-Royal, was not merely a satire on *Andromache*, but a vicious, underhanded attack on Racine the man. It enjoyed notoriety and success, no doubt because it attacked Racine and his work; spectators of all ages and of all times seem to revel in the sport of condemnation.[3]

Racine, who had now entered life's mainstream, must have realized that bitterness, jealousies, rancor are all part of man's world. He had to learn to cope with these mishaps, to become impervious to excoriating statements as well as abrasive forces permeating the air. Popularity sets its price, frequently a high one. Though already accustomed to cutting innuendoes and outright slander, and quite adept at indulging in cruelties in his own right, Racine was not one to bare his breast and await the daggerthrust of his enemies.

Encouraged by the fact that Henriette d'Angleterre, the King's sister-in-law, had become his protectress, he decided in his preface to *Andromache* to subject the critics to their own type of perverse medicine. He systematically planned his counterattack. Pithily he argued against the most outlandish remarks enunciated by those who considered themselves experts in matters of drama.

To the critics who felt he had violated the sacrosanct rule of *vraisemblance* by taking liberties with history, Racine pointed to his sources: Virgil's *Aeneid*, Euripides' *Andromache*, Seneca's *Troades*, Homer's *Iliad*. Though Racine openly admitted modifying certain minor facts, he did not, he affirmed, alter his characters' "moral attitudes" in any way. Such changes as were made by him were justified and in conformity with the temper of the times and his own personal vision of the events and the people he treated in his play. In Euripides' drama, Astyanax is dashed from the walls of Troy by Greek soldiers, Hector dies, Andromache is taken prisoner by Pyrrhus and has a son by him, Molossus. Hermione, in love with Pyrrhus, is determined to kill Andromache, of whom she is jealous, and Molossus. In Racine's version Molossus does not exist; Astyanax does not die but is brought along with his mother to Pyrrhus' kingdom; Andromache only knows one husband, the dead Hector. A mother bemoaning a husband's fate, fearing the death of her only son, Racine declared, is far more dramatic than if she had two of each.

Critics also assailed Racine for having turned Pyrrhus, the "ferocious" Greek hero, into a gallant and "sweetish" lover.[4] Racine admitted he had softened certain harshnesses present in Seneca's portrayal of Pyrrhus because such a cruel being would have been offensive to seventeenth century audiences and would certainly have violated the rules of *bienséances*. Other defamers accused Racine of the opposite crime: of having created an overly ruthless Pyrrhus. To these detractors Racine stated flatly that he did not seek to transform the Greek hero into a honey-sweet, Romanesque figure, a Celadon, a shepherd type depicted so frequently in the novels of the time.[5] Furthermore, he asserted, had Pyrrhus been a *perfect* hero, such a creation would have violated the precepts Aristotle set down for tragedy in his *Poetics* and that were adhered to rigidly by seventeenth century dramatists. A tragic hero, according to Aristotle, could neither be completely good nor totally bad. If he were the former, the punishment dealt him would give rise to indignation on the part of the spectator rather than pity, an absolute requisite for tragedy; if he were the latter, pity could certainly not be elicited because no one would feel sorry for an excessively evil being. Some weakness, therefore, some "flaw" within the hero's character is imperative for tragedy—he must fall upon evil days through some *fault* of his own. Only under such circumstances can "pity and not detestation" be aroused. Racine concluded with a particularly apt quotation from a commentator on Sophocles' works, who stated:

> One must not delight in cavilling at poets for the few changes they may have made in the legend; but rather strive to consider the excellent use they made of these changes, and the ingenious way in which they have modified the legend to suit their theme.[6]

✻   ✻   ✻

Andromache takes place in a chamber in Pyrrhus' palace, situated in Buthrotus, a town in Epirus.

Act I. Pyrrhus would like to marry Andromache, whom he has taken prisoner. She, however, is dedicated to the memory of her dead husband Hector. Her only desire in life is to bring up her son Astyanax. If Pyrrhus marries Andromache, he would be rejecting Hermione, daughter of Helen and Menelaus, who has been sent to his court to become his bride. The Greeks, fearing that Astyanax will one day try to rebuild Troy, demand he be delivered to them. Orestes tells his friend Pylades that he has had himself appointed Ambassador of the Greek cause in order to see his beloved Hermione once again. Though she has always rejected him, Orestes is still passionately in love with her. Pyrrhus wants to force a decision from Andromache and to this end threatens her: he will hand Astyanax over to the Greeks if she does not marry him. Andromache hesitates. Pyrrhus becomes irate.

Act II. Hermione informs Orestes of her intention to follow him on his journeys if Pyrrhus marries Andromache. Orestes rejoices. Pyrrhus, angered with Andromache because of her extreme attachment to her husband's memory, informs Orestes of his decision to deliver Astyanax to the Greeks and marry Hermione.

Act III. Orestes, depressed over the outcome, plans to take matters into his own hands. He will kidnap Hermione. Andromache, beside herself with fright, pleads with Hermione to help save Astyanax. Triumphant now, Hermione rejects Andromache's pleas. Disconsolate, Andromache throws herself at Pyrrhus' feet, beseeching help from him. He repeats his proposition: marry him or lose her son. Andromache rushes to Hector's tomb to seek counsel.

Act IV. Andromache agrees to marry Pyrrhus, but plans to kill herself after the ceremony. Hermione, rejected by Pyrrhus, will marry Orestes if he kills the monarch. Orestes, abashed by such a request, anguishes.

Act V. Andromache and Pyrrhus marry. Orestes kills Pyrrhus after the ceremony. When he informs Hermione of his deed of valor she heaps imprecations upon him rather than the praise he expected. Hermione rushes forth toward the dead Pyrrhus, stabs herself and falls on his corpse. Orestes goes mad. Pylades leads him away. Andromache is greeted by the people of Epirus as their new Queen.

I

Andromache's focal point is love. All in this drama revolves around this single motif. It is endowed with prismatic nuances, gradations ranging from mother love, love for a dead past, erotic love, to blind passion, sadism, masochism—with ramifications such as loss of identity and alienation.

✓ ✓ ✓

Andromache is a fully developed female figure. She is resolute, pragmatic, strong, a most humane mother.[7] She has experienced love as Hector's wife and as Astyanax' mother. In this most important realm she is fulfilled. She seeks to prevent any further mishap, and is determined to do everything within her power to keep her son Astyanax with her. The danger she runs is meaningless. She takes and makes her stand courageously.

The fact that Andromache's life is devoted entirely to the rearing of her son Astyanax can be interpreted in two ways: from a personal as well as from an impersonal point of view. The former implies the very natural love a mother bears her son. The latter may be looked upon in a broader manner, Astyanax representing things to come. The child as the fruit of the union of two individuals is considered to be a positive and productive force—the man of the future.

The drama's immediate conflict arises as a direct result of the two above-mentioned attitudes: the Greeks versus Pyrrhus–Andromache. Andromache sees Astyanax as an individual child. The Greeks look upon Astyanax as a symbol, a collective figure, the harbinger of future creativity which is negative in their case. Since he represents the city they have destroyed, he is to be feared. Troy's possible resurgence plagues them. Such a possibility can come to pass if Astyanax were to grow up and become the hero his father had once been. The Greeks, therefore, are adamant upon destroying him.

The question arises as to why the Greeks are so fearful of Astyanax' power. In this drama they are seemingly tired of their formerly vigilant and intense attitude. Such alertness as is demanded of a society in danger can and does, in the case of the Greeks, make for a positive outlook. The Greeks during the Trojan war kept abreast of social, economic, and political movements. Overly worn attitudes did not corrode their society. Now, however, they want to relax their attention, rest on their laurels by ridding themselves of a potential danger in the form of Astyanax. They fail in their mission because they are *prisoners* of their attitudes rather than masters of them.

Strangely enough, though Andromache is the only real *prisoner*, she is also the only *free* person in the drama. She is a truly queenly type and is treated as such by Pyrrhus' people after his death:

> Andromache is now in sole command;
> They treat her as their queen and us as foes.[8]

Andromache is not ego-centered nor does she succumb to her passions as the other protagonists do. She can, therefore, maintain a cerebral attitude toward events provided they do not inflict danger upon her one sensitive spot, her love for her child. She is fully cognizant of Pyrrhus' love for her and because she is not involved emotionally she can parry astutely his every advance. She suggests that a powerful man such as he must not possibly be so feeble as to permit "so great a heart" to "show so much weakness."[9] Moreover, she knows when and where to flatter: he is far superior to the Greeks, she tells him, and should not accept their way. Because of Andromache's energy, her lucidity, and the force of her convictions, she succeeds in injecting a vital spirit into Pyrrhus' heart. She is the one to set off the spark which smolders within him, which forces him to act and take notice of the world about him, to reject the archaic traditions rampant in his court.

Andromache's steady ways stand out most authentically when contrasted with Hermione's demeanor. Unlike Hermione, she does not suffer from inflation, nor is she vindictive, nor does she resort to subterfuge and hypocrisy except when it is a matter of protecting her child. When Andromache pleads her cause to Hermione (III, vi), enlisting her help to escape with her son to some distant island, she speaks tenderly and in terms of motherhood.

> But I still have a son. You'll know some day
> How strong upon a mother's heart his sway;
> But you will never know, may Heaven forbid,
> The mortal cares a child can make us suffer,
> When of so many blessings we might taste
> He is the sole remaining—and is threatened.[10]

The haughty, vengeful Hermione refuses to furnish any aid, suggesting instead that Andromache use her own power over Pyrrhus to foster such help. Andromache and Hermione have no common denominator. They live worlds apart.

Only once does Andromache lose her self-composure, when Pyrrhus resolves to hand Astyanax to the Greeks (III,vi). Her anguish reaches an acute pitch. Instinctively, she rushes to her husband's grave in order to seek counsel: "Come to my husband's tomb to seek his guidance."[11] The idea of returning to Hector's tomb is, both philosophically and psychologically, one of the most captivating moments in the drama. Symbolically, the tomb can represent the unconscious, indicating, in Andromache's case, a rejection of a rational and conscious approach to her problem, and opting for irrational guidance. Such indwelling (or such a state of regression) is salutary in Andromache's case. Her energies had formerly been directed outward. Now, aware of the failure of such an extraverted way, she turns inward. All extraneous activity, therefore, is rejected by her and, like the Buddhist, she permits her unconscious to have dominion. Such concentration of thought as she now experiences acts as a stimulant, renewing the activity within her unconscious. As the dynamism increases so does the turbulence. The unconscious, therefore, experiences a kind of "reshuffling," whereby certain contents are pushed forth into the conscious mind, creating a different attitude. The parable of Jonah and the whale, for example, is a most fitting illustration of this procedure. Jonah, like Andromache, also withdraws from the world temporarily, in his case into the whale's stomach. There, symbolically speaking, he sinks into the past, into those primitive and arcane regions which all men share in common—the collective unconscious. Within this realm, where life is both born and destroyed, where Andromache as well as Jonah experience a linking up with the *prima materia,* additional strength and energy is derived; contents from a world of potentialities, from an area in eternal ebullition are assimilated by the conscious mind. When Andromache rushes to her husband's tomb, she is in effect taking a dark journey to the realm of the dead; such contact permits her to experience a *participation mystique* with universal forces, infusing her with the strength and insight necessary to face her new stuation.[12]

Andromache's dead past has actually come to life and imposed itself upon her present situation. It is her past which dictates her decision to marry Pyrrhus and to do away with her own life after the ceremony. Looked upon in this manner, Hector, though dead, remains very much alive, and a powerful figure. Now that Andromache's road has been revealed to her through an immersion in the past, she can travel it with relative ease. With no thoughts of vengeance or anger, Andromache, mistress of her actions, emerges victorious from her dilemma.

Andromache is unique in Racine's theatre. A woman who acts with compassion, humility, tenderness, and extreme understanding, she conducts herself throughout the play with dignity and grace. Andromache knows what life really means and is willing to make the supreme sacrifice—herself—for her "unique treasure,"[13] her child, the creative force, the promise of the future. Within his limbs rests man's hope.

✦ ✦ ✦

Hermione is a *shadow* figure for Andromache; that is, she is the bearer of Andromache's inferior characteristics. The rejected maiden, the recipient of unrequited love, she is filled with feelings of inferiority. These negative aspects present in her personality are repressed by her rather than understood and accepted as part of a *whole* personality. Because they are rejected and not given the proper attention, they react like a starving animal and become destructive and vicious. Hermione is starved in that same way: lacking love, unable to understand her feelings, she has become half a human being. Andromache represents the positive aspects of the collective and fruitful mother principle; Hermione, the unfulfilled virgin daughter.

Hermione is a "rootless" being, in that no one wants her and she belongs nowhere. Her father had sent her away to marry Pyrrhus, who rejected her. She is, therefore, like an unstable weather vane standing high on a church steeple, acting and reacting to given situations whichever way the wind blows. Because of this lack of steadiness, which would have given her a sense of harmony and balance, she is the victim of extremes: hatred, love, rage, etc. Her quixotic nature compels her to act impulsively, irrationally. Frequently, she comes to regret her deeds and suffers deeply because of them.

Reason, therefore, is not Hermione's dictating force, it is not *sui generis*. Thinking, analytical assessments of situations are never undertaken. Feeling is Hermione's dominant function. Violent emotional reactions, indicative of an infantile, archaic psyche are always in order. Because of her extreme affectivity, Hermione is given to extreme ambivalence: one minute she adores Pyrrhus; the following, she considers him her enemy. Such confusion as she experiences between love and hate indicate clearly that these feelings are still undifferentiated. They are, therefore, experienced only unconsciously and have not yet reached the light of consciousness.[14]

Hermione's unconsciousness, her utter blindness to her situation, is acute. Yet, interestingly enough, she frequently considers such a state to be a panacea, a means of alleviating her suffering at least temporarily. To obliterate sight or consciousness is most certainly a form of escape when pain becomes too difficult to bear.

> Why must you stir the embers of my anguish?
> I fear to face my heart in my sad state.
> Try and forget all that you have seen;
> Believe I love no more and praise my will;
> Believe my heart is hardened in its hate;
> Ah! if you can, make me believe it too.[15]

Hermione not only does not want to look at her situation realistically, but elicits her servant into playing this dangerous game of truth-veiling: persuading her that she no longer loves Pyrrhus. Hermione opts, then, for illusion over reality.

Hermione is a complex figure. Inwardly she is riddled with feelings of inferiority; outwardly she wears a mask (a *persona*) displaying *hybris*.[16] The love-sick Orestes viewing her outer countenance considers her "inhuman," unapproachably proud, condescending, inexorable, domineering, ungrateful, disdaining. When Hermione confronts her audience (II,i) and casts off her persona, she reveals an altogether different type of creature. Filled with shame and pain, disgraced by Pyrrhus' public rejection of her, she gives the impression of being rather pathetic.

Always in a state of flux, Hermione would like to annihilate all those feelings of inadequacy, of ineffectiveness, of failure which she feels most forcibly within her. Only one method is capable of destroying such sentiments: counteracting them with overpowering rage.

> Ah! let me have some time to feed my fury
> And steel my heart against my enemy.
> I wish to leave him weltering in my loathing.
> He'll do his best to welter—faithless wretch![17]

The enormous quantities of psychic energy she musters through anger, momentarily at least, eradicate her excruciating sense of shame.[18]

Racine depicts with great depth and understanding the gamut of emotions leading up to Hermione's violent bursts of rage. When, for example, she sees Orestes for the first time (II,ii) she describes herself as a "sad princess"[19] and tries to evoke sympathy and pity from him. She even goes so far as to inform Orestes of the possibility of her loving him.

> Yes, you whose love, engendered by their spell,
> First taught them the full meaning of their power;
> You, whose great virtues forced me to esteem you;
> You, whom I pitied and would like to love.[20]

Totally amoral, irresponsible, egotistical, primitive, she lives in her own primeval and wildly ego-centered world. Only when Orestes acquaints her with the truth, that Pyrrhus loves Andromache and not her, does the shock of reality become too violent for her to bear. She cannot think of herself as disdained, as rejected. Her ebullient emotions converge, blocking out whatever vision she might have mustered. Anger blazes forth. Hermione spews venom like an animal and demands vengeance every step of the way.

> Go, arm the whole of Greece against a rebel:
> And let him pay the price of his rebellion;
> Let's make Epirus yet another Ilion.
> Go—can you now persist I love him still?[21]

Only when Pyrrhus decides to marry her does her extreme desire for vengeance abate.[22] Then she regresses into a passive state, that of the dutiful daughter who foregoes personal joys for the sake of political reasons. In this instance too she acts in bad faith; she is unwilling or unable to look at her situation lucidly, to probe. Her joy knows no bounds and mounts to the heights of jubilation. She is ready to fly forth in a cloud of heavenly bliss. When Andromache comes to her on bended knees asking her for help, Hermione abrupt, arrogant, clings to her pleasure. The moment Pyrrhus reverses his decision, however, announcing his plans to marry Andromache, Hermione transforms her wounded pride into an aggressive and destructive weapon—vengeance again. The hybris which has led her to crave for extreme violence now compels her to seek blood.

Hermione goes one step further. She suffers from a virtual madness: *alienation*. Such a state occurs when the ego has been severed from the *Self*. Nothing can hold Hermione down at this point. Her wildest exigencies must be satisfied by the only one who loves her and the one person she reviles: Orestes. When he recoils at the thought of killing Pyrrhus she accuses him of cowardice, of being unworthy of her. In a frenzy of emotion, accelerating with every verbal gyration, Hermione offers herself as the prize for Pyrrhus' murderer.

Hermione's alienation intensifies. She suffers, momentarily, from an eclipse of consciousness. She questions: "Where am I? What have I done? What more must I do?"[23] So totally removed from reality is she that she begins to err, confessing:

> I am consumed by passion, torn by doubt.
> I wander, aimless, buffeted by fate,
> Shall I know never if I love or hate?[24]

When Orestes has accomplished the murder, Hermione who, during her virtual state of amnesia, has forgotten her command, labels his action monstrous, accuses him of parricide. Her state of despair is now so acute that she again experiences alienation. Anguish settles over her. Her *raison d'être* has vanished. She rushes off-stage where Pyrrhus' body is being carried forth and there raises her eyes toward the heavens, stabs herself, falls dead upon his corpse.

Hermione, the virgin princess, is never allowed to develop. Unconscious of her situation, she sees the world about her only through her own distorted eyes. She proceeds through feelings alone, irrationally and instinctually. Experiencing bouts with inflation and alienation, she suffers the fate of all those who live out unreal situations (Icarus, Phaeton): rising to the heights and falling to the depths.

As a negative image of Andromache, or a shadow figure, Hermione represents the unacceptable characteristics of an unfulfilled and rejected human being. She is all the more destructive in this capacity since her emotions are released through anger, condemnation, vengeance, and extreme cruelty. Such a monstrous, amoral, and unregenerate creature as Hermione cannot survive.

✓   ✓   ✓

Pyrrhus, the King, possesses few of the qualities befitting a monarch. He has neither sound judgment nor self-control. On the contrary, he behaves irrationally, reacting affectively to external stimuli when these concern him directly. A division is apparent in Pyrrhus' personality, somewhat similar to the breach in Hermione's psyche but less pronounced. When, for example, he is dealing with questions of war, conquest, strictly masculine entities, he proves himself to be strong, sanguinary, and a fighter. In Andromache's presence, on the other hand, he is emotionally bound and seems unsure of himself. Weak, vacillating, he is very nearly effeminate.

The split within Pyrrhus' personality, which Racine dramatized with such clarity, is fascinating to analyze. In the domain of force, vigor, heroism, battle, Pyrrhus is certainly Achilles' son, in that he knows no peers.

> The whole of Greece now threatens me with war;
> But even were they to traverse the seas
> With a thousand vessels, clamouring for your son;
> Were all the blood to flow that Helen shed;
> Were I to see my palace in all ashes,
> I will not hesitate, but speed to save him:
> I'll shield his life at the expense of mine.[25]

When describing his battle against Troy, the carnage, the devastation, the anger, and excitement implicit in this mass murder, he does so with zest. Courage is also his when confronting Orestes. He belittles the Greeks who fear Astyanax' future strength. Pyrrhus is able to experience this kind of vigorous approach to war and to his enemies because he is in full rapport with all those unconscious contents which belong to the masculine, virile domain.

Pyrrhus' force, however, suddenly vanishes in Andromache's presence. He becomes sheepish, subservient, uses any and all means to try to win her affection, though he may appear ridiculous in the process. He flaunts his might at first, hoping to impress her, to instill in her a sense of admiration for his heroism. He boldly asserts that he will never give up Astyanax to the Greeks, though such refusal might mean war. Moments later, he adds his conditions meekly: if Andromache acts in a more "kindly" manner toward him.

> Will you refuse to look on me less coldly?
> Hated by all the Greeks, on all sides hemmed,
> Must I by your reproach be still condemned?
> I offer you my sword. Have I some clue
> You will accept my heart that worships you?
> In fighting for you, may I feel sure, please,
> You'll not be ranged among my enemies.[26]

It is certainly clear that Pyrrhus does not know how to handle his feelings. When he does express such sentiments he does so in a most infantile manner. He belittles himself unwittingly in her eyes, achieving the opposite from the desired effect. Because he fails to elicit a change of heart within her, he resorts to insults and threats: calling her "cruel" and warning her that Astyanax' life is in danger. Moments later, he begs her to accept his adoring love. Even Andromache is taken aback by such obsequiousness, which seems all the more surprising in view of his heroism as a military man. What does this fundamental weakness within him mean? she questions.

> Why must so great a heart show so much weakness?
> Do you want so fine, so generous a plan,
> To be scoffed at as just a lovesick whim?[27]

The fact that Pyrrhus is so awkward in his rapport with Andromache indicates an undeveloped feeling (eros) function: that is, he is unable to relate to others as far as his feelings are concerned.[28] Such a lack on his part fosters a sense of disquietude, failure, and rejection, in a way similar to Hermione's. He becomes hyper-sensitive, is easily hurt, and takes umbrage instantly when Andromache does not respond to his affection. A play of opposites (enantiodromia) develops within his psyche. If he is unable to dominate a situation or person, he despairs and angers; if, on the other hand, he feels all have acquiesced to his desires, he becomes unrealistically overjoyed, more than the situation warrants.

As the play progresses we see a change in Pyrrhus' attitude. The instability which dominates his relations with Andromache begins to invade that strongly masculine aspect of his personality: his warrior, heroic, kingly side. What he had once been capable of viewing objectively and relating to with ease now becomes dominated by his overwhelming passion for Andromache. This new focus dictates his political decisions.

The governing principle with which kings are supposedly endowed generally places them above and beyond subjective and sensual considerations. In Pyrrhus' case, the opposite results. He has now become subservient to them. His relationships and his political stand will be motivated not by reason but by his archaic world of instincts. There is, therefore, little rationale in his behavior. Pyrrhus' actions become very nearly mechanical. When, for instance, Andromache draws away from him, he seeks out Orestes, promises to deliver Astyanax to the Greeks and marry Hermione. Since his ego cannot bear the loss of Andromache, which would be interpreted as failure on his part, his attitude becomes more and more aggressive and defiant. He boasts, as had Hermione to Orestes, of having overcome his love for Andromache and predicts that this haughty Trojan lady will fall on her knees before him, concluding by declaring his intention to see her again if only to express his hatred for her. He revels in the thought of being master now. Inflation takes hold of him. When Andromache rejects him, the pendulum swings the other way. Like Hermione, Pyrrhus never seeks to sound out his problems and is continuously living within a web of illusion, swerving from love to hate, from joy to sorrow.

Though Pyrrhus suffers because of his unrequited love for Andromache, he does not hesitate to act harshly and, therefore, to hurt Hermione. He has no understanding or interest in her pain. He treats her as an object, the butt of his own moods. His decision to speak truthfully to her and to inform her of his projected marriage to Andromache is not motivated by any great moral deliberation, but rather by an immediate desire to gratify himself, to rid himself of his anxieties and to finalize matters.

Pyrrhus is unaware of his own situation and personality. As a result, he cannot objectify his feelings. His sense of cognition concerning others does not function adequately. He is incapable of relating to women except on a most primitive level, his *eros* function being underdeveloped. He is a person of extremes: overly sheepish toward Andromache or extremely harsh with Hermione. Such emotional instability prevents him from assessing the higher values at stake in the political situation. Pyrrhus has a counterpart in antiquity: Epimetheus. Like his ancestor, he never analyzes his acts or thinks out the import of his words *a priori*. Only after they have been enacted or enunciated does he become aware of their implications and come to regret them.[29] A slave of his disjointed being, Pyrrhus becomes a sounding board for his "rootless" moods. Like Hermione, he can never enjoy independence of spirit and is a being incapable of molding destinies. His unregenerate attitude, therefore, cannot survive.

↗   ↗   ↗

Orestes is the most tragic figure in the entire drama, because he is totally helpless. Undeveloped, immature, daemon-driven, his passivity is his undoing. His role (an ambassador, a messenger of sorts sent by the Greeks) symbolizes his personality: he is a carrier, a medium type, not an innovator.

Orestes is the direct psychological descendant of Eteocles and Polynices (*The Theban Brothers*). He lives in an archaic domain. Like a child, he experiences *participation mystique* with the forces of the universe and cannot, therefore, differentiate or understand his outlook. His vision is submerged in the dismal recesses of his unconscious. He knows only one reality: his obsessive love for Hermione.

Orestes is totally dominated by the Hermione archetype: the virgin goddess, alluring and cruel. Despite the fact that his potential is great, that he is a Prince and, therefore, many roads are open to him, he is unable, as are many heroes under the dominion of a destructive feminine principle (Attis, Pentheus), to re-orient himself. His undoing began before the outset of the play—the moment he surrendered to Hermione. The more she reviles him and compels him to suffer the indignities of the enslaved and dominated male, the less chance he has to grow and to assert his masculinity.

Racine reveals to his audiences the gradual undoing of such a personality—the perfect tragic figure—in whom the "fatal flaw" has been personified. In the beginning of the drama Pylades describes Orestes (I,i) as a melancholy person, a passive young man.

> Would you indeed, enslaved as you are now,
> Entrust the issue of your life to love?[30]

Orestes first hesitates, then confesses his overpowering passion for an "inhuman" person and his inability to overcome the daemon corroding his very being. Indeed, he is prepared to give up the fight against his daemon-love, though the perils are great.

> Since all my strivings to resist are vain,
> My destiny now sweeps me blindly on.
> I love: and come to seek Hermione,
> To win, to snatch her, or else die before her.[31]

Like the men described by Plato in his "Allegory of the Cave," Orestes is unable to see the light; his world, as is theirs, is circumscribed, and he is enchained by it, powerless to cope with it.

Orestes is double: dominated by his affects and, at the same time, able to speak lucidly on political matters. For example, he tells Pyrrhus in logical terms his reasons for coming to Epirus. On the other hand, when it is a question of winning Hermione's love, he melts in her presence, confesses his suffering, and manages, as does the King, to appear ridiculous. He cannot alter Hermione's course any more than he can his own. He must follow the path marked out for him by his destiny, his inner being. The continual belief he has in the successful solution to his problem mars his vision. He therefore sinks ever more deeply into his inextricable situation.

Hermione's repeated rejections of Orestes affect him deeply. His feelings become turbulent. The energy accumulated by such motion flows inward, into his unconscious. It is never lived out realistically or channeled in some positive work. As a result, the unconscious is filled, so to speak, with masses of chaotic contents. At certain points, these become so dynamic as to spill over into the conscious world in the form of fantasies. During these periods Orestes' eyes dilate and his actions and words become uncontrollable.

Orestes' loss of lucidity is "progressive." It began with his inability to see his situation clearly and reaches a climax when Hermione demands he kill Pyrrhus. At first he recoils from such a horrendous thought. To sacrifice for Hermione was within his plans—his own life, if need be—but to take another's seemed anathema to him. In the end, however, Orestes becomes totally submissive to Hermione. He becomes the vehicle, symbolically speaking, of the destructive female figure. She is, in effect, acting through him. Having thereby shed his own personality, his ego has regressed to the point of being virtually non-existent. A breakdown then has taken place between the conscious and the unconscious worlds: outer and inner are one. Differentiation is absent. Orestes is now living in *primal waters*. He commits the crime. Afterward Hermione reviles him, calls him "monster": author of a "parricide." The shock of her castigations brings Orestes back to reality. Consciousness reappears momentarily and, at this point, he comes to realize the magnitude of his crime. Guilt ensues and grows to the point of paranoia. When he hears of Hermione's suicide, a total and prolonged eclipse of consciousness occurs. The forces of Orestes' instinctual world have free rein; they are autonomous contents now. Totally unaware of what is transpiring, of what he is saying, of where he is, Orestes claims he knows only one thing—that he must expiate his crime. Then he sinks into oblivion.[32]

Racine's description of Orestes' gradual insanity is extraordinary. By using archetypal imagery, he lifts Orestes from a personal and rational world to that of a collective and irrational one. In so doing, he impels his readers to march downward with him, to the frightening realm where serpents slither about, and where Medusa and Gorgon-like forms—all incarnations of Hermione—writhe.

> But what do I see? Hermione kiss his brow?
> She comes to snatch him from the threatening blow?
> Ah gods! what vampire looks she hurls on me!
> What fiends, what serpents in her company?
> Ye hellish daughters, come, tear me in shreds!
> See, see, those serpents hissing round your heads.
> For whom do you bring these engines of affright?
> Do you come to drag me down to eternal night?[33]

Orestes' fantasies rise spontaneously from beneath the turgid waters of his unconscious. Monstrous women with claws of brass, hair of masses of living and hissing serpents parade before him in their ghastly horror, each personifying Hermione in her most crushing aspects. These negative female forms turn upon the helpless hero and like devouring vultures suck his blood, his life, and his heart.

The extreme force of Orestes' speech rests not only on Racine's splendid use of archetypal imagery, but on the contrasts he injects into this soliloquy, the rhythms of his clauses, the alliterations and onomatopeias; for example, the famous line "Pour qui sont ces serpents qui sifflent sur vos têtes." The orchestration of these various elements is superbly blended and makes Orestes' descent into nigredo that much more formidable.

Orestes seeks to expiate his crime. His sacrifice in this connection is nearly, but not totally, complete. He loses his sanity, but not his life. In a sense, he is like King Lear, whose suffering is also intense, whose blindness vis-à-vis his own daughters is as total as Orestes' toward Hermione. Both have to experience bouts of insanity and a submersion into the collective unconscious, there to be cleansed of failings, washed of sins, and, years later, reborn into a new existence and a reoriented world.[34]

The symbol of the *serpent*, which Racine uses so effectively in the above-quoted passages, implies rebirth. Though the snake is itself a complex and ambivalent entity, destructive because of its bite, associated with matter since it slithers along the ground, it also has its positive aspect. The snake sheds its skin, implying resurrection or rebirth. It has also come to represent energy, wisdom, and the infinite mysteries of the universe. Indeed, Philo of Alexandria considered the snake the most spiritual of animals. The Orientals (Buddha) drew analogies between the serpent and the wheel of life.[35] The fact that Orestes has now been placed in direct rapport with such a vital entity and that he has not been destroyed by it, as were Pyrrhus and Hermione, implies that a rebirth of consciousness will occur after he has experienced submersion within the primal waters.

Like Ixion, Orestes will suffer the tortures of punishment (in his case, insanity). Bound to the underworld (the unconscious), as Ixion was tied to the fiery wheel which turned about in space, both experience the flaying of an aimless and rootless existence.[36]

II

Racine's characters are no longer "buds," but beings endowed with sufficient consciousness to experience suffering of the most excruciating kind: rejection, shame, pride, anguish. Yet, these same figures lack the lucidity to apprise their own situation and account for their turmoil. They are, therefore, under the dominion of a daemon which eats away at their every organ.

The characters in *Andromache* do not develop in the true sense of the word. They do, however, live in a world of frenetic activity. Each time they unleash their venom, they do so with force and vigor, creating enormous suspense and excitement. This dynamism inherent in Racine's creatures sets forth a particular rhythmic pattern in the drama which ranges from *immobility*, resulting from their inability to alter their course or behavior, to extreme *acceleration* of pace, when their emotions burst forth as they try to alter their way. Such antithetical movements also affect the protagonists' moods, giving rise to heights and depths, tragic immobility and moments of extreme elation. During the course of the play, Racine uses a variety of tempos as a dramatic vehicle, as a means of keeping his viewers enthralled—creating, in this manner, concomitant rhythmic patterns within their own psyches.

This same rhythmic mode is also present in *Andromache's* structure, as it will be, to a greater or lesser degree, in all his future dramas. *Andromache* opens at a critical juncture in the lives of the protagonists. All is static. An expository scene usually outlines the situation: a *crisis*. In this case, Orestes acquaints his audience with his situation, relating certain incidents to his good friend Pylades in terms of past, present, and the likely future. Activity now occurs and consists in finding a solution to the problem posed at the very beginning of the drama.

Racine ignites potential situations by his use of symbols. The flamboyant images used in *Andromache* are not merely the stylistic requisites of a baroque writer, but are the very life force of this drama. The images themselves—flame, fire, blood—though used in previous works (*The Theban Brothers* and *Alexander the Great*) have never been incised into his creatures with such force as in *Andromache*.

Pyrrhus, for example, speaks of burning, consuming, blood, remorse, regret, iron. Such descriptive nouns and adjectives denote the conflicts devouring him. Like fire, the outcome of his decisions can take on a destructive or constructive turn. Moreover, his incendiary emotions are forever exploding and consuming in the blaze. Each time they gnaw and plague his soul. Unable to hold firmly to a single decision he has made, he is forever vacillating, carried forth like fire by a strong wind. As a result of his indecisiveness, he experiences an overwhelming sense of ineffectiveness, gutted with feelings of remorse. Immense distances separate him from the "iron" being he would like to be. Hermione and Orestes also speak in terms of bruising pictorial images when under stress.

Racine pays particular attention to the *eye* symbol. It is of primary importance in his panoply of images because it is looked upon philosophically as well as dramatically. The eye—the "inner eye"—is the source of light and, by implication, intelligence, understanding, and spirituality. The Egyptians refer to the "divine eye" as the one "which feeds the sacred fire or the intelligence of Man."[37] Eyes for Racine were in effect repositories, urns, mirrors leading down to the twisted depths of man's soul, and sources of his actions and sentiments.

Racine makes expert use of the eye image in various ways. Orestes, for example, looks upon the eye at times as a weapon to be "defied," to be mastered. Hermione's eyes, he declares, no longer trouble him because he has overcome the glare of her gaze.[38] Actually, what he is declaring in this instance belies the facts. In vain does he try to overthrow this potent force of love, which seems to concentrate all its energies in Hermione's eyes. He fails to do so. Later, he realizes to what depths love has reduced him and he refers to his lack of sight, his "blindness," his impotence.

Eyes can, paradoxically enough, act as masks and impede vision. Orestes claims that this is true in Hermione's case: "Your eyes have not experienced (understood) my constance?"[39] On another occasion, when Orestes is seized with rage, Pylades begs him to dissimulate his gaze.

> Dissimulate; control your agitation,
> And also make your eyes maintain the secret.[40]

Orestes is in fact helpless. He cannot dictate to those doors, "his eyes," which open on to his inner world.

Eyes are also vehicles which look out upon the future. When, for example, Orestes gazes into Hermione's eyes, his fate seems to materialize before him: "seeking in your eyes elusive death."[41]

Images, generally speaking, are used by Racine not only as vehicles to enhance the drama implicit in certain characters and situations, but as a means of eradicating man's rational attitudes toward time and space. For example, images associated with past experiences suddenly burst forth into present tirades, becoming part of an *actual* situation. This intense activity or interchange destroys the limiting linear conception of time and space of which most Occidentals are victims. Another dimension, thereby, comes into being. Characters no longer live in fixed realms, but float into uneasy ones, fluctuating ceaselessly in an expanded universe in which present, past, and future merge.

Andromache is very much aware of the dimensionless world which she inhabits. Her past is forever being injected into her present with glimmers into the future.

> Must I forget them, if he'll not remember?
> Forget my Hector's loss of funeral rites,
> His body dragged defeated round our walls?
> Forget his father cast down at my feet,
> His bleeding body clutching at the altar?
> Think, think, Cephise, of that cruel night,
> Which doomed a nation to eternal night.
> Imagine Pyrrhus, with his glistening eyes,
> Entering in the glare of our blazing mansions,
> Kicking aside my brother's mangled corpse,
> And slaked in blood inciting to fresh slaughter.
> Do you hear the victors' shouts, the wounded's groans,
> Choked by the flames or dying by the sword?
> Do you see Andromache distraught with horror?
> Such is the way I first set eyes on Pyrrhus;
> Such are the exploits that have crowned his fame;
> Such is the husband you would thrust on me.[42]

Pyrrhus also relives his deeds of valor during the Trojan War and several times during the play, juxtaposing the fearless hero aspect of his personality with his weakly structured lover side.

This non-linear concept of time and space can be transformed into a dramatic technique and used with extreme impact by modern directors. Past events such as certain battles described by Pyrrhus could be flashed onto screens located either in the acting area or any place within the theatre; Andromache's fears of future catastrophes can likewise be concretized. In this manner the protagonists—and the spectators empathetically—can be thrust into the vast expanse of time, compelled to experience their impotence and shuddering at the thought of the infinite possibilities which await them.

In this world of magic, nightmare, and consistently glowing and abrasive images, Racine has recourse to a symbolic representation of the entire drama: the *circle*. Pyrrhus, Hermione, Orestes form a circle: each loves the other and is loved by another. Only Andromache stands aloof, beyond the circle, her attachment to the other protagonists consisting only in Pyrrhus' passion for her. The circle in this case represents the primordial or original psychological state of man, the "uroboric" stage of development in which consciousness has not yet come into being or at least not in sufficiently forceful doses to be meaningful. Andromache is the only conscious being in Racine's drama. She survives the ordeal intact, indicating, in part, how vitally important lucidity is in living one's earthly existence.

III

Andromache is a work embedded in a truly earthly realm, and for this reason the love-passion is experienced on a most primitive and instinctual level. Only Andromache rises above the norm, and does so because her notion of love is better balanced: it is both spiritual and physical.

Andromache represents the trans-personal female principle in her maternal, forgiving, and faithful aspects. She is perhaps a composite of Racine's ideal woman, his Beatrice. Her portrait might have been modeled in part on Mother Agnès de Sainte-Thècle, Racine's aunt whom he loved and admired; in part on his sister Marie, gentle and loyal; and also on the beautiful Mlle du Parc. Racine's protagonists, however, are active *Gestalten*. They are really not identifiable with anyone living in his time or entourage.

Pyrrhus, Hermione, and Orestes are all shadow figures to a greater or lesser degree. They dwell in archaic regions, unable to discern, and so act impulsively. They are not lightbearers nor are they intrinsically evildoers. Given to bouts of inflation or alienation, they react at times like glandular cases. Hopelessly embroiled in the inchoate waters of their unconscious, they are perpetually thrust forth with the flowing tide. Reacting intensely to violent undercurrents and volcanic tremors, they emerge from the drama as useless entities, unable to change their course, incapable of *will* or *sight*. Orestes alone, the perpetrator of the only real crime, is the single person worthy of redemption. He is the only one truly to sacrifice and thereby earn pardon. Neither Pyrrhus nor Hermione ever feels guilt; they are unaware of morality.

So far as writing brings unconscious contents to consciousness, one may conclude that *Andromache*, symbolically speaking, is a mirror image of an inner drama being lived subliminally by the author. Though one cannot relate certain events or characters appearing in the drama to those actually experienced by Racine in his daily life—the source for these remaining inscrutable and unfathomable—one can affirm that Racine has reached another stage in his emotional development. He is now able to express feelings of *love* and *relatedness*: eros. Heretofore, he could only exteriorize certain antagonisms (*The Theban Brothers*) and heroic elements within his personality (*Alexander the Great*). Now that love is personified in its multitude of gradations, the implication is that the repressed and enmeshed forces within his psyche are welding together. Such a process makes for growth. *Andromache* is a sincere and poetic outpouring of one who is ready and able to involve himself with the world and its people.

4

Britannicus

> "I must assure myself
> a port in the tempest . . ."[1]

SHORTLY after *Andromache's* stunning success, Racine permitted himself the luxury of writing a light and witty comedy, *The Litigants*, suggested to him by Aristophanes' *Wasps*. This was to be Racine's only comedy. He considered the genre inferior to tragedy. Moreover, tragedy seemed to suit his temperament better, particularly at this juncture of his life, so fraught with anguish.

✦ ✦ ✦

Ever since Racine had met La Du Parc, he had grown increasingly possessive of her. Causes for his extreme insecurity might be proposed. She was a fine actress, exceptionally beautiful, charming, and endowed with great finesse. Her gracious ways served to attract many men to her orbit. The Chevalier de Genlis sought her hand in marriage.[2] Racine must have been racked with jealousy. His growing sense of doubt as to her fidelity was soon replaced by anxiety, then dread, and finally utter despair. La Du Parc died suddenly in the month of December, 1668.

The events leading to her demise were and still are shrouded in mystery. In fact, it was not until November 21, 1679 that certain details concerning La Du Parc's death were revealed, at the trial of Catherine Des Hayes Voisin, known as "La Voisin," a notorious murderess who had played the pivotal role in one of France's most horrendous criminal cases, "L'Affaire des Poisons."

La Voisin, the mistress of Paris' public executioner, had won for herself a formidable reputation for her practices in chiromancy and necromancy, witchcraft, infant sacrifices, poisonings, and abortions. During the course of her trial, two thousand cadavers of newborn infants and their charred remains, burned in an oven built for this purpose, were unearthed in her garden.

La Voisin had attracted to her home in the Quartier St. Denis people of all walks of life, aristocrats in particular. These believers in the occult, determined to rid society of people they considered undesirable, wishing to win or maintain the affections of others, visited her, paid dearly for her concoctions: magic powders and black masses. The Abbé Guibourg, a defrocked priest, usually performed the masses. First he filled a chalice with the blood of an infant he had killed, then placed it on the nude body of the person imploring the aid of supernatural powers, after which he would enunciate and then chant special prayers.[3]

La Voisin was tried in the Chambre Ardente, a court specializing in such cases, condemned to death and burned alive on the Place de Grève. Certain highly placed officials and aristocrats with national reputations were also convicted of ignominious acts along with La Voisin: the Marquise de Brinvilliers, who had poisoned her father and brothers and very nearly succeeded in killing her sister-in-law; the Princesse de Tingry, Mme de Dreux, the Maréchal de La Ferté, the Maréchale de Luxembourg, the Duchesse de Bouillon. . . . Even the name of Mme de Montespan, Louis XIV's mistress, was linked to this nefarious affair. She had been accused of having ordered black masses to be held to win and keep the King's affection. Four hundred and forty-two people were summoned to appear before the Chambre Ardente; two hundred and twenty-eight were imprisoned.[4]

When La Voisin testified at her trial, she accused Racine of having poisoned La Du Parc for reasons of jealousy. She and the actress had been close friends, she asserted. Racine had done his best to separate them and had gone so far as to forbid her to visit La Du Parc during her moment of need at the end, though she called for her continuously.

Opinion today, however, generally favors another view. Most scholars feel that La Du Parc died as a result of an abortion. It has been asserted that Racine had made her pregnant again (their first child, a daughter, was being raised away from Paris and in secret) and that she was the one to insist upon an abortion. According to certain indications, the Chevalier de Genlis had asked her to marry him, and another pregnancy at this time would have voided such "fine" plans.

A second theory forwarded is that Racine was the one to insist upon the abortion. The birth of a second child would have compromised his future with the aristocrats, a class whose support he was determined to maintain. Certainly, many members of the higher classes, including the King himself, would have looked askance at such an ill-assorted couple: a thirty-five year old actress with the rather "scandalous" reputation accompanying practitioners of this profession, and a twenty-nine year old poet at the outset of what was considered by some to be a brilliant career. Moreover, such a marriage would have placed terrible financial burdens upon Racine. La Du Parc had three children and a mother to support. Racine's drive and ambition might certainly have been reason enough to cancel such ideas of marriage and to suggest an abortion.

According to Brossette, La Du Parc "died in childbirth" and La Voisin's testimony was completely false. Yet the two reasons forwarded as possible causes of death (poison and abortion) might, in the light of medicinal practices in the seventeenth century, both be acceptable. Poisons were frequently used to bring on abortions. La Voisin could very well have furnished such drugs to La Du Parc. These sometimes occasioned violent stomach spasms with ensuing hemorrhages and death. La Du Parc, who might have taken these poisons for medicinal reasons, might also have succumbed as a result of continuous bleeding. It has even been suggested that Racine's preoccupation with poisons, bloodshed, and violence in *Britannicus* perhaps stemmed from the trauma he had experienced as a result of La Du Parc's death.

Whatever Racine's role in this affair, there is no question but that he suffered intensely. He had not only lost his loved one, but the ideal interpreter for his female roles. According to the testimony revealed by Béatrice Dussane, Racine was present at La Du Parc's deathbed and wept. At her funeral, the gazeteer Robinet described him as "half dead" with grief.[5]

✦   ✦   ✦

Little is known concerning Racine's private life from the time of La Du Parc's death to the opening of *Britannicus* on December 13, 1669. Though they were not happy months, it can be assumed they were productive ones.

Racine dedicated *Britannicus* to the Duc de Chevreuse, a man friendly to Port-Royal and a member of one of the most powerful French families.[6] Racine welcomed the warmth and understanding ex-

pressed by the Chevreuse family all the more intensely after the castigations leveled at *Britannicus*. The dramatist Edmé Boursault expressed his opposition to Racine's characters and plot line in smarting
terms.[7] Saint-Evremond also aimed his acidulous remarks at Racine,
condemning the entire subject as unfit for theatrical production.[8]

When Racine wrote *Britannicus*, he seemingly kept Corneille's
criticisms of his former works in mind. In the *Epître au Roi*, Corneille
had implied that Racine could treat only the theme of *love* in his dramas; *politics*, which is the basis for "real" and "substantial" dramas,
was anathema to the newcomer. Racine must indeed have pondered this
situation because *Britannicus* depicts the political climate in Rome under Nero's reign with vigor and insight.

Racine, angered by the callousness of the remarks leveled against
his work, answered his enemies in two prefaces to *Britannicus* (1670–
1676), really a defense and an explication of his theatrical point of
view. To those who considered Nero's character too cruel or too kind,
as the case might be, he declared:

> But here he is a budding monster. He has not yet set fire to Rome. He
> has not killed his mother, his wife, his tutors. But apart from that it
> seems to me that he lets through enough cruelties to prevent anyone
> from mistaking his character.[9]

To others who claimed that Britannicus was too young to be truly
heroic, that Junie did not resemble the historical figure, Racine asserted
that Britannicus' youth inspired "compassion" and that Junie was true
to Seneca's portrayal of her. To critics who claimed the play should
have concluded with Britannicus' death, Racine replied that by so doing he would have violated the all-important unity of action which was
required of seventeenth-century playwrights. Racine understood this
unity as meaning "the imitation of a complete action," acquainting
audiences, therefore, with the fate of *all* the protagonists involved.
Other remonstrators accused Racine of writing in too simple and natural a manner. To these, he retorted with great aplomb.

> Instead of a simple plot burdened with little matter, such as a plot that
> takes place in only one day must be, a plot which progresses step by
> step to its end, which is only sustained by the interests, the sentiments,
> and the passions of the characters, it would be necessary to fill this very
> plot with a heap of incidents, which could take place only in a month,
> with a great number of theatrical tricks, all the more surprising for be-
> ing less probable, with countless declamations in which actors are
> made to say precisely the contrary of what they should say.[10]

✓ ✓ ✓

Britannicus takes place in Nero's palace.

Act I. Agrippina has connived to have her son Nero made Emperor of Rome, and his half brother, Britannicus, dispossessed of his rightful heritage. As the play opens, Nero seeks to discourage his mother's intrusion into his life. To this end, he counters her orders and has Junie, whom Agrippina had promised in marriage to Britannicus, brought to the palace. Burrhus, the stoic and Nero's teacher, justifies the Emperor's act.

Act II. Narcissus, Britannicus' tutor, but secretly working for Nero, encourages the Emperor in his repudiation of Agrippina. Nero then exiles the freedman Pallas, friendly to his mother, repudiates his wife Octavia, chosen for him by Agrippina, and plans to marry Junie. One obstacle, he learns, stands in his way: Junie loves Britannicus. He orders her to lie and tell Britannicus she no longer loves him. Nero will be standing in the shadows listening to their conversation to make certain she carries out his orders. Britannicus' life is now at stake. He is stunned by his beloved's revelation.

Act III. Surprised by Nero's sudden bid for independence, Burrhus tries in vain to dissuade him from indulging his passion for Junie, which he considers immoral since she has been promised to Britannicus. Agrippina is angered over her son's willful ways and joins forces with Britannicus. Junie secretly confesses her true love to Britannicus while Nero, informed by Narcissus, intrudes upon them. Britannicus is arrested, Junie and Agrippina are held virtual prisoners.

Act IV. Agrippina pleads with Nero to become reconciled with Britannicus. The Emperor accepts, but only outwardly. He admits to Burrhus his plan to have Britannicus killed. Burrhus tries and believes he has dissuaded him from perpetrating such an evil act. Narcissus, however, advises him otherwise.

Act V. Agrippina is pleased over what she believes to be a reconciliation, but Junie foresees an ominous end. Burrhus enters and announces Britannicus' death by poison. Junie escapes from the palace into the Temple of the Vestal Virgins, where she will spend the rest of her life. Narcissus, in his attempt to prevent her from reaching her destination, is killed by the Romans. Nero's despair at having lost Junie verges on madness.

I

The main theme of *Britannicus* revolves around Agrippina's over-powering domination of her son Nero and his equally strong resolve to rid himself of his mother's treacherous tentacles. Sub-themes in the form of antagonisms also come into prominence: love and hate, stoicism versus pragmatism, past and present, virtue and vice.

✤   ✤   ✤

Agrippina is a manifestation of the Terrible Mother archetype: negative, evil, and devouring. She cannot, therefore, be looked upon merely as Nero's individual mother, nor he, by the same token, as merely her personal son. They must be considered as symbols.[11] The power which Racine breathed into this primitive and disturbing creature likens her in some respects to the Greek earth mother Gaea; more so, however, to India's terrible Kali in her death struggle with her creation. Kali, like Agrippina, was intent upon subduing and capturing her prey, holding him within her clutches. The impact of this collective force, Agrippina in Racine's drama, adds to the play's mythical qualities and its dynamism, enlarging, thereby, the scope and ramifications of its main theme, the internecine war between mother and son.

Though the mother image had figured in *The Theban Brothers* in the person of Jocasta, it was relatively insignificant, a very nearly passive role. In *Alexander the Great*, the maternal aspects of the female principles were nonexistent as such, though elements of these qualities were infused into Cleophilia. In Andromache, we find the first portrayal of a positive mother figure: a composite of all the helpful elements expected of such a type. Agrippina, whose name can be transformed into the French word *agripper*, meaning to grip, to attach oneself, to hang on to, to clutch, defines her personality perfectly. She is the antithesis of Andromache.

The conflict to be lived out in *Britannicus* is, on a collective level, the one every male must undergo in one way or another, if he is to liberate himself from domination by the mother principle. If he succeeds in his battle, independence results. He becomes capable of living his own life, of passing from adolescence to maturity, from a parasitical to a productive existence, from unconsciousness to consciousness.

Nero's wrenching away from his mother's grasp is experienced by her as a Calvary. Indeed, Agrippina's trial is summed up most succinctly by her servant in the opening passage of the drama. She waits expectantly before her son's door.

> While Nero sleeps,
> Must you stand waiting here for him to wake?
> And wandering through the palace, unattended,
> Must Caesar's mother watch beside his door.[12]

The door, a separation, shuts her out of her son's world. Her anguish mounts and she paces. Her steps resound throughout the palace and become that much more frightening with the inclusion of such images as "wandering," "watching". . . .

Feelings of impotence have intruded into what she had formerly considered her infallible domain, her dominion over her son's life. The more her security wanes, the more turbulent become her emotions. Frightened, she expresses the need of assuring herself some kind of "port in the tempest." Intuitively, however, she knows this to be impossible and foresees her future: "Nero will cut adrift, if not thus tied."[13] Tense, summoning her strength in a concerted effort to halt her son's swiftly growing personality, she begins what will develop into a death struggle.

Agrippina is so involved in maintaining her control over her son's actions and thoughts that she is unable to assess her situation with clarity. She is, therefore, forever attributing the wrong reasons to her acts and is misguided in her efforts. The ignominious crimes she committed in the past (the lies, the deception, the torture, even her husband's murder, for example) were all perpetrated, she claims, for the benefit of her son. Unconsciously, she considers herself a regulator of destinies, a kind of goddess, a powerful being placed above and beyond the human realm.

Agrippina's obsession with power and the resulting dynamism develop only one side of her personality while destroying another. She can, for example, relate to people only in one manner, by dominating them, by manipulating their every act. The tension expended in thus exercising her *will* impedes her faculty for thought, for tenderness, for humanity. As a result, she is unable to understand, to explicate, to come to terms with anyone. Most important, Agrippina is incapable of love. She is caught in a vicious circle. To compensate for her *arid* relationships with people, she builds up, unconsciously, the primitive and infantile aspects within her personality. These manifest themselves in the form of extreme possessiveness, which in turn further impedes her ability to love.

Her extremely one-sided nature leads to an unbalanced outlook upon life in general and the person or persons she focuses upon in particular. Any slight alteration in her rapport with her son, for example, throws her into a frenzy, the anxiety being out of proportion to the deed. The greater the distress, the more securely she tries to hold on to the object of her desire. She has, in essence, become victimized by that very object she seeks to dominate.[14]

Agrippina's unconscious attitude toward Nero, it can be asserted, is a negative one. It is also static. She persists in trying to keep her dominion over him, in forcing him to remain her "little son." Intuitively, however, she feels the utter impossibility or unnatural nature of her desires. In this connection she speaks in terms of a giant animal moving about in her limbs, preparing to exit from her being. Later, she declares: "Deep in my heart I felt the dreaded omen."[15] Conflict rages within her: her will to dominate versus the glimmer of reality which reveals the impossibility of such an attitude. The dynamism aroused by her chaotic thoughts stirs her affectivity to terrorizing dimensions.

Agrippina is like a giant maw who once gave life and is now determined to withdraw it. Artfully she goes about trying to destroy her son. First, she attempts to elicit a sense of guilt within him. In crescendoes she blurts forth, telling him that he "owes" her everything: that she murdered, stole, poisoned for him alone. How wonderful things used to be, she declares,

> . . . when Nero, young,
> Sent me the prayers of an adoring Court;
> When he left all affairs of State to me,
> When at my word the Senate would assemble[16]

Agrippina can look upon Nero only as a child, actually as an object, since love is never at stake here. Her attitude toward her son and toward men in general never alters. She looked and still does look upon them as vehicles to satisfy her whims, as a *phallus*, symbolically speaking. She is in essence Agrippina, the *Magna Mater*, the *container*; and men, Nero in particular, the *contained*. If he remains in this condition, all development is going to be stifled. He is only able to experience his mother on an unconscious level, never in the light of consciousness or rationally. No genuine or authentic relationship, therefore, is possible.[17]

Agrippina's second step in her attempt to mutilate her son, preventing, thereby, any development within him, is to castigate him. She has noticed, she informs him, that even as a child he possessed highly unpleasant qualities: deceit, pride, savagery, furor. These traits she considers so ignominious that she has kept them secret, unwilling to let the world know the demoniac nature of her son. Belittling him as best she knows how, she seeks to crush all the *élan* which might be aroused within him.

Yet she is thwarted in her attempts to castrate her son. Burrhus, seemingly, has turned against her. He gives his reasons for so doing. He explains to the Queen that her son is no longer her exclusive property, that he is not her "personal" offspring, but lives now in a "collective" realm, he is Emperor. "He's no more son, but master of the world . . ."[18] Though Burrhus tries to illuminate Agrippina on this subject, it is to no avail.

> They would have made him grow old, still a child.
> Then, Madam, why complain? We reverence you.
> We swear by Caesar and his mother too.
> The Emperor, true, no more comes every dawn,
> To place the Empire at your feet and fawn.
> But should he, Madam? Should his gratitude
> Shine clearly in his servitude?
> Must Nero always humble, always tame,
> Not dare to be a Caesar but in name?[19]

The Queen's third attempt at destroying her son results from jealousy. When she discovers Nero's love for Junie, her dread and anger know no bounds. A symphony of gradations, in Racine's extraordinary study of jealousy, is now articulated.

> Can you not see how far I am abased,
> Albina? Upon me he foists a rival.
> If I do not soon snap this fatal bond,
> My place is filled and I become a cipher.
> Till now Octavia, with her empty title,
> Powerless at Court, could be ignored by it,
> Rewards and honours, showered as I saw fit,
> Drew to me all the selfish prayers of men.
> Another woman captures Caesar's love:
> She'll wield the influence both of wife and mistress.
> The fruit of all my cares, great Caesar's chance,
> Will soon become the prize of her one glance . . .
> All flee my presence. . . . I'm alone . . . distraught . . .
> Even if I hastened Heaven's most dread decree,
> My thankless son . . . His rival comes to me.[20]

Agrippina's flame-like personality reaches fulminating force. She is at an impasse. Junie poses a real threat to her. It is she, Agrippina feels, who will "replace" her in her son's world. Deflated, her ego fights for its life. The Queen's frenzy is commensurate with that of a vulture, screaming its anguish. Overwhelmed by the frightening tempo of her passions, she is unable to decide which of the two paths she should tread to win Nero back. Should she try to dominate him as is her custom? Should she listen to Burrhus who suggests she take Nero's personality into consideration, to act with kindness and understanding? Only through proper handling can she halt the growth of this evil excrescence which is her son.

Fear now crystallizes about the object of her desire. Agrippina approaches Nero, talks to him in one of the most gripping scenes in the entire drama (IV,ii). All the wiles at her disposal are used to manipulate the coveted being. Depicting herself as the self-sacrificing mother, she proceeds to list her activities throughout her life, all designed for the welfare of her "beloved" son: her marriage to Claudius, her wish to leave the throne to Nero, the marriage she arranged between Nero and Claudius' daughter, Octavia, to insure his kingship, Claudius' legal adoption of Nero, Britannicus' exile, Claudius' murder.

> I sought his hand, obsessed with but one thought
> To leave you on the throne where I should sit.[21]

Her endeavors are to no avail. As she struggles to win her battle against her son, so Nero's personality suddenly begins to burgeon forth. He sees through his mother's machinations, her pragmatic ways, her constant desire to gratify her ego. Indeed, he curtails her power, forces her to remain virtually captive in the palace. And he declares outspokenly:

> You previously—if I dare plainly speak—
> Have only worked, in my name, for yourself.[22]

Nero keeps hammering the nail into his mother's heart with agility and force. "But Rome demands a master, not a mistress,"[23] he asserts.

Perspectives are lost, logic has been dispersed as Agrippina struggles for survival. She grasps at the nearest safeguard, heaping her son with accusations. She charges him with ingratitude, deception, perfidy. In a frenzy, she calls upon the heavens for help.

> I have but one son. Heaven, that hearest me,
> Have I, except for him, asked aught of thee?
> Nothing could daunt me, remorse, dangers, lies;
> His scorn I swallowed and I shut my eyes
> To the dread horror then foretold to me;
> I've done my all.[24]

Blinded by affectivity, Agrippina is unable to discern her son's final and masterful coup, his clever use of the lie. He wants a reconciliation, he informs his mother. Nero is in effect fostering a climate of illusion, agreeing with the Queen's demands. He will befriend Britannicus, make his mother "arbiter" of his love, he declares. Agrippina's intense joy becomes all the more frightening in the face of Junie's extreme sense of doom. Agrippina, lunging forth, sings her son's praises.

> If you had only seen with what caresses
> He had pledged to me his earnest faith afresh!
> With what embraces he has just detained me!
> He could not take his arms away from me;
> With patient goodness, shining in his face,
> He told me, first of all, the smallest secrets.
> He was my darling son who came to rest
> His proud head on my broad, forgiving breast . . .
> He asked my aid in great affairs of State . . .
> Rome soon will know her Agrippina again![25]

When Agrippina is informed of Britannicus' death, her lofty position is suddenly cut asunder. The shock of her downfall opens her eyes, at least partially. She sees Nero for the first time as an individual in his own right, not as an adjunct to her own personality. His evil nature, his saturnine ways are articulated.

> Go on. You have not done this deed in vain.
> Your murderous hand, beginning with your brother,
> Will, I foresee, reach even to your mother.
> Within your inmost heart I sense your hate;
> You'll want to snap our bond and seal my fate.
> But I wish my very death to burn your breast.
> Do not think, dying, I shall let you rest . . .
> Remorse shall rend you, like the raging Furies,
> That you'll appease with fresh barbarities;
> Your frenzy, ever growing as it goes,
> Shall see, as each day dawns, some fresh blood flows.
> But I hope, at least, Heaven, weary of your breath,
> Will add to all your victims your own death;
> That after weltering in their blood and mine,
> You'll have to shed your own, in moan and whine . . .[26]

Agrippina's divinations and the imprecations she heaps upon her son are, interestingly enough, a resume of her own life experience as projected onto her son.

Agrippina, a woman at the mercy of a supra-personal force or power within her, has rejected all the womanly qualities of tenderness, goodness, loving ways. Because of her power drive, she has unconsciously fallen victim to a predatory daemon, an archetype within her.[27] She is swollen with an invincible egotism and because of such characteristics has no regard for anyone's welfare. Only at the end, when suffering has provoked some semblance of vision, does she realize wherein she has failed in maintaining mastership over her son. Never once, however, does she look within herself, assess her situation, her world, her point of view. Her depths always remain murky.

✶   ✶   ✶

It can be said that Nero is his mother's son, vicious, violent, anguished, passionate, weak. Caught up in his undeveloped personality, he slashes about like a storm which both his mother and his tutor seek to calm. Just as Agrippina must be looked upon as a collective figure, so must Nero. He is "all" those sons trying to liberate themselves from the Terrible Mother archetype. He never succeeds, however, in attaining independence; he merely veers from one sphere of influence to another; first Agrippina, then Burrhus, then Narcissus. His "evolution" into the monstrous Nero of history can be measured and evaluated in terms of the particular influence to which he succumbs.

When falling within the scope of Agrippina's daemon, Nero is child-like, hovering within his mother's orbit. The seeds of revolt, nevertheless, slumber within him. The question remains as to how he will accomplish his bid for freedom. Secret and deceptive means will be his. Such a path clearly indicates a cowardly nature. He is never able to face his mother's gaze, rather he shies away from it. He cannot bear the fixity of her stare. His "clouded" demeanor reveals his indecisiveness, his innate fear or inability to fight strongly and forcefully for his beliefs.

Nero is first prodded into assuming control over himself by his tutors: Seneca, the Stoic, and Burrhus, also a Stoic and commander of the pretorian cohorts (guards). Had he not succumbed to their influence, he might never have endeavored to sever ties with his mother. The outcome of his tutors' teachings, however, is unfortunate as he never really understands the profound meaning of their philosophy. Nero turns the "moral" lessons of the Stoics into insidious vehicles for destruction.

Stoicism taught control over passions and desires, renunciation of pleasure and pain, detachment from the external world. The Stoics further believed that emotions were evil and must be overcome by cognitive means (logos), that ethical progress was a matter of reason and knowledge; morality, a personal question; virtue, a matter of will, and the means of true happiness. Stoicism flourished in Rome at a time when this city was in a state of decay, when license bloomed, when social and religious structures were crumbling. It had gained impetus, to a great extent, as a counterforce.

What are the psychological implications of Stoicism? Was this philosophy suited to Nero's personality? Was it a "wholesome" way of life? Stoicism, an ego-centered way, is based on the pride of virtue. It is an abstract system which goes contrary to nature in that it disregards human frailties. The cognitive view of life advocated by the Stoics does not take into account man's instinctual world, which is part of the "whole" of man. It essays, rather, to suppress this aspect—man's entire affective side—which it considers weak (these include love, affection, relatedness). To suppress this part of a human being is tantamount to starving him. As a result, the animal within him rages, hungers, loses control, destroying all balance within the personality.

The Stoics then were trying to destroy what they considered to be man's inferior characteristics, his instincts. What they did not take into consideration was the fact that when instincts are properly tended to (understood) and accepted, they act in harmony with the other aspects of the personality and as such are positive forces. When unattended, however, they crave for what is rightfully theirs and become virulent and destructive. Not to take into account man's earthly half (physis), merely to cultivate his godly or spiritual side (logos), is to cut him off from life, to create a topheavy being whose illusions and delusions will cause him to crumble, to grovel in the most turbid of mires.[28]

The life of the historical Seneca, Nero's most trusted adviser between the years 54–57, illustrates perfectly the tricks that the suppression of instincts can play within the personality. Seneca's instinctual half, crushed by his cognitive side, blazed with fury in his tragedies, *Hercules, Troacles, Medea, Phaedra, Thyestes*, etc. These are marked by the most violent and the goriest characters in any theatre. Seneca, however, was fortunate because as a poet he could channel his instincts, liberate them through the medium of his art. Nero's plight was less auspicious. He had no outlet but his fellow men.

To impose the Stoic philosophy upon Nero was suicidal. It fostered the growth of the "monster" in him. When Agrippina chose Seneca and Burrhus as her son's tutors, she did so with the firm belief that they would teach him virtue. Neither she nor Burrhus nor Seneca (who does not appear in the drama, but whose name is mentioned and whose presence is keenly felt) were in any way aware of the effects of their teachings (instilling in him a sense of pride, a desire for independence, a notion of Empire and rulership) on their ward. What they were actually accomplishing, however, was disastrous. They were inflicting a predetermined simulacrum upon him. Burrhus and Seneca were molding Nero to fit their image of what an Emperor should be. Never once did they take into account Nero's personality, his needs, and attempt to build around these. They succeeded in stifling him, in rejecting Nero the individual in order to create Nero the collective figure. For this reason, in essence, his innermost nature could never develop. He could not possibly integrate the various aspects of his personality into a cohesive whole since he was forever rejecting some part of himself. He remained infantile in his behavior, therefore, and merely passed from one state of dependency to another.

When carefully examining Burrhus' relationship with Nero, we witness a step-by-step deterioration of the Stoic teaching.

The first time Burrhus is aware of the ineffective hold Stoicism has upon his pupil occurs during a conversation which centers around love, that very aspect of human nature which he denigrates. Because he has been "well" taught, Nero looks upon love as an evil rather than as something natural: "the evil is without remedy." Yet he cannot cure himself of his weakness: "I must love, finally."[29] Burrhus, rigid in his attitude, decries Nero's lack of control. A cognitive attitude toward love, as toward anything else, must be applied, he asserts. The will, like a muscle, must be exercised constantly if it is to remain flexible.

> Above all, if avoiding Junie's eyes,
> You would, a few days, stay away from her:
> Be sure, however much one seems to love.
> One loves not if one wishes not to love.[30]

Burrhus only later has a glimmer of insight into his pupil's character. He realizes that the evils he thought he had crushed remain, virulent, undaunted, ready to emerge with tornado-like intensity.

> Burrhus, Nero lays bare his inmost soul.
> This savagery you thought you might control
> Is ready to break loose from your weak bond.
> To what excesses it may spread beyond![31]

Now Burrhus loses composure to a certain degree. And since Seneca is not in Rome, he turns to Agrippina for help. He implores her to grapple with a cause he feels he has lost, to use gentleness in confronting her son and winning him to the side of virtue. So intent is Burrhus in imposing his dictum that he fails totally to see Nero in the light of his own development. Only when he confesses his treachery outright to his tutor, "I'll hug my rival, but to smother him,"[32] does Burrhus react strongly and positively. He again explicates his ethos, declaring that the Emperor of Rome should be virtuous, should be an image to his people, should be loved and admired. Nero, however, intent upon achieving his own ends at this point, grows weary of abstract formulas. Exasperated, he makes a *tabula rasa* of his past.

> What? Must I ever, chained by my past fame,
> Retain before my eyes some nameless love
> That Chance gives us and takes away in one day?
> Slave to their wishes, tyrant of my own,
> Merely to please them do I wear the crown?[33]

Nero overthrows everything now. Desirous only of gratifying his instincts, suppressed for so long, he luxuriates in a world devoid of anchors and chains. Because Nero has never been given a chance to develop, he cannot seem to relate to family or friends; he is considered always as a pawn or as an object. His personality rests on no solid foundation and for this reason he falls a prey to any domineering force surrounding him. Britannicus' tutor, Narcissus, his next master, inculcates within him the arts of treachery and deceit in their most blatant forms.

Narcissus' name describes his personality. Like the young plant god who was under the dominion of "mother earth," he is undeveloped, effeminate, virtually emasculated. Narcissus seeks out the easiest paths, whether right or wrong. Morality is unknown to him. He is neither evil nor good. To be one or the other implies a sense of consciousness, at least in terms of one's acts. Narcissus lives in a nebulous and clouded underworld where differentiation has never taken place.

Interestingly enough, it is to Narcissus and not to Burrhus that Nero first describes his love. He must have felt, intuitively, that Burrhus would not understand the meaning of those emotions he considers base. The feeling realm, which is not within Burrhus' scope of reference, is the only world in which Narcissus can really function.

Though Narcissus may not fully comprehend Nero's reasoning concerning his love, he does not undervalue the power of the Emperor's passion (instinctual realm) for Junie. He is in fact excited by it and encourages the Emperor in his courtship. A basic jealousy between Burrhus and Narcissus might also account for the lavish advice he offers Nero, all counter to Stoic teaching: "Lord, love does not always await reason,"[34] he states.

Narcissus goes one step further. He does his best to incite trouble and to this end confirms Nero's suspicions concerning Junie's love for Britannicus. He urges his master to win his beloved's affection; the glitter of an Emperor's love, he intimates, will dazzle this maiden. "Command she love you and you will be loved."[35] Excited by the very thought of a conflagration, Narcissus encourages Nero to reject his mother's vigorous control over him by stirring his misguided sense of pride: "Must you forever cower beneath her tutelage?"[36] And, he adds:

> Live for yourself and reign. Why reign for her?
> Are you afraid?[37]

Suddenly Nero sees himself as he really is: a fearful, cringing boy where his mother is concerned. He begins to articulate his anguish, admitting his weakness.

> Safe from her eyes, I threaten, I command,
> I heed your counsels and I dare approve them;
> I rage against her and I try to brave her.
> But—I am laying bare to you my soul—
> As soon as, by ill-luck, I'm in her sight,
> Whether I dare not yet deny the power of
> Those eyes, where I have so long read my duty,
> My strength against her I in vain assemble:
> My startled Genius before hers must tremble.
> And so to free me from this servitude,
> I shun her everywhere, am even rude,
> From time to time inciting her to rancour,
> So that she may avoid me as I shun her.[38]

Nero is now under Narcissus' sphere of influence. Not completely, however, since he recoils with horror at the tutor's proposition to have Britannicus poisoned. Such a decisive response indicates a desire to emerge from the archaic and primigenial world in which he lives. He cannot accomplish his goal unaided.

Junie, Agrippina's opposite, plays a primal role in Nero's life. Agrippina, it can be said, is a projection of Nero's bestial side, whereas Junie symbolizes his spiritual aspect. Nero is never able to relate to either force. When under his mother's dominion, he is fully dependent upon her. When within Junie's orbit, he cannot rise up to the realms inhabited by such a perfect and ideal being.

Nero is so unrelated to Junie that he cannot even conceive of her as a whole female figure, but merely as half of one, an all-spiritual force, a hallucinatory vision. She lives within his being as does the moon, as a nocturnal shadow moving about his zone of influence. The tears she sheds when passing through the great hall to her apartment (II,ii) symbolize the evanescent, ephemeral entity which she is. As such, she lacks body and depth and exists only as a fantasy, a dream, a figment of Nero's distorted imagination, a being living in a uterine paradise. Nero craves for Junie, since she compensates for the beauty, gentleness, and love he has lacked throughout his life.

Nero's inability to speak with Junie as she passes through the hall (II,ii) reveals the unreal nature of his relationship. Later, when his aphasia disappears (II,iii), his words to her appear awkward. He compliments her first, hoping that well-placed phrases will serve to attract her. They have the opposite effect. Junie avoids and evades what she considers to be his unpleasant manner, and as she does so his passion mounts. Unsure of himself, fearing he will lose the only beauty in his life, he resorts to threats. He informs her of his intention to banish Britannicus unless she tells his rival that she no longer loves him.

Nero watches Junie's torment as she carries out his orders. A sense of power and achievement floods his system for the first time. He is acting *like a man*. He considers himself master of situations, life's supreme manipulator, as his mother had once considered herself. His ego dilates. Certain critics have considered Nero's reaction to Junie's and Britannicus' pain, expressed in the following lines, as proof of his sadistic propensities.

> But I will seek my joy in his despair.
> I keep a charming picture of his smart . . .[39]

Though this may be so in part, the Emperor's joy also stems from a feeling of relief: that is, he finally no longer feels helpless, he now considers himself a true Emperor capable of giving orders and fashioning futures. Such a sense of fulfillment, though false in essence, sustains his pleasure and is more rewarding than the momentary satisfaction of sadistic penchants.

To complicate Nero's situation, however, Britannicus, who had merely been a vehicle for Agrippina's power lust, an excuse for Narcissus' presence in the palace, becomes a very *real* threat to his plans: his rival. Britannicus comes to represent everything that Nero is not. Like Junie, he is tender, moral, kind. When Britannicus tries to confront Nero, he succeeds only in arousing his anger. The Emperor recoils at his own impotence, realizing at this point the precarious nature of his situation. The extreme pride he had felt moments before now vanishes as he succumbs to pain and, with it, to desires for vengeance. "I must be respected, I must be obeyed!" he declares.[40] The very fact that Nero feels he must insist upon obedience indicates the weak image he has of himself. A strong person would enforce obedience through demeanor and actions, not verbally alone.

Nero is no more able to establish a relationship with Junie than he is with any other individual in the drama. He has always associated her with the highest of realms; she is, therefore, never really part of this earth. Because of her unreality, she is able, at the end of the play, to escape from the palace to the Temple of the Vestal Virgins, there to fulfill her destiny as *spirit*.

Nero, condemned to a state of silence and solitude, is compelled henceforth to *indwell*. His madness, however, is in no way comparable to Orestes'. The Roman monarch's journey inward is not in quest of redemption as it was with the Greek youth, but rather a wild fury at the thought of having lost Junie. His eyes, glassy with emptiness, unable to focus, are never tormented with any moral question. Submersion into oblivion, into *mystery*, is the outcome of his adventure.

II

Britannicus can be described as a type of sudden and explosive gushing forth of Racine's inner world in the form of antithetically colored fantasies given shape and flesh. These aggrandized shapes shuffle about on stage, bellow their burdens, confront each other in chromatic color tones, prod and stir viscerally all those with whom they come into contact.

The antagonisms basic to the creatures in *Britannicus* are brought into sharper focus by an extraordinary visual technique inherent in Racine's text and based on the interaction of light and dark, black and white. Such juxtaposition serves to usher in a whole new and mysterious atemporal realm, adding, thereby, another dimension to Racine's outpourings. A stunning example of this optical method is achieved in Act II, ii, when Nero hides in the shadows of the great hall and watches Junie pass before him into her own apartments, bathed in reflected light. The contrasting color tones immediately implant in the onlooker's mind a sharp delineation between the carnal world, represented by the Emperor, and the spiritual realm, symbolized by Junie. The eerie hues which move about the stage take on concrete shapes, flooding the atmosphere with an inexplicable sense of dread and terror.

> Stirred by a curious desire,
> Last night I watched her brought into the palace,
> Her sad eyes, wet with tears, to Heaven raised,
> Sparkling through all the glittering arms and torches;
> Beautiful, unadorned and simply clad,
> Befitting beauty just borne off from sleep.
> Indeed, I do not know if this undress,
> The shadows, torches, cries, and midnight silence,
> And the wild aspect of her bold abductors,
> Enhanced the frightened sweetness of her eyes.
> However that may be, by all entranced,
> I wished to speak to her, but lost my voice:
> I stood there rooted, as though wonderstruck,
> And let her pass beyond to her apartments.
> I passed into my own. There, all alone,
> I sought to drive her image from me.
> Obsessed with her, I thought to soothe her woe;
> I loved the very tears I caused to flow.[41]

The dramatic opposition of color tones in this scene is realized as follows. Nero stands invisible on the side of the great hall which is cast in blackness. In sharp contrast to this penumbra is the dazzling light arising from the flaming torches, rendered even more striking by their reflection upon the metal armaments hanging about. As Junie walks through the room, she slips into and out of Nero's orbit, into an aura of spectral glare. Tears shine from her eyes. These, pure in their transparency, enhance her immaculate nature, transforming her, in Nero's eyes, into an essence, a dream, a phantasmagoria.

Racine calls upon the auditory sense to further increase the antithesis between Nero—immersed in blackness or its counterpart, the harsher hues emanating from the fiery torches, indicating passionate and unregenerate urges—and Junie, entranced in lunar-like reflections, standing for the impalpable world of the spirit. Sounds, or the lack of them, "screams and silence," pound forth in rhythmic reverberations and serve to implement the sharp division already existing between two clashing worlds: the inaudible as revealed by Junie and the audible by Nero.

The evanescent, ephemeral Junie is set far above Nero's earthly dominion of brutal contrasts. He, *physis*, can never hope to unite with his opposite, *nous*, any more than black and white can fuse in a differentiated world. For this reason he fails "to enclose Junie in his shadow." Though Nero is unaware of his fate rationally, he seems to sense it unconsciously. No balance, no wholeness, no *complexio op-positorum* is or could ever be forthcoming. Junie fulfills her destiny as spirit, Nero his, as flesh. The perception of such an outcome shocks him into a state of immobility and aphasia, of virtual paralysis. He knows now he cannot impede the march of events.

The mysterious and awesome forces called into play in this scene by both visual and auditory means also succeed in shattering the cognitive triad of past, present, and future. Future developments impose themselves upon the present and Nero's immediate reaction to these previews of things to come. The linear conception of time disappears, as it had in certain instances in *Andromache*, and protagonists and onlookers alike are plunged into an endlessly cascading *pleroma*.

The symbols used in *Britannicus* ally the visible with the invisible world, the animate with the inanimate, present and future. A limitless realm is thereby created which injects a mythological quality into this work. Moreover, what had been rationally explainable in terms of character and situation, now becomes nebulous, ambiguous, mystical—creating a fitting atmosphere for the entrée of Racine's creatures.

The two symbols most frequently called upon by Racine in *Britannicus* are the palace and the eye.

The palace symbol fixes the locale, circumscribes the action, increasing the depth and potency of the emotions and events depicted. Though *Andromache* and *The Theban Brothers* also take place in a palace room, never prior to *Britannicus* does the King's domain assume the force of a protagonist. In the former dramas, the palace acts as a background, an adjunct, a means to an end. Now, however, though the palace serves as decor, it becomes also basic to the action, revelatory of the personalities inhabiting its secret corridors and recesses.

The palace implies many things. It can be looked upon as a screen, a mask, a facade, a device capable of preventing communication between an exterior and visible domain and an inner world, that of the living mystery. As a separating device, the palace intensifies the already vicious antagonisms at play. It "watches" Agrippina wandering through the corridors,[42] *shut out* from her son's world by a "door." Rejected, shorn of her life's goal, she is fearful, as Nero pursues his solitary way. Because of its constricting nature, the palace for Junie has always been a vehicle for destruction. When, for example, Nero imprisons her within its folds, it stifles her growth, wrenches her very heart from her.

Since it is a vessel-like entity, a container of sorts, the palace has been associated with the womb. It is, therefore, a fecundating object, able to give birth to a "monster." Once an active participant in Agrippina's life, she speaks of the palace with nostalgia as a protective, comforting entity, enclosing her within its being as Nero had once lived within his mother's limbs.

> Within the palace, where, behind a veil,
> Invisible and present, I became
> The almighty spirit of that mighty body.[43]

The palace is a microcosm; within its enclosures there exist emotions on the verge of exploding, a whole subliminal world within which personalities are reduced to their component parts. A repository for emotions, the palace is frequently personified and becomes a living and flexible object able to hold all the feelings and emotions projected upon it. When, for example, Narcissus informs Britannicus of the futility of his pursuits and supplications, he does so in terms of the palace. "In vain this palace echoes with your sighs."[44] The Emperor's abode in this instance has been transformed into an instrument capable of absorbing and consoling the pain of others.

Because the palace is personified, it is endowed with the capacity to feel. The differences, therefore, existing between inert and animated matter are abolished. When Junie tells Britannicus that "These very walls . . . perhaps have eyes,"[45] one has the impression that this royal abode has been transformed into a hydra-like animal, able to peer at its victims from all sides. These many-seeing eyes gaze with the vigor of a deity, injecting a sense of doom and fright into all the corners of what has now taken on a spaceless and timeless dimension. Man, small, frightened, crawls about, his despair increasing to the point of suffocation.

The eye symbol plays a primordial role in this work. Just as the palace represents two worlds, the outer and the inner, the concrete and the amorphous, so does the eye. The eye as a sphere, hollow on the inside, with a dark center covered over by a vitreous element, is in essence not only a mirror capable of reflecting outer action but a container in which all past events and feelings repose. Because of these qualities, the eye can also be considered as an urn in which archaic and inchoate feelings, sensations, and memories repose.

When, for example, Junie's eyes are "sad," though events themselves seem to be working in her favor, they function as prognosticators.

> Why, as you hear me, do your sweet, sad eyes
> Gaze far away from me into the skies?[46]

The eye senses an ominous portent living within the multiple time sequences reposing in her being. Dismal color tones tinge her expression in cloudy and blurred gradations.

As an "observing consciousness," the eye illuminates what might remain dark, the inner world.[47] When, therefore, Britannicus seeks to discover the truth concerning his situation, he asks Narcissus to observe the eyes of his partisans as well as their words. He infers in this passage the existence of a dichotomy between the expression as revealed by the eye, an organ of perception and therefore truthful, and the understanding of rationally conceived speeches, a vehicle of the mind and at times an instrument for deception.

Eyes, to Nero's way of thinking, are so powerful an instrumentality that they have assumed auditory qualities. They are, in this respect, capable of screaming out their vision. "The glances you think dumb I'll overhear."[48] Frequently these staring objects overpower Nero, paralyze his every fiber, as they do that of the primitive.[49] Such an instance occurs in Agrippina's presence, when he speaks out his dread for her spellbinding black orbs, her spheres of influence: "Those eyes, where I have so long read my duty."[50] His mother's eyes are like magical and hypnotic forces, dispensing their evil powers with crushing intensity.

As "mirrors" of his inner world, his eyes project its turbulence. When Nero learns of Junie's flight from his palace, these cavernous entities of his can no longer veil his sorrow. They have taken on the hardened gaze of the criminal. Unsettled, they shift about, assuming an expressionless stare, as though life itself had been drained from them.

The spacelessness and timelessness achieved by Racine through his color tones and his imagery serve to dislocate his characters' and his viewers' entire frame of reference. The ordered, reasonable universe they had once known has given way to a boundless region in which beings are propelled by staccato-like rhythms and whirlwind forces. In this world of intangibles, life is experienced as if in a state of suspended animation, each entity a foil or a buttress for eternally erupting impulses.

III

Britannicus burgeoned forth directly out of Racine's unconscious. To try to point to specific instances in Racine's life which might have led to the formation of certain personalities and situations in this play would be to severely limit its scope. One may assert, however, that certain preoccupations on Racine's part (the Jansenist ascetic life which still weighed heavily upon him, the sorrow experienced from La Du Parc's death, his ever mounting difficulties furthering his career) were projected into this drama, contributing to its climate of dread, despair, and hopelessness. All the protagonists in this work are doomed: Agrippina and Burrhus fail in their endeavors, Narcissus and Britannicus are killed, Junie escapes into the land of the spirit, Nero, unable to face his ordeal, seeks oblivion. Racine's inner turbulence, it would seem, was too powerful a force to be contained. It erupted with whirlwind intensity, transmuted in the work of art.

5

Berenice

"To search for myself,
to recognize myself . . ."[1]

*B*ERENICE was performed for the first time on November 21, 1670. Eight days later, Corneille's *Titus and Berenice* opened at the Palais-Royal. Many people have wondered whether the simultaneous productions of these two plays treating the same subject was coincidental.

Some theorists have felt that Henriette d'Angleterre's pathetic story had inspired Racine to create his *Berenice*. She had married Philippe duc d'Orléans, Louis XIV's brother, for reasons of state, though in love with the monarch and he with her. Fontenelle, however, in his *Life of Corneille*, suggested that Henriette d'Angleterre had proposed the topic to both Corneille and Racine. In this fashion, the rivals she felt would fight their literary duel in the open. L'Abbé du Bos and Louis Racine, however, suggested that Henriette d'Angleterre, who was the protectress of both Molière and of Racine,[2] had proposed the subject to Racine alone. When Corneille's friends heard of this happening, they informed the aged writer of the situation, who went ahead and wrote his own version of the play. Others have suggested that Racine usurped the idea from Corneille.

A further hypothesis has been forwarded: Louis XIV's love for Marie Mancini, Cardinal Mazarin's niece. Because the Cardinal had other plans for the King of France (he was arranging his marriage to Marie-Thérèse of Austria), he likewise concluded other wedding arrangements for his niece (the Connetable Colonna), forcing upon each of the participants a painful separation.

It was not, however, unusual for two writers to create a play on similar subjects. Such a situation had already arisen with Racine's

Alexander the Great, performed at the Palais-Royal, and Abbé Claude Boyer's *Alexander the Great*, given at the Hôtel de Bourgogne.[3] Moreover, neither Racine's nor Corneille's plays were the first French renditions of Titus' love for the Jewish Queen. Magnon had written a *Titus* (1600), Jean Regnault de Segrais an incomplete novel (1648, 1651), Scudéry included a long passage on Berenice in *The Illustrious Women* (1642).

Though the play's genesis is uncertain, what is definite is the fact that Racine's work earned a "succès de larmes." Corneille's *Titus and Berenice* was performed twenty-one times and, considering the average number of performances for the time, was not looked upon as a failure.

Berenice was successful; yet it did not escape attack. The anti-Jansenist Abbé Montfaucon de Villars harangued against it in his *Critique of Berenice* (1671). He condemned Racine's play on several counts: it did not adhere to the rules (the first act was useless; the action in general was halting and reduced to a series of "madrigals and elegies"); the historical inaccuracies were appalling (the Consuls could not come to see Titus as indicated in the play since at the time of Vespasian's death there were only two Consuls, Vespasian and his son); the characters did not resemble their original counterparts (Racine's Antiochus was foolish, Titus dishonest; Berenice was lacking in dignity, the letter she wrote to Titus in Act V being ridiculous); Racine's style was too familiar; Berenice, the Jewess, could not possibly "attest to the Gods." Racine must have taken some of the aforementioned criticisms quite seriously. In subsequent editions, he modified some sections of his play, omitting, for example, the text of Berenice's letter to Titus and having her invoke "heaven's" help rather than the gods.

Racine was not one to shrink before opposition. He answered his disparagers forcefully in two prefaces to *Berenice*. The topic itself, he indicated, had been drawn from Suetonius' *Lives of the Caesars* and was ideal for the theatre because of the "violence of the passions it could excite."[4] To those enemies who asserted that there was no blood or death in his drama and, therefore, no tragedy, he remarked:

> It is by no means essential that there should be blood and corpses in a tragedy; it is enough that its action should be great and its actors heroic, that passions should be aroused, and that everything in it should breathe that majestic sadness in which all the pleasure of tragedy resides.[5]

Moreover, the various emotions experienced in the Berenice-Titus liaison were indeed of a "touching" nature and, therefore, conducive to tragedy. To those who condemned his play because of the simplicity of its action, he made an obvious thrust at Corneille and his followers.

> There are some who think that this simplicity is a sign of lack of invention. They do not reflect that on the contrary all invention consists in making something out of nothing, and that all that multiplicity of incidents has always been the refuge of poets who did not feel in their own genius either enough fertility or enough strength to hold their audience through five acts, by a single plot, sustained by the depth of the passions, by the beauty of the sentiments, and by the elegance of the expression.[6]

The theatre's cardinal rule, Racine explained, was "to please."

✓   ✓   ✓

Shortly before La Du Parc's death, a young actress, Marie Desmares, called Champmeslé, married to the actor-author Charles Chevillet, arrived in Paris. After playing in a pastoral by Boyer, *Venus' Feast*, and in Quinault's *The False Tiberius*, she signed a contract in 1670 with the Hôtel de Bourgogne. It was La Champmeslé who starred in Racine's *Berenice*.

Unlike La Du Parc, who dispensed her favors judiciously, La Champmeslé was more responsive to demands made upon her. She and her husband, it was said, were prone to infidelities and neither was jealous of the other. Several men, including Charles de Sévigné and Jean Racine, were linked to her. When Louis Racine, the author's son, wrote his *Memoirs* on Jean Racine's life, he denied any existence of a liaison between his father and the celebrated actress. Their relationship, he asserted, was strictly of a working nature. His father spent a great deal of time training La Champmeslé in the art of recitation, diction, gesticulation, etc. Since she had a poor memory, he explained, her parts had to be taught her first, before any tonal or rhythmical devices could be superimposed. Indeed, Racine taught her so well that people were convinced she had been created to portray his characters. Such felicity of style as she displayed on stage was due to the hours of work Racine had spent training her. Mme de Sévigné, in a letter to her daughter (March 16, 1672), echoed the opinion of many of her contemporaries, that Racine wrote his plays for La Champmeslé.

Racine had learned the art of declamation at Port-Royal from his teacher Antoine Le Maître. Because of his feeling for language and the expert training he received, he infused his speech with great musicality and knew just how to modulate his voice. In time he gained such expertise in this field that Louis XIV made Racine his official reader.

✓ ✓ ✓

Berenice takes place in Rome, in a vestibule between the apartments of Titus and of Berenice.

Act I. After a week of official mourning for the Emperor Vespasian, Titus is to marry Berenice, Queen of Palestine. Antiochus, King of Commagene, who has been secretly in love with her for five years, now declares his passion openly. He knows such an act to be hopeless and so intends to leave Rome directly after his confession. Though Berenice is surprised by his feelings, she is preoccupied with her own problems and wonders why Titus has been avoiding her for the past week.

Act II. Titus, unbeknown to Berenice, has decided to ask Antiochus to take her back to Palestine. He cannot marry her because of Roman hostility to monarchies and Berenice is a Queen. When Titus sees her, he lacks the courage to speak the truth. Intuitively, Berenice feels something is wrong.

Act III. Antiochus finally carries out Titus' will. He informs Berenice of the separation which must take place between her and Rome's future Emperor. Berenice cannot believe the news and is convinced that Antiochus has been motivated by jealousy. Hurt, he decides to leave but before doing so wants to make certain of Berenice's future.

Act IV. Berenice, in a state of extreme agitation, awaits Titus' arrival. Torn between his love for her and his obligations to his country, Titus finds sufficient strength to reveal the situation to her. Berenice despairs. She is determined to kill herself. Titus, also in a state of anguish, consults the Senate once again, hoping for a reverse decision.

Act V. Antiochus learns of Berenice's intentions to leave Rome. He despairs and longs to end his life. Meanwhile, Titus discovers Berenice's letter in which she informs him of her decision to commit suicide. He threatens to do likewise unless she attempts to understand his point of view and the necessity for a separation. Once Berenice is assured of Titus' love for her she finds the strength to leave Rome. Antiochus also departs, but alone.

I

Titus is unlike any of Racine's other heroes. Having already experienced all the violence possible in the domain of love and war, he is purged of his volatile qualities and longs for an inherently stable life. In *The Theban Brothers*, Racine introduced two heroes, Polynices and Eteocles, who burn themselves out because of their "internecine" bat-

tles. Pyrrhus (*Andromache*) is destroyed because he permits himself to
be led by the one he loves and never assumes any kind of kingly attitude. Orestes (*Andromache*) who goes mad from remorse, never develops his own personality, but remains wholly dependent upon the
female principle. Nero (*Britannicus*), broken in spirit, withdraws into
his inner realm. Titus is the only hero so far who sees his course with
lucidity, who knows what his way must be, and who activates his will
in order to assume and maintain a cognitive attitude.

In certain ways Titus is a Cornelian hero who is not only conscious
of his obligation to a higher authority (the collective), but who does
his best to carry out its decision. He is also a Sartrian hero who not
only develops during the course of the drama, but in so doing *creates*
himself.[7]

The concept of "creating" oneself, of "turning oneself" into a being whose principles and goals in life are lofty, has etiological significance. Berenice is rejected by the Roman Senate as a Queen, not as a
woman. Kingship (Queenship) is of a hereditary nature and, as such,
does not fit into the Romans' system of things. To be King implies no
initiative, no extreme tension on the part of the participant, a title
which comes to an individual through no force or incentive of his own.
An Emperor, on the other hand, is a person who "earns" his title and
who is proclaimed by the people. The word "imperator" was a title
Roman soldiers bestowed by proclamation upon a general who had
won a victory, after which it was ratified by the Senate. Julius Caesar
was Rome's first Emperor. Titus, therefore, like his predecessors will be
forced to earn the title of Emperor, which means that he must transform himself from the love-sick adolescent whose sole preoccupation
has been war and love (before the play begins), to a mature personality
whose view of life is based on sound judgment and encompasses all his
people, not merely himself.

Considered from a philosophical point of view then, the theme of
"love" may be looked upon as an obstacle Racine sets in his hero's
path, like the labors of Hercules. Titus must sacrifice his love, he must
pass through his ordeal (initiation) if he is to step from youth to manhood. His drama resides then in the crossing of the barrier which
separates one phase of life from another. Berenice and Antiochus, from
this point of view, are merely agents, hurdles set in his path, preventing him from journeying through passage.

Titus is one of Racine's most complex heroes. Since he seeks by
definition to transform himself into a mature human being (an Emperor), he must of necessity abandon the love which has been the
primal force of his existence. He is then sacrificing his ephemeral and

personal life as Berenice's lover for an eternal and collective state as Emperor.[8]

Let us examine Titus' situation in greater detail, first the historical figure (40–90 A.D.) who was called by his people "the delight of humanity" and by the Jews "the wicked one."[9] Titus was the son of Vespasian. Since he had been brought up in Nero's Court, it is understandable that he would have been exposed to Stoic philosophy, to Mithraism and to the license inherent in Roman society at the time. In his youth Titus fought valiantly in Germany and Great Britain, and had followed his father to Judea. He laid siege to Jerusalem in 69, saw to it that the Temple was destroyed and, according to Josephus, sacked the city to such an extent that one would never have known that it had once been inhabited. It has been estimated that as many as 1,000,000 Jews perished. Titus, who succeeded his father in 71, was an able administrator. His career was cut short, however, when he died of a fever only twenty-seven months after he had become Emperor.

Titus was very much influenced by Mithra worship. Such a philosophy, replete with energy and asceticism, is not only present in his actions, but embedded in the imagery of his dialogue.

The worship of the bull-god Mithra was not new. According to the *Gathas*, it had been suppressed by Zarathustra, but returned all the more brilliantly some years later. At this juncture, the bull became the symbol of the springtime sun, an energetic and fecundating natural force which tried to rid the world of darkness and sin. Indeed, certain hymns speak of this animal as having a thousand ears and ten thousand eyes. When Mithraism was an intrinsic part of Persian religion (during the period of Cyrus and Artaxerxes), Mithra votaries would go through a series of purification rituals, washing themselves for three days, enduring beatings of all sorts, sacrificing cattle and birds.[10]

As Mithraism spread to Babylonia and Greece, the bull became associated with the god of victory and war, he became *Sol invictus*.[11] Nero was initiated into this cult as were the Caesars of the first two centuries. Titus, brought up in the very heart of Nero's court, cannot help but be immersed in this sect in which energy, fire, and asceticism play such a prominent role. As a youth, he had the energy of a bull, functioned instinctually, and in battle forged ahead, a conqueror.

According to Racine, Titus' life can be divided into two phases, a flamboyant youth and a studied, even ascetic, maturity. The disruptive element which caused the change within his personality was the death of his father, the Emperor Vespasian. This loss was instrumental in bringing about Titus' mysterious evolution from a primitive and child-like state of dependency in which the cult of energy was uppermost to an existence filled with responsibility, with the inclusion of the more ascetic aspects of Mithra worship.

In certain individuals, transformation never occurs. Nero is a case in point. His instincts never evolve positively, they stagnate within him, regress. For this reason he is forever recreating childlike or infantile milieux for himself. What Titus experiences with his father's death is shock and, with it, the impact of responsibility. A collision has taken place within him between instinct and ego consciousness. At first he experiences his battle passively, by running away from it, never confronting the real issue in the form of Berenice. He is always asking someone else (Antiochus) to carry out his plans. Had he not taken the situation in hand, he would never have passed the hurdle and would have smothered as Nero did. Titus, therefore, has to act aggressively and break the bonds which impede him from fulfilling his destiny. He succeeds and turns into the image the Romans projected on their Emperor.[12]

As *Berenice* opens, the adolescent stage of Titus' development (his Dionysian side with all its frenzies, though a positive force in the first half of life) is coming to a close. The mature man (possessing the Apollonian qualities of judgment) is being born.

To earn the title of Emperor, however, will be difficult for Titus. Like Pyrrhus, he is a man divided. Fiery, brilliant, courageous when it comes to war, he seems very nearly pusillanimous when confronting Berenice. The mere thought of cutting ties with her is too painful even to articulate.

> I'm going to leave her and forever.
> I have not only just abandoned hope;
> I made you speak, I listened to your words,
> So that your zeal might secretly succeed.
> In countering my love that still would speak.[13]

What makes his plight all the more tragic is his analytical assessment of his own situation, his lucidity.

> I loved and sighed for her when all was peace;
> Another ruled the empire of the world;
> Captain of my fate, and still free to love
> I was accountable to me alone . . .
> I felt the burden that had fallen on me;
> Far from belonging to my love, I knew
> I had to renounce my very self.[14]

When Titus confesses "I had to renounce my very self," he is in effect admitting to the need of rejecting his personal existence in order to fulfill a collective image. By becoming identified with his office he is divesting himself of his individual personality and life.[15]

What changes occurred in Titus during his period of transformation? The creation of a personality which had little or no basis in reality, which existed solely in the minds of the Roman populace. Titus donned a mask, a *persona*, effecting in this manner a compromise personality designed to mediate between the individual (himself) and the society (he hopes to represent). This kind of transformation usually results in extreme inner chaos, the man behind the mask struggling with the outer being. Titus does not escape such torments. In the process he becomes a solitary figure, divesting himself of everything that is real and alive, opting for the imaginary and the abstract.[16]

Early in the drama Titus realizes that the image he seeks to create for himself is antipodal to the inner man he is; as Lao-tzu once said, "High rests on low." The dichotomy in Titus' personality between the external man, whose *persona* gives the impression of strength and courage, and the inner man, the victim of melancholia and extreme timidity, becomes all the more apparent. Titus is perfectly aware of his inertia. Indeed, he is ashamed of it. Unable to cope with his situation, he seeks to escape from it and asks Antiochus to bear the message of separation to Berenice.

> I'm waiting for Antiochus to entrust
> To him this precious charge I cannot keep.
> I want him to escort her to the Orient.[17]

Even his confidant is astounded by Titus' pusillanimity. That a conqueror of nations should be incapable of speaking out to a defenseless woman is virtually unbelievable.

> And that the conquering hero of the nations
> Would soon or late know how to conquer self.[18]

The very same points debated in *Britannicus* between Burrhus' virtuous, reasonable philosophy of love and Narcissus' pragmatic attitude are again taken up in *Berenice*. Though greater understanding of the human *feelings* involved in love relationships is present in the latter work, the consensus still remains the same: when seeking to become Emperor (a public figure) strength must be expressed in all domains.

Titus reaches moments of exasperation as he tries to "create" the public figure he seeks to become. He rebels against the burdens placed upon him, angers at the thought of what must be sacrificed in order to fulfill his destiny.

> Beneath fine names, how cruel is my honour!
> Ah, how much finer would my sad eyes find it,
> If it were to confront me but with death![19]

The more Titus analyzes his plight, the more despondent he becomes and the greater is his inertia. Once the shock resulting from his father's death and the ensuing realization of his life's course has subsided, a type of introverted lethargy sets in, rendering him incapable of all action. He begins to question his goals. He wonders why he is so preoccupied with the Emperorship, with honor and dignity. After meditation, he realizes that Berenice nurtured these ideas of "honor" and of "fame," that she introduced them to him. As a youth, he had never thought in these terms though he did display an innate sense of justice. Suetonius tells us that Titus was present when his good friend Britannicus was poisoned. He was so distraught by this crime that he drank the rest of the liquid in the glass and became very ill. His feelings of decency exhibited in this youthful act were implemented, later on, by Berenice. For these reasons he cannot hurt her. His devotion to her will not permit such a callous attitude to prevail.

> I owe her all, Paulinus. Harsh reward!
> All that I owe her is to crash on her.
> All price of all my fame and all her virtue,
> I'll say to her "Depart, see me no more."[20]

Since Berenice was in part the instrument of his evolution, since it was she who instilled ideas of virtue and honor within him, to reject her would submerge him in guilt feelings. The weight of his crime seems too great. "Come, think, no more,"[21] he says to himself.

When finally Titus does face Berenice (II, iii), as he must, he suffers from aphasia, as had Nero when confronted with the vision of Junie walking across the palace hall to her apartment. Titus is incapable of uttering a word concerning her departure. Shocked by his own incapacity, he seeks out Antiochus and declares, "I only want to borrow your voice."[22] And he pursues:

> Then go to her and tell my troubled silence.
> Explain, above all, I must not see her.
> Be the sole witness of her tears and mine;
> Bid her farewell from me and bring me hers.
> Let us both flee, the tragic meeting flee.[23]

Never is the dichotomy between Titus the Emperor (*persona*) and Titus the individual brought out more forcefully.

> Pity my irksome greatness.
> As master of the world, I rule its fate;
> Kings I may make and I may unmake kings,
> And yet I am not free to give my heart.[24]

The most traumatic moment of the play occurs when Titus becomes his own conscience, judge, and executioner. To assume such a role is tantamount to playing God and requires superhuman strength. He confronts Berenice with the painful news in a speech constellated with words such as "force," "tear," "duty," "glory," "pain," and concludes with the notion that he, as Emperor, must be an example to the masses and she must comport herself like a Queen.

> I beg you fortify my heart against you,
> And help me dam its weakness, if I can,
> And hold back tears that spring continually;
> Or if we are not master of our tears,
> Let honour then at least sustain our sorrows,
> And let by all the world be clearly seen
> An Emperor's tears and the tears of a Queen.[25]

Titus has taken the giant step. He has liberated himself and cleansed his conscience. Such a forward act is usually followed by a regressive one. Titus is no exception to the rule. The image of Berenice's grief stirs his passions once again and, in so doing, dims his rational outlook. Fear, tenderness, anguish seize hold of him. Crying, groaning, and trembling, he explains himself still further.

> Yes, Lady, it is true, I weep, I sigh,
> I tremble; and yet when I claimed the Empire,
> Rome made me promise to uphold her laws;
> And I must now uphold them.[26]

Moments later he recoils at the brutality of his act. Guilt, self-hate, envelop his being.

> No, I'm a savage brute.
> I loathe myself. Even the hateful Nero
> Never drove his cruelty so far.
> I will not suffer Berenice to die.
> Let Rome say what she will. I shall defy
> Her.[27]

Confusion mars his speech. He can no longer remain the divided being he has become: the strong Emperor and the weakly structured inner man. He searches desperately for the answer. "To find myself, and to recognize myself."[28]

In an act of escapism or of gallantry—both interpretations are conceivable—Titus asks Berenice to choose his course for him. He forces her then to assume the responsibilities for their futures. He so belittles himself at this point, even in his own eyes, that he threatens to take his life if she does not understand and accept the depth of his love.

Titus has run the gamut. He has revealed himself as a rational, strong man worthy of assuming the Emperorship; also as the subservient, tender, and sensitive being unable to realize himself. When Berenice does choose to leave after being assured of Titus' love, the real Emperor is born.

Titus could not realize himself alone. He needed a strong hand to steer him in the right direction. Berenice, magnanimously, extended hers.

*   *   *

According to Suetonius (*Lives of the Caesars*), Tacitus (*Histories* II), and Flavius Josephus, Berenice was not a Palestinian queen but an Oriental princess. She was a domineering, intriguing, beguiling woman. According to Juvenal (*Satires* VI), she was the essence of immorality. It seemed that she was already at least forty years old when she first met Titus; she had been married three times when Emperor Vespasian first arrived in Judea. According to Tacitus, Berenice, the granddaughter of Herod the Great, helped the Roman cause, and Vespasian was quite attracted to her. Titus, who had been commanded by his father to continue the campaign in Judea and who was twelve years younger than Berenice, was smitten with her charms. After the capture of Jerusalem, Vespasian ordered his son back to Italy (71 A.D.) and the Titus-Berenice affair was ended. Eight years later, after Vespasian's death, Berenice arrived in Rome intent upon renewing her liaison with Titus. Though he was not so inclined, Suetonius implies that Titus was still in love with Berenice when he sent her "far from Rome in spite of him and in spite of her."

Racine has transformed the sensual, alluring, and captivating Oriental Princess into a selfless woman, deeply in love. Life for her has no meaning without Titus. Yet, despite the impression of victimization which she inspires, she does have another quite fascinating trait in her personality.

Before Berenice came to Rome, a stranger in a foreign land, she seemed to be the dominating factor in her relationship with Titus. It is she who has molded him, who has elevated him to a realm above that of immediate sensual gratification, who has taught him the ways of the world. Indeed, it could even be asserted that Titus, in some respects, plays the role of son to Berenice. Though she is a potent force in Titus' life, she is also an important power in her own right.

Endowed with extraordinary perception, she feels more keenly the nuances in her love relationship with Titus. It is as though her subliminal world is ever vigilant, warning her of dangers lurking near by. Berenice is an intuitive type, so sensitive to temperaments that the slightest changes which occur in her relationship with Titus are divined by her immediately. As a result, she is forever seeking an inner reason for such variations. Any transformation from the normal or ordinary worries Berenice. In this respect she could be labeled a misoneist.

When Titus proclaims a long period of mourning after his father's death, his entire demeanor toward Berenice changes—inexplicably so. She is determined to search for the reasons behind such a modification of attitude.

> This mourning Titus laid upon his court
> Included the suspension of his love.
> No longer did I have his warm attentions
> That made him spell-bound pass the days with me.
> Silent and troubled and with tearful eyes,
> He only greeted me with sad "good-byes."
> Imagine then my grief, as you well can,
> When my whole heart loves in him but the man,
> And far from all the grandeur of his birth
> Would choose his heart alone and seek his worth.[29]

Intuitively, Berenice realizes that Titus is slipping from her grasp. She refuses, however, to believe the warnings flashed from within. Indeed, her admiration and passion for him grows in direct proportion to the impression she has of his diminishing love for her. Titus is now described by her in apocalyptic terms, as Emperor, as a creator of nations, very nearly as a god figure. She realizes and even accepts the fact that he is no longer exclusively hers, but one who must be shared. Moreover, she indicates her willingness to relinquish the role she held for so long in their relationship, as dominating partner.

> Titus, all powerful, loves: he need but speak . . .
> The people crown with flowers his every image;
> Have you not seen the splendor of last night?

Did not his greatness captivate your sight?
The night of crackling flame, the pyre, the torches,
The eagles, faces, people, soldiers, arches,
The consuls, senators, the crowd of kings,
Whose brilliance all from my beloved springs;
The gold and purple, glittering with his glory,
The laurels witness to his triumph's story;
The myriad eyes one saw from every side
Gazing their fill at him, unsatisfied;
His royal stance, his fascinating airs;
With what respect, what reverential stares
Did all in secret pledge their loyalty![30]

As Berenice's passion and admiration for Titus grow, her behavior becomes concomitantly more subservient, her thoughts increasingly confused. She can no longer separate the *man* from the *office*.

Berenice idealizes Titus. Such a state can be interpreted as an unconscious flight from reality. The further she strays from her immediate situation, the greater her inner dynamism, the dimmer her vision. Only a *potential* world is observable to her now. When confronting Titus in this state of passion, a whole muted and forbidding world bubbles forth in such words as "solitude," "alone," "secret." Titus keeps his distance and reserve. Slowly Berenice's excitement wanes and she is submerged in opposite feelings, those of solitude and dejection. She develops the mannerism of the exile.

Because Berenice is the intuitive type, she feels her role as foreigner at court that much more keenly. Her sense of isolation and rejection palls on her to such an extent that she loses her ability to communicate with her beloved. Like Titus, she suffers from aphasia: "I remain voiceless and without resentment."[31] Prior to his change of attitude, Berenice had never wanted for words. However, now that their common denominator, their love, has been wrenched from them, a void has set in.

Though Berenice's heart and feelings are subtle barometers for measuring the variations in their rapport, she still refuses to believe them. Rather than accept her fate, she further belittles herself by remaining in Rome, awaiting a word, a nod, a sign, a gesture, anything emanating from Titus: "A sigh, a glance, a word from your mouth."[32]

When Titus does not muster the strength to speak to her frankly and sincerely, he is in effect yielding to the past once again, to the time he experienced the mother-child relationship. He longs for his youth, that carefree period when he roamed throughout the world.

> Ah, would to Heaven my father were alive!
> How happy I should be![33]

Berenice, reacting to Titus' sudden, regressive ways, believing in his love and the possibility of their remaining together, becomes a willing dupe. An unreal situation is conjured forth.

After passions have dimmed, Berenice ponders his actions and his words. Contents from her unconscious seem to surface. She listens to the inner voice which warns her of the meaning of Titus' silence, his muted tones and the mystery enveloping each of his words. She juxtaposes his past and present actions and words, tries to assess her situation, evaluate all the nuances of the flexible relationship.

> The more I call the past to memory,
> From the time I saw him first to this sad time,
> Too great a love has been my only crime.[34]

Still Berenice declines to believe reality, attributing the change in his demeanor to her overly possessive nature.

Even when Antiochus delivers Titus' message, informing Berenice of the necessity for her departure, she refuses to accept the interdict. Her desires are at war with her inner voice, ever vigilant in its warnings. "Alas, I do my best to shut my eyes. . . ."[35] The conflict is too great. An avalanche of emotions burst forth: anger, pity, anguish, love, suspicion, tenderness, envy. Her turmoil now expresses itself in concrete terms. She is in a state of physical disarray. Her confidante wants to help her smoothe her garments and comb her hair.

> Let me re-do these veils that slip from you,
> And these loose tresses that conceal your eyes;
> Let me repair the havoc of your tears.[36]

When Berenice finally does confront Titus, she feels the extreme weight of shame, disdain, and rejection. Looking upon her existence as that of being reduced to ashes, herself as the most pitiful of Queens, she can envisage only one way out, to end her life. In one of the most dramatic moments in the entire drama, Titus, suddenly wrenched from his state of verbal lethargy by her tears, reveals his feelings. He lays his heart bare, expresses his willingness to sacrifice the throne for her, to follow her to the ends of the earth. Indeed, his attitude has altered considerably at this point, giving the impression that he is willing to grovel at her feet, to once again assume the child role in their relationship. As Titus abases himself, the balance in their relationship shifts and so does Berenice's attitude. Her pride no longer destroyed, certain of his love and respect, she accepts the sacrifice she knows she has to make in his behalf. Berenice has mustered the strength to face her ordeal. Now she expresses contentment with the thought of living with the memory of her once resplendent love.

> Titus loves and forsakes: I love and flee.
> Your sighs and bonds take from me far away.
> Farewell. Let us—all three of us—portray
> To all the world the sweetest, saddest love,
> Whose painful tale it ever will preserve.[37]

✓ ✓ ✓

Antiochus is an artificially conceived character, one of Racine's weakest. He has no substance and assumes no real place in the drama. He is a buffer set into the play's network in order to effectuate the minimal plot line. He neither inspires pity nor horror, nor sympathy, nor any other emotion.

To a certain extent, however, Antiochus can be looked upon as Titus' double. Both are fine warriors, both are timid in their rapports with Berenice, both vacillate as to their course. In war, for example, Antiochus (like Titus and his predecessor Pyrrhus) is heroic. He crushes rebellions in Judea, saves Titus' life. Indeed, Titus appreciates his courage and declares it openly. When, however, Antiochus wishes to reveal his passion for Berenice, he finds himself incapable of forthrightness. He remains silent, does not assert himself, succumbs, as he puts it, to his "melancholia."[38]

Antiochus is a passive human being, a sounding board for everybody's emotions. He is Titus' spokesman and Berenice's confidant. His feelings and outlook fluctuate in direct relation to the climate of emotions set forth by Berenice and Titus. When he believes he has a chance of being accepted by Berenice, he declares his "surprise is extreme"[39] and is uplifted and wafted by clouds of joy. When, on the other hand, he sees his love as unrequited, he treats Berenice as an "ingrate," as "cruel."[40] He is always shifting the blame on to others, dispelling, thereby, his own feelings of utter weakness.

Antiochus is psychologically impotent. He neither changes nor develops. He never looks within for an explanation of his situation, nor can he act decisively. He seems to be a pawn of destiny, shunted here and there without ever really understanding his position or his personality.

II

Berenice is a meticulously fashioned play. Indeed, it is constructed like a building, each block superimposed one upon the other, a series of parallel scenes leading up to a peak of intensity. No extraneous events, no artificially created situations mar the simplicity of the lines.

Racine's contemporaries, accustomed to the plays of Corneille, the novels of the Scudérys and of Honoré d'Urfé, were used to a variety of peripeteia in each work, in addition to lengthy analytical studies. Racine, on the contrary, had closely controlled the vicissitudes in his drama. Unless they were directly involved in the play's action, he rejected them as so much extraneous material. He focused his insights on very limited terrain and there, like Proust, dissected his protagonists, their every emotion. Like Proust also, he had recourse to images each time he sounded out the mysterious and unuttered forces inhabiting man's inner world, noting visually their responses to the various stimuli which always came to plague them in one way or another.

Because of *Berenice's* dual nature, its outer condition of stasis and its inner dynamism, a Kafkaesque quality encompasses the drama. The characters give the impression of being caught in a vise, of being mysterious and solitary, unable to communicate with one another, victims of their torments which grow and tighten until the point of suffocation.

Berenice's setting is as directly involved in the play's action as that of *Britannicus*. Antiochus describes the locale at the very outset of the drama, two doors on opposite sides of the stage. One door leads to Titus' apartment, the other to Queen Berenice's. The decor is then a visual counterpart of the inner action occurring in the drama, two opposing ways of life succinctly expressed by Antiochus' verbal allusion to them.

> This door gives access to his private chamber
> And that door opens on the Queen's apartment.[41]

The esoteric world Racine reveals through visual and auditive means has never been used more strongly than in *Berenice* (flame, torch, torrent, brilliance, and their opposites: blackness, shadow, somber, dark). A clever director would certainly intensify the impact of this already intense drama by concretizing the various elements included by Racine in his verbal gyrations. Words such as "secret," "silence," "obscurity," "solitude," "voiceless," "murmur," "tomb" underscore the torments within the play. These inchoate sensations can be given form, after which they assume the role of protagonists fighting their way across the stage into the spectators' very hearts.

III

Berenice marks an enormous advance in Racine's roster of dramatic situations. With the exception of *Alexander the Great*, which, as we have seen, is not a typically Racinian work, no positive outcome had previously emerged in the various conflicts arising in his plays. Titus is the only hero so far to have evolved during the course of the play, from a dependent adolescent to a man of stature, conscious of his obligations and prepared to exercise his will. With the birth of judgment and the will to power to carry out his plans, the Emperor was given life. Titus is Racine's first hero come of age.

Berenice is a play reflecting the "calm" which has set in after the extreme "turbulence" experienced in *Britannicus*. The drama, wholly inner, may be a reflection of Racine's own mellow mood at this juncture of his life. Having experienced the traumas of love with La Du Parc, he was now perhaps beginning to bend to circumstances, to acquire wisdom in his relationships. The furor of his passion (the second is usually not so intense as the first) seemed to have been less fierce. Experience, understanding had come to his aid in divining the human heart. *Berenice* is like an operatic score; the infinite personality modulations are noted with particular care and precision—the silences, the crescendoes, the diminuendoes—as each protagonist sings forth his miseries and joys in profoundly moving tones.

6

Bajazet

"What am I . . ."[1]

BAJAZET was performed for the first time at the Hôtel de Bourgogne in January (probably the 5th or the 6th) 1672. It was well received by audiences who were fascinated by the play's Turkish theme. Indeed, anything and everything Turkish had been à la mode in Paris since 1670, when the Ambassador from this "exotic" land and his retinue paid an official visit to Louis XIV.

Though Bajazet was acclaimed by both public and the majority of critics, vituperative remarks against this work were still made. Mme de Sévigné, for example, was convinced that *Bajazet* had been written for the actress La Champmeslé,[2] with whom Racine was then in love, and "not for the centuries to come," that his work on the whole was inferior to Corneille's thrilling dramas, that the Turkish mores depicted in his work were not accurately portrayed.[3] The poet Segrais reported a confidence made to him by Corneille, who criticized the liberties Racine had taken in describing the play's locale, Constantinople, and in depicting the characters who were in essence French and certainly not Turkish in mannerism or sentiment.[4] The ironic and querulous critic Donneau de Vizé included in his newspaper *Le Mercure galant* a severe criticism condemning the play on the basis of its historical inaccuracy.[5]

Racine must have been inured to adverse criticism, at least to a certain extent, because his two prefaces to *Bajazet* were remarkably reserved. Never once on the defensive, he declared unequivocally that *Bajazet's* plot had been based on actual events which had occurred in 1638 and were reported by M. de Cesy, France's Ambassador to Constantinople. Furthermore, he stated his complete fidelity to Turkish mores.

The main thing I was concerned with was not to alter anything in the manners or customs of the nation.[6]

To those critics who had condemned *Bajazet* on the grounds that modern topics were unsuitable for tragedy, he pointed to Aeschylus' *Persians*, which not only dealt with a current subject, but introduced Xerxes' mother, who was still living at the time, into the play. Imaginations could be stirred and passions kindled, Racine maintained, no matter what the date of the events depicted in the work, provided the locale was set in some distant land.

The distance in place makes up in some sort for the too great nearness in time. For ordinary folk treat in much the same way what is, so to speak, a thousand years away from them and what is a thousand leagues away.[7]

Though Racine declared that the plot for *Bajazet* had been drawn from incidents related by the French Ambassador to Constantinople, he might also have been inspired by an event which took place at Fontainbleau on November 10, 1657. On that day, the Marquis Jean de Monaldeschi, former favorite of Queen Christina of Sweden, was strangled in conformity with her orders and very nearly in her presence, as punishment for his jealous actions aimed directly against her latest lover, Captain of the Guards Sentinelli. Queen Christina was asked to leave France after this shocking incident.

✦ ✦ ✦

Bajazet's plot, though not as trim as *Berenice's* is, nevertheless, still simple.

Act I. The Sultan Amurat, far from Constantinople, is warring against Babylonia. To make certain his power is secure at home, he gives orders to Roxana, whom he has left in charge, to have his younger brother Bajazet killed. The Sultan's Grand Vizier, Acomat, fearing for his life, plots against his master by fostering a passion on Roxana's part for Bajazet. Roxana is now intent upon marrying Bajazet. Athalida, a princess of royal blood, and Bajazet have been secretly in love ever since childhood. To make matters even more difficult, Acomat is intent upon marrying Athalida, hoping to secure his position in so doing.

Act II. When Roxana informs Bajazet of her wish to marry him, he hesitates at first by pointing to the fact that such an alliance would go against tradition. Roxana turns white with anger and decides to have the procrastinating Bajazet killed. Both Athalida and Acomat, fearful for Bajazet's future, prevail upon him to agree to marry Roxana.

Act III. After Bajazet follows Athalida's orders and acquiesces to Roxana's demands, his beloved is struck with jealousy. To reassure Athalida, Bajazet receives Roxana coldly. She now swells with anger. Meanwhile, Orcan, the Sultan's servant, arrives with a secret message for Roxana, announcing Amurat's return and requesting a confirmation of Bajazet's death. Bajazet's erratic behavior makes Roxana suspect some kind of infidelity on his part.

Act IV. Roxana tests Athalida's feelings by revealing the contents of the Sultan's letter to her, informing her of her decision to obey his command. Athalida faints, thereby revealing her love for Bajazet. When a note declaring Bajazet's passion for Athalida is found on her person, Roxana's frenzy knows no bounds. She meditates vengeance.

Act V. Bajazet is to be killed by Roxana's slaves, the Mutes, when he steps out of the main room. But first, Roxana forces him to choose: marry her and watch Athalida be put to death or be killed himself. Bajazet, unwilling to pay such a price for his freedom, confesses his love for Athalida and offers his life to save hers. Athalida does likewise in a parallel scene. With extreme aplomb, Roxana utters the famous word, "Leave." Bajazet walks out of the main room and is killed. Moments later Roxana is assassinated by Orcan, who is carrying out the Sultan's secret orders. Orcan is then put to death by Acomat's men. Athalida kills herself on stage. Acomat flees in the galley ship he had prepared for such an eventuality.

I

Bajazet is a drama in which the power drive manifests itself through hatred, lust, vengeance, deceit, and murder. It is a subtle and frightening account of a mysterious war being waged between matriarchal and patriarchal forces.

The patriarchal society is represented by the Sultan who, like a transpersonal divinity, stands remote, awesome, all-powerful. The matriarchal society as exemplified by Roxana, the Sultan's delegate, symbolizes the earthly and material realm. Her domain is the castle (harem), an enclosed vessel-like area, chaotic and turbid, over which the Feminine Principle reigns. Here, all is felt and surmised in half tones. A binary division exists within the matriarchal society, between nascent male forces and crushing female dominion. The male to all intents and purposes is excluded from this society as an independent individual, but grasped within its clutches as a dependent and subservient being.

The ruling force in the hierarchical picture offered us in *Bajazet* is the Sultan. He is a solar emanation, an energizer, the subtle initiator of all action. Everything radiates outward from him, the source of light and spirit. He is then the seminal force setting into motion the infernal machine which is played out in this drama. Though he is far away, fighting some nebulous war against the Babylonians, dwelling in some spaceless and timeless region, his power and personality impregnate every facet of this play. His presence, like that of divinity, is made known in mysterious ways, through two messages.[8] He is the one who has placed Roxana in charge and who orders Bajazet's death. Everything that occurs in this exitless world of the castle (harem), over which Roxana reigns, is dependent upon him. He is described by the various protagonists as cagey, suspicious, ruthless, sanguinary, barbaric, a rather frightening father image in a patriarchal society.

The Grand Vizier Acomat is an old man[9] whose powers have been virtually wrested from him by the Sultan.

> The army he commands; and leaves to me
> A pallid power in this deserted city . . .[10]

Acomat is a sexless, eunuch-like, useless being, whose sole function in this drama seems to be to foment trouble among its participants, to try in his own weak and quasi-castrated way to destroy the all-encompassing father image by working surreptitiously with its female counterpart. His intention of marrying Athalida is purely political, it lies fallow in a field of dried wheat. None of his plots or counterplots succeed, and since he is actually extraneous to the play itself he is the only one who sails out of it alive.

⚹   ⚹   ⚹

Bajazet is a seventeenth century Pentheus who tries in vain to extricate himself from the matriarchal society of which he is a victim. He has lived in the Sultan's palace, a prisoner, ever since he was a child. As a result, he is weak, indecisive, vulnerable, and identityless. He sums up his own character adequately when he questions, "What am I?"[11] Never having developed beyond the adolescent stage, he is unable to commit his symbolic act of destruction which would have severed him from his past and from the matriarchal environment, the feat each hero must accomplish to earn his freedom. He is, therefore, never conscious of his own masculinity. Indeed, what makes the situation ever more critical is that Bajazet, a structureless being, is not only Roxana's victim, but the pawn of his beloved Athalida. A prisoner of a female world, his actions and emotions fluctuate, as do those of women, at a rapid tempo and in direct rapport with the situations motivated by both Roxana and Athalida. Unlike the Sultan, Bajazet is not the initiator of actions. Rather, he is their victim. His life, consequently, is wholly dependent upon external circumstances.

Despite the fact that Bajazet is aware of his situation, in that he knows he would like to fight back and to take matters into his own hands, he is nevertheless so emasculated that distances between what he imagines he would like to accomplish and what he is capable of carrying through are too vast to permit him to actualize his wish. Bajazet's several heroic statements during the course of this drama are merely braggadocio, they do not ring true.

> I do not deem death the supreme misfortune

or

> I would prefer to leave, with bloody blows,
> Than bear her husband's name against my will.[12]

His words are gestures, masks, a facade behind which there is a void. Never once does he plot or plan or make the slightest attempt to overthrow the matriarchal society. The "burning" love which he claims to feel for Athalida becomes in effect meaningless, since passion needs nourishment to keep it alive. Such tending can only come from the masculine aggressive force which is seemingly nonexistent within Bajazet. As he shuttles from Roxana's to Athalida's directives and back again, he never takes command of the situation, but rather becomes the sounding board for their feelings, the bearer of their wills. Bajazet is an obedient servant rather than a heroic lover.

The feelings of ineffectiveness which Bajazet experiences as a result of his weakness are translated into psychological terms as guilt. As the play proceeds, Bajazet finds himself ever more deeply enmeshed in an inextricable situation and he becomes possessed by pangs of despair. A real dread of becoming the victim of some unknown and shattering punishment for his deceit, the lie he has been living vis-à-vis Roxana, is the basis of his excruciating feeling of guilt. An urgency to liberate himself from the false situation he has been experiencing manifests itself through confession: "Heaven punishes my sham . . ."[13]

Like a parasite, he has always lived through Roxana's or Athalida's

personality and never as an individual; he has remained an adolescent,
unable to extricate himself from the grasp of the dominating female
figure, from his mother-dependency type of existence. He resembles
his psychological forefathers: Pentheus, whose mother Agave tore him
to pieces unwittingly, or like Narcissus, Hippolytus, Attis. It is no
wonder then that his contemporaries described Bajazet as "insipid."

✓ ✓ ✓

Roxana is the head of the matriarchal society depicted in *Bajazet*.
She is the personification of the destructive aspect of the Great Mother
archetype. A lunar force, she is the all-powerful ruler over the palace,
which is in effect a microcosm of the world. Vicious, lustful, she wields
her strength possessively as did her historical counterparts, Agave, Ino,
Cybele. And her love is all-consumming and all-destructive.

> That I have sovereign power upon your life,
> That you may only breathe as long as I love you,
> And that but for this love your frowns offend,
> Do you not know, you would long since be dead?[14]

Roxana looks upon Bajazet as her "product," her "object." She
seeks to mold him as she sees fit. Indeed, she pontificates, she was the
one who brought him forth from "nothingness."[15] She is his creator
and his very life depends upon her whims. She forces him to choose
marriage to her or death. Actually, there is no choice; both alternatives
are synonymous. Marriage to Roxana would be tantamount to a living
death, an enslavement to the forces of the Great Mother archetype.

Nuances and gradations of personality are perceptible at times
within the framework of Roxana's personality, moments when compassion and a semblance of tenderness seem to shimmer forth from her
smoky depths. For example, during those seconds when love for Bajazet is uppermost, she considers herself weak and defenseless, very
much of a woman.

> Would you have thought it, Madam? His quick return
> Would make so much love follow so much rage?[16]

Quickly, however, shame envelops her. She hurriedly withdraws this
vulnerable aspect of herself, resuming her role as crushing empress
figure, with such utterances as:

> His woe or weal depends upon his reply.[17]

Unbending, vengeful, and vindictive emotions mark Roxana's features. When thwarted in her desires, her hatred is unrelenting. If she cannot possess Bajazet, then no one else will, certainly not her rival Athalida. She will see to her demise as well as to that of her lover.

> In righteous rage I'll spy upon the traitor;
> I will surprise him with his Athalida;
> And stabbing both of them with the same dagger,
> Will stab myself and from their union stagger.[18]

When Roxana learns of the insidious plot leveled against her by both Athalida and Bajazet, she bares her fangs like a hunted animal. Shaken to the very foundations of her being, iced, shivering, trembling, burning, she swears destruction on the very one she loves.

> O knave, unworthy of the life I threw to you?
> I breathe once more: and I exult to find
> The traitor has, for once, betrayed himself.
> Free the cruel cares I would have grasped,
> My icy anger harbours but revenge.
> Kill Bajazet! Avenge me. Run. Seize him;
> See the hands of the mutes prepare his doom.
> They come armed with those fatal bowstrings
> That squeeze the life out of betrayers like him.[19]

A prey to ambivalent notions, a complex of sado-masochistic feelings, Roxana savors those "sweet" sensations of vengeance and despair. Dizzied and limp with lust, Roxana imagines yet another torment to force upon Bajazet, to compel him to watch Athalida put to death. When he recoils from such plans, Roxana calls upon her Mutes to kill him. They are posted outside her door and the moment Bajazet steps forth from her presence they have orders to cut him down.

These Mutes which Racine has introduced into his drama are powerful figures because within them an entire hidden world smolders, repressed. Unable to express themselves verbally, they can exteriorize their feelings only through gestures. Maimed, emasculated, they become the evil ones, implementing the subliminal matriarchal forces. When, therefore, Roxana screeches her "Sortez"[20] to Bajazet, knowing that the moment he steps forth he will be killed by the Mutes, the calculated force with which she commands him to depart indicates the vigor of her sadistic intent. Indeed, Roxana nearly carries out the Sultan's secret orders to the last syllable, "Show not your face without his head in hand,"[21] an image emphasizing most strongly the "devouring" aspect of this archetypal mother figure and comparable to Salome, whose cruelty was also carried to the extreme.

✼ ✼ ✼

Athalida is Roxana's paler counterpart. Double female personages often figure in Racine's works (Iphigenia and Eriphile etc.). Athalida, to a far lesser extent than Roxana, manipulates the strands of Bajazet's destiny, and he very docilely carries out her orders. Unlike Roxana, however, Athalida's love is tragic from the very beginning because it can never be realized. "My only hope is in my despair,"[22] she declares. If she wants Bajazet to remain alive, which is the most she can hope for, given the circumstances, she must resign herself to his marriage with another. Courageously, therefore, she attempts to give him up. "Let him marry her . . . rather than die."[23] In Racine's cosmogony, however, his creatures are very rarely masters of their cerebral attitudes, they are rather marked by their instinctual world. Athalida is no exception.[24] Despite her intentions, she becomes the very instrument of her lover's death. "I could not overcome my jealousy,"[25] she remarks. Her apparent comprehension of her plight transforms her feelings of ineffectiveness into a viable force within her. Like Bajazet then, she is crushed by guilt and begs the divinities to pardon her for her artifice.

> O Heaven, if our love is condemned by thee,
> I am most guilty: slake thy wrath on me![26]

Indeed, she even goes so far as to blame herself directly for Bajazet's death. "I can blame his death only upon my madness."[27]

Athalida's character is marked by a strange complexity. On those occasions when she feels herself master of a given situation, she is transformed into an authoritarian female figure. At the time when Bajazet's death seems impending, Athalida assumes a posture of strength and orders him to marry Roxana. "That you still live, indeed because I wished."[28] When, on the other hand, events seem to slide forth from her grasp, she experiences doubt, guilt, fear, agitation, pain, and tears. After Bajazet has carried out her orders and agrees to marry her rival, Athalida cringes with jealousy and confesses: "It is no pleasure to increase my pain?"[29] as if oblivious of her former command. Later, certain of Bajazet's love, she again transforms herself into a dictatorial figure, asking him to pursue a hypocritical course. In this instance, she is the manipulator of the entire situation, attempting on her own to convince Roxana of Bajazet's love. "He still loves you,"[30] she declares.

Athalida's constantly vacillating attitude points up the tragedy of her inextricable situation. She is the most human of the protagonists.

II

The symbolizm in *Bajazet* further increases the excoriating nature of this drama.

The fact that *Bajazet* takes place in an exitless area (a palace in Constantinople) increases the virulence of its momentum. Certain intrusions from the outside world, in the form of orders, penetrate this claustrophobic locale, rendering the entire atmosphere that much more awesome and terrifying.

The *palace* in which the action takes place can then be looked upon as an occult and mysterious world, that of the unconscious with its secrets and its treasures. It is a lunar and chthonic kingdom, a complex of converging and merging instincts. Nothing is clear in this tenebrous domain; for beneath each facade, sign, and portent lies a frightening network of primal forces.

The palace becomes an entity unto itself, isolated in its magnificence. The moment Roxana begins wielding her power, she cuts it off from the rest of existence with such utterances as:

> Do you not know you're lost except for me?
> That I, above all, am the one to please?
> Do you not know I hold the palace gates,
> That I may open or forever shut them?[31]

or when she orders the doors to the palace shut:

> Let the seraglio be shut.[32]

The matriarchal (unconscious realm within the castle) has now been severed from all contact with the patriarchal world (conscious forces outside the castle). No communication, therefore, exists, symbolically speaking, between the conscious and unconscious attitudes. Such a state of affairs indicates a loss of equilibrium followed by a total submersion into the tidal waters of the unconscious, resulting in certain death.

The death struggle now begins, between a rigid and decaying society as represented by the "prostitutes" in the harem (that is, by Roxana) and the emergence of a new and creative world which could have been born from the union of Bajazet and Athalida. Roxana, however, like Astarte or Kali, encircles her prey, extinguishing its life flow.

Associated with *Bajazet* is the metal mercury. The protagonists are mercurial, as are the events and situations which are of their making. They are forever changing from one attitude and state to another, and with unparalleled fluidity. Athalida, for example, notices Bajazet's sudden change, "Bajazet could have worked so quick a change?"[33] Such modifications of orientation are due to the fact that the protagonists are not flesh and blood human beings, but rather dynamic entities. They exist as potentialities. Like mercury, they never attain any kind of form or solidity. They are shapeless and frequently assume extremes in their points of view, depending upon the magnetic pull of the moment. For example, Roxana's prodigious hatred for Athalida, Athalida's distorted jealousy of Roxana when she thinks Bajazet has fallen in love with her, Bajazet's insistence upon meeting death rather than agree to marry Roxana, etc.

The mercurial nature of these protagonists, indicated by their constantly changing emotions (furor, anger, hatred, tears, love, lust, etc.), also indicates the enormous quantities of psychic energy (libido) at their command. Such energy would have been salutary indeed had these beings been able to channel their instincts and mold them into some ascending shape or pattern. Racine's creatures, however, are unable to stabilize themselves, to achieve balance. Totally immersed in their "sense" world, they never live wholly.

The strange "fire" which burns hard within each protagonist is not in *Bajazet* a source of illumination, but rather of annihilation. A symbol of fecundity, fire corresponds at times to the Heraclitan "agent of transmutation" since all things emerge from it and return to it. In *Bajazet*, however, fire is not a regenerative force, but rather an actively destructive one. There is no Prometheus here, but rather an Empedocles, a man who jumped into the living crater of Mt. Etna. Roxana and her cohorts are all embedded in a living volcano.

To underscore the destructive aspect of the fire images with which Racine splashes his canvas (enflamed, blind, dazzling) he has recourse to other equally crushing types of image, "devour" and "cruel feast," indicating the aggressive nature of the entities involved. To tear apart, to split asunder, to dismember as Agave and Set had done, implies the extremes to which these creatures go in order to be reborn, to be transformed from the split individuals they are into the whole human beings they seek to become. Racine's insistence, for example, upon facial attributes (mouth and eyes which, as we have seen in previous plays, are capable of revealing secret intentions) is yet another device used to reveal the desperate urgency of his protagonists' orientations.

III

Like a Greek tragedy, *Bajazet* is a myth, an externalization and collectivization of a personal inner experience. It is Racine's version of a Great Mother myth, that of Pentheus, for example, or Phaeton, Hippolytus. Powerfully and turbulently, Racine's protagonists spew forth their torments in language so violent and so vicious at times as to cut the spectator, like vitriol eating away at the soft fiber of flesh.

Roxana's statement, "Go back, back to the void I snatched you from,"[34] sums up most effectively *Bajazet's* theme. Roxana, as the archetypal mother, is the one who draws Bajazet out of what the mystics refer to as "nothingness," that world of potentialities and creativity, that undifferentiated kingdom where conflicts are nonexistent, contrasts and opposites unknown. Bajazet is ruthlessly ejected from this world of primordial unity, of nonobjective reality, and brought forth unequipped into a realm of conflict and dissension. Here, he can either sink or swim, liberate himself by committing his heroic deed or be submerged into an irretrievable identification with the archetypal mother. Neither Roxana nor Bajazet nor Athalida are able to ascend into a world where coherence of attitude exists, where independence makes for growth; and so they sink into the quagmire of primal waters. The Solar world, through which independence could have been achieved, had closed its doors.

When Madame de Sévigné wrote in a letter dated March 16, 1672 that "Bajazet was an icy character," that the mores of the Turks were poorly observed, and that the end of the play was badly prepared, she was in part justified in her appraisal.

Bajazet is in fact an icy character, congealed in his own powerlessness, unable to act except when forced to do so by outside parties, and, as ice, he melts into nothing during the heat of the performance. As for being unfaithful to Turkish mores, Mme de Sévigné is again correct. *Bajazet* goes far beyond being merely a social tragedy. It is a work which introduces spectators and readers to a world of primordial relationships and universal concepts as fundamental today as they were three hundred years ago. Racine's personal problems, as projected in *Bajazet*, have become collective ones. That the play's conclusion was poorly prepared is, however, an unjustified evaluation on Madame de Sévigné's part. The finale is evident from the very outset of the drama when Roxana declares:

> For the last time, I shall consult him now.
> I must know if he loves me.[35]

The moment Roxana's attentions are focused on Bajazet, she never permits him to escape her clutches. Even Roxana's death does not come as a surprise. When patriarchal forces hold sway, they overwhelm all within their sight.

7

Mithridates

"If this torrent pulls me,
it will inundate everything . . ."[1]

MITHRIDATES[2] was presented at the Hôtel de Bourgogne on January 12, 1673. It earned Racine an immense success.[3] Even the critics, formerly so acidulous in their commentaries, were won over, for the most part, by the poet's verbal powers. Robinet called this work "clever" and "the subject well treated."[4] Mme de Coulanges, writing to her friend Mme de Sévigné, called *Mithridates* a "charming play" worthy of "admiration."[5]

Racine's greatest joy came about perhaps as a result of Corneille's downfall. Corneille's latest heroic comedy, *Pulchérie* (1672), performed at the Théâtre du Marais, had not been well received. The old lion was seemingly losing his vitality. Paris knew it. Racine must have reveled in it. As Corneille's star dimmed, so Racine's rose. Concomitantly he was relieved of financial burdens. For some time now he had been living modestly on the Rue Saint-Dominique. A year after the production of *Mithridates*, however, he moved to the Hôtel des Ursins on the elegant Ile de la Cité in Paris. Only people of a certain class were permitted to inhabit these spacious and attractive buildings. Racine was one of them.

✦ ✦ ✦

Mithridates takes place at Nymphaeum, a seaport on the Cimmerian Bosphorus in the Crimea.

Act I. After fighting the Romans for forty years, Mithridates, King of Pontus in Asia Minor (Anatolia), has suffered his first defeat. It has been rumored that he has been killed and, therefore, will not marry Monima, a beautiful Greek girl living at his court. His two sons, Xiphares and Pharnaces, are also smitten with her. The former, following in his father's footsteps, is Rome's bitter enemy. The latter, betraying his father, hopes the Romans will help him win Monima. She, however, despises Pharnaces and secretly enlists Xiphares' aid. Xiphares, believing his father dead, confesses his love for her. Mithridates, the originator of the false rumor, returns. Pharnaces asks Xiphares to help him in his rebellion against their father. Xiphares refuses.

Act II. Monima is too sad to greet the King upon his return. Mithridates, consumed with love for her, is jealous of Pharnaces, whom he believes she loves. Secretly, however, Monima confesses her passion to Xiphares but demands that he avoid her since she is honorable and seeks to remain faithful to the King.

Act III. Mithridates decides to battle the Romans again. Xiphares agrees to his plan. Pharnaces' response is negative. Mithridates suspects Pharnaces of loving Monima, and to dispel his doubts orders him to marry the daughter of the King of Parthia. Pharnaces, believing his brother to have betrayed him, denounces Xiphares' love for Monima. Mithridates, tortured with jealousy, seeks to discover the truth. He tricks Monima into confiding her love for Xiphares. Now, he ponders a horrendous vengeance.

Act IV. Xiphares warns Monima of the King's anger. She realizes she has been duped. The King wants to marry her and angers over her indecisiveness. Meanwhile, Mithridates learns of his enemy's arrival on his shores. Pharnaces has been aiding the Romans in their venture and, he now surmises, perhaps even Xiphares.

Act V. Monima, who believes Xiphares has been killed, tries and fails to hang herself with the royal head band. She then receives orders from the King to poison herself. Just as she is about to imbibe poison she learns that Mithridates is dying and that Xiphares has routed the Romans. She rushes to them. Before the monarch's demise he unites Monima and Xiphares.

I

Mithridates is essentially a political play, treating themes Racine had already sounded out: the rival brothers (*The Theban Brothers, Britannicus*), unrequited love (*Andromache*), jealousy and fury. For the first time, however, he chose an old King as his central figure. Mithridates is more than a reigning sovereign. He assumes the posture of a suprapersonal figure, an archetype, that of the Terrible Father. It is interesting to note in this connection that whereas *Bajazet* depicted a matriarchal society, *Mithridates* focuses upon a patriarchal world. This change of focus may indicate two things. Outwardly, Racine might be writing a political play, a "masculine" drama in order to vie with Corneille. The variation in emphasis may also indicate his own willingness to confront forces which had formerly frightened him, the multiple father images he had known at Port-Royal.

An old King (Mithridates is seventy-two years of age) usually symbolizes a being endowed with extreme wisdom, superior consciousness, virtue, and sound judgment. Such a figure is frequently associated with a person who has achieved the ultimate point in his career, a true victor. Mithridates fits few of these requirements. He is courageous and heroic in war, but as the play begins he has lost to the Romans, implying a negative attitude. As an unproductive force he is the victim of his instincts (anger, jealousy, hate). Moreover, he remains unloved by Monima and succeeds in inspiring awe in his entourage only when he fulminates.

In many respects Mithridates is as blind as King Lear. Since he has forever been looking *outward* (symbolically speaking, as a conqueror), trying to acquire unto himself and, in so doing, leading the life of a youthful warrior, he has never peered *within* in order to assess his situation, as would a mature man. He is, therefore, unaware of the utter folly of vying with his sons for Monima's love. Reason can only emerge after he has experienced the excoriating sensations of jealousy and defeat.

The historical Mithridates was a forceful, energetic King. Known as Mithridates VI Eupator Dionysos, he was surnamed The Great (135–63 B.C.). At thirteen he succeeded his father to the throne and it was at this age that he withdrew from the social world. He remained in solitude to escape the countless attempts made upon his life. During this period of introversion he hardened himself to the task of destroying Rome. To serve his political needs, he had his mother, his tutors, and his wife assassinated. A mighty soldier, he seized all the lands bordering the Euxine (Black Sea), then presented himself to the rulers of the provinces of Asia Minor (at that time under the domination of Rome) as the great liberator. Ten thousand Roman citizens were massacred during the course of Mithridates' battles. After he sent an army to Greece and took the Aegean islands, he married Monima. The Roman consul and general Lucius Cornelius Sulla, nearly seventy at the time, headed an army which forced Mithridates back to Asia. Licinius Lucullus, another Roman general, pursued him to Armenia; but, when Lucullus was recalled home, Mithridates reconquered his realm. Pompey, when sent to battle him, won the war on the Euphrates.

Racine's Mithridates is also a conqueror—like Caesar or Napoleon—who inspires fear, anguish, and hatred. When he first arrives on the scene after having spread the false rumor of his death, his entourage is surprised, as well it should be (II, ii). He depicts himself as a supreme monarch, a "judge," with very nearly god-like attributes, a remote and heavenly father image.

> But as your judge, you have a loving father,
> You took as true, rumours I spread myself;
> I hold you guiltless, since you wish it so.[6]

Mithridates seeks to maintain the power he now enjoys but is unsure of succeeding. To this end he is forever setting traps to test his sons' characters. Such underhanded activities certainly indicate a lack of confidence in himself and a lack of insight into the dominion of others. For this reason Mithridates is vulnerable. He is forever over-reacting to situations, far too easily hurt by Monima, overly angered by whatever his sons may think or say.

To maintain control over everyone, Mithridates fights all change whether it be on a political or a social level. In so doing he seeks to project his inner state onto a realm which cannot be limited by his own conceptions and categories. The world changes; Mithridates does not. He has not developed since his youth, when his Roman obsession took hold. For this reason he is unwilling to release his stranglehold on his sons, on Monima, and on life in general.

Such an intense desire to dominate banishes any kind of love-bond which might develop between himself and his sons or himself and Monima. Indeed, Mithridates (like Agrippina in her capacity as mother and wife) has either forgotten or never knew the real meaning of the word "father" or "lover." His possessiveness, which stems from feelings of insecurity, intrudes upon all his relationships. This builder of nations and destroyer of kingdoms is as unsure of himself on the social and personal level as is a child when confronting a giant.

The more insecure Mithridates feels, the greater is his desire for conquest. Over and over he tries to prove the same thing, that his power has not diminished, while at the same time dispelling his feelings of ineffectiveness. Interestingly enough, as he describes past battles, some new elements enter the picture. Mithridates is suddenly infused with extreme dynamism. Indeed, his entire countenance alters. The fulgurating intensity of past glories gives him the energy to face present ordeals. Words sizzle as he depicts battles, soldiers in disorder, their alarm, death:

> Harsh cries retorting harsher from the rocks,
> The endless horror of a midnight fright . . .
> You see me burning with the self-same love;
> Nourished by blood and hungering for war,
> My heart enchained, despite my heavy years
> And woes, drags everywhere its love for Monima.[7]

His speech is aflame with vitality and, as he stands before his terror-stricken entourage, it is as if his onlookers were watching a transfiguration, the man changing into a god. Like a tornado, he is propelled by his own gusto, creating a further dichotomy between illusion (past) and reality (present). Emotions dilate his every thought. Hybris takes hold. Like Jupiter, Mithridates' jealousy and anger are boundless. He loses his identity and sees his sons as "rivals." He plans more battles with the intent of ridding himself of them.

As a leader of men Mithridates is an activator of cosmic forces, arousing them from their lethargy, leaving the hot and stilled sands of his static kingdom for the churning sea which will take him to Rome. There he will capture his monstrous enemy.

> The preparations of a mighty voyage,
> My ships that must be ready to set sail,
> My soldiers, whose forbearance I must tempt,
> Demand my presence at this hour.[8]

Mithridates dreams of the sea which stimulates his already intense nervous system. His language is studded with nautical terms, references to sea ways and geographical areas, to lands unconquered, rival monarchs, merging waters, inundations, torrents, ports, raging floods, ships, drownings.[9]

> Never shall Rome be conquered but in Rome.
> In her blood, I'll drown her that nation slow;
> Burn down the Capitol where I was due,
> Trample her honours, tear out from her maps
> A hundred royal shames, and mine perhaps;
> And, flame in hand, I'll sear out every name
> That Rome hung there for everlasting shame.[10]

Mithridates still feels like a lion, as virile in his old age as when young. He has neither simmered down with the passing of years nor has he developed consciousness. He is totally unaware of the age differential between himself and Monima and is therefore thoroughly shocked by her coldness. His ego denuded, he begins to suffer the chill of abandonment and the iciness of solitude.

Unlike Pyrrhus or Titus, however, Mithridates has the courage of his convictions. He is unafraid of Monima and so manipulates her like an "enemy," with cunning. First he inspires her with confidence, then lavishes what she believes to be affection and understanding upon her. He goes so far as to suggest she marry Xiphares who is really a "replica of himself." Taken aback by his sudden change of attitude, Monima believes in his sincerity and confesses her love for Xiphares.

The play could have ended at this point, with Mithridates' pride devastated, his ego crushed. It did not, however, because the situation had not yet been resolved. The monarch was unwilling to withdraw from life's flow, his point of view was still negative. He could not accept the fact that he had failed to win Monima's affection any more than he could consent to defeat in battle. When Monima, however, fatigued of the struggle, asks to be judged and condemned for her "rebellious" act, Mithridates clothes his feelings of destitution with rage. In so doing he reverts to his role as distant monarch. Breaking all earthly ties with Monima, he ascends to that remote world of the Terrible Father archetype, the judge of man, God. Anger inundates his being. A severing occurs between his inner and outer worlds, somewhat similar to that suffered by Orestes, but less violent and prolonged. "Who am I?" he questions.[11] He fails to recognize Monima. The pattern of life he had once known has been shattered. His behavior becomes irrational. It is in this frame of mind that he decides to immolate his enemies (Xiphares, Pharnaces, Monima). In his folly, strangely enough, he comes into contact with a more profound reality. As his vision expands, he sees Xiphares as his double and is unwilling to kill him (symbolically speaking, himself). When some semblance of consciousness returns, however, he evaluates his situation, this time pragmatically, and realizes that Xiphares is his most powerful fighter and must be spared.

> A son whom Rome fears? who can avenge his father?
> Why shed a blood that I so greatly need?[12]

Only when he learns that his son Pharnaces is leading the Roman troops against him does real pain intrude upon his life. It is so excoriating that he is moved to tears. "The King, himself deceived, bursts into tears."[13] The blow is too powerful for him to bear and he plunges his sword into his breast. Now, for the first time, Mithridates functions on a human level. The tears not only offer him release, but succeed in wrenching him from the heights of unreality and power to which he had risen as a youth and upon which he had determined to remain. The artificial and static climate which he created for himself crumbles. With his descent to earth, so to speak, the gossamer veil vanishes, permitting Mithridates to gain the wisdom and self-knowledge which usually accompany age. Like Lear, after his bout with insanity, so Mithridates after struggling with pain, can experience the joys of the world in terms of love and understanding.

> Such service can be recompensed alone
> By the most splendid jewel of my throne!
> But all my empire, all my crown is you;
> You are my only gem: let me give you;
> And all the pledges I exacted, please,
> My heart entreats them all for Xiphares.[14]

Unlike Pyrrhus, who died before any inner transformation could occur, or Titus, whose change depended upon Berenice's reactions toward him, Mithridates' illumination results from a series of shocks which permit him to experience self-fulfillment at the end of his life with the knowledge that his "beloved" son has succeeded him as conqueror, a domain which properly belongs to youth.

No play written so far by Racine reveals more clearly the tendencies an overly possessive father exhibits when he fails to experience life's process fully; that is, its intensity when a youth and its more subdued and ponderous aspects when mature. As a man unwilling to relinquish his authority, Mithridates represents a negative father image for both his sons. Like a child, he seems devoid of the sense of time and because of this outlook encourages a condition of stasis at home. His life, therefore, becomes a series of negative acts in both political and psychological domains. The perpetual pirate which Mithridates has become is shocked into a new state of awareness by his son's treachery. The tears he sheds shake him to his very foundations, so to speak, "reshuffling" unconscious contents, enabling these to burst forth into the light of his rational world. With the birth of this new frame of reference comes the understanding that each man has the right to leave his imprint upon the sands of destiny. Now it is his son's turn.

ʳ   ʳ   ʳ

The rival-brother theme has been treated by Racine in *The Theban Brothers* when he confronts his audiences with an internecine war ending with the demise of both Eteocles and Polynices; in *Britannicus,*

when Nero has his brother poisoned; in *Bajazet* when the Sultan succeeds in having his brother killed. Whereas the good brothers are killed
in the former works, the opposite situation occurs in *Mithridates*.
Pharnaces, the evil one, is done away with by the Romans. Other differences are also present.

In *Mithridates* we are introduced to a triangular situation,[15] far
more complex than in any previously mentioned play. The fact that the
King (Father) seeks to maintain the *status quo*, both politically (on the
battlefield) and sexually (through Monima), creates an illusory and
rigid situation as we have seen. To be unwilling to relinquish one's
stranglehold over people, to refuse to turn over the Kingship to a
younger and more malleable force, is to assume omniscient and om-
nipotent qualities which do not rightly belong to man but rather to
God. Mithridates had considered himself (unconsciously certainly)
and was considered by those about him as a suprapersonal father
image.

Xiphares is blinded by his father's immense radiance and force. A
dutiful son, he has always bathed in his shadow, as the moon to the
sun. Enjoying the *order* of his father's rule, he has never asserted himself and has, therefore, been unable to develop as an individual. When
news of Mithridates' death is brought to him, he is seized with ambivalent feelings, a sense of release from the domination he has known
throughout his life and a feeling of fright, now that he must make his
own way.

Xiphares is only now faced with serious problems. What has been
repressed for so long in the secret silence of his inner world, his hatred
for his brother and his love for Monima, surges forth. Indeed, he expresses his passion for her without compunction. The propulsion of
these catapulting emotions shakes his balanced outlook. Moreover,
their onslaught leaves little feeling left with which to mourn his father.
He gives the impression, therefore, of being callous and wonders himself why he should feel so little from such a loss. Upon hearing of his
father's safe return, guilt at his behavior comes to the fore.

> I know what is my crime and know my father;
> And worse than you I have my mother's crime;
> But whatsoever love may have bewitched me,
> When Father once appears, I must obey.[16]

Mithridates assumes once again his role as ruler and his son as
the one ruled. To regress to a former state, however, is far more difficult to accomplish once the fruits of liberty have been partaken. Conflict arises within Xiphares' heart for the first time. His obligation to

his father and country are at war with his personal love for Monima and his hatred for his brother. He succeeds in crushing the conflict and in withdrawing to the obedient son position. When, however, he suspects Pharnaces of winning Monima's affections, he goes to pieces. He intimates that he could accept his father's passion for Monima, but not his brother's. He is, thereby, identifying with his father to such an extent that he would be living through the monarch as Monima's lover. Symbolically speaking, he would be pursuing his shadow existence.

Xiphares' feelings of obligation toward his father indicate a highly developed sense of morality. The vise in which he is caught leads at times to his utter despair, when he realizes that a shadow existence cannot possibly lead to self-fulfillment. During these moments he toys with the idea of committing suicide, as had certain of his predecessors: Berenice, Antiochus, Titus. His undeveloped personality has been so crushed by what his father represents (authority, law, order) that he cannot even find the strength to carry out a final negative act. When finally his father asks him to fight alongside him against the Romans, he flushes with excitement and acquiesces.

It might be concluded in Xiphares' case that he is hiding behind the "old order," as represented by his father, escaping thereby from the exigencies required of those leading their own existences.[17] Indeed, it is much simpler for him to obey his father than to rebel against him and create his own life. As long as Mithridates lives, Xiphares cannot.

✓ ✓ ✓

Pharnaces is of a different ilk. He has rejected the Terrible Father image which would have forced him to lead a parasitical existence. Like Abel, he refuses to follow the old order and forges ahead to create the new by allying himself with the Romans. Aggressive, courageous, ready to attack, he is in this respect like Nero, who also wanted to annihilate those forces he felt were stunting his growth. Nor is Pharnaces fearful of expressing his love to Monima. He seeks to persuade her to flee with him away from a static and regressive situation, to new lands. "That but reminds you of your slavery."[18]

When Pharnaces hears of his father's death he feels no sorrow and certainly no guilt. Indeed, it encourages him to fight for freedom. Moreover, he can rightly assume his father's role since he is the elder brother.

> My father leaves me master of this realm;
> It falls to me now to fulfill his word.[19]

But when he learns that his father is very much alive, he frenzies at
first over his precarious situation. As always, however, he resorts to
his wits to help him overcome dangers. A son rebelling against a family situation is, of necessity, independent and self-sufficient, or should
be so. Pharnaces is no exception to the rule. Ingenuity is his exclusive
weapon. He warns Xiphares of the dangers involved for both of them.
They will be considered "criminals" by their father, he warns, for having expressed their love to Monima and for having taken matters in
hand.

> The more his love, his hate is even more!
> Be not too sure he'll love you any longer,
> His jealous fury will be all the stronger,
> Consider well. You have the soldiers' hearts,
> And I'll have aid that I shall not impart.
> Be led by me. Let us assure our grace;
> Let's make ourselves the masters of this place,
> And warrant, he to us can but prescribe
> Such terms as we are willing to suscribe.[20]

Pharnaces suggests total rebellion against Mithridates. This idea
is anathema to Xiphares. First, because he is a dutiful son. Second, he
feels that little would be accomplished by such a move. He would be
victimized by his older brother rather than by his father. Moreover,
if his father were not alive to maintain a semblance of balance between
the two, the situation might grow even more serious for him. In either
case, he lives a parasitical existence.

Pharnaces, unlike Xiphares, is amoral. He would stoop to anything to wriggle out of a dangerous situation. When, therefore, his
brother refuses to rebel against Mithridates, it is he who betrays him
and informs his father of Xiphares' love for Monima. In the end, however, he is caught in his own trap and dies.

Pharnaces, the unwanted brother, is determined to lead his own
life by rejecting the authoritarian father spirit that spells stagnation
for him. Rebellion is usually followed by a period of solitude that engenders meditation. Pharnaces' dynamism, inherited certainly from his
father, dispels such an outcome. Had he been forced into isolation, he
might have looked inward and been illuminated. A sense of responsibility and a moral code might have developed. He never succeeds,
however, in creating an ethic for himself. His acts, therefore, remain
negative and his death at the end—the reward he receives as betrayer
of father and country—comes as no surprise.

✓ ✓ ✓

Monima is the only female figure in *Mithridates*.[21] A descendant of Antigone, of Junie, Monima is gentle, kind, honorable, and courageous. Unlike her predecessors, however, she has no identity. She is rooted to no soil nor to any ideal.

> No relatives, no friends, forlorn, afraid,
> Queen long in name, in practice prisoner,
> Now widow, without knowing any husband.[22]

When Xiphares confesses his love to her she listens with contained joy. She not only responds, but experiences an inner glow, comfort, a sense of belonging. She wants to become part of his life now.

Monima, like Xiphares, has a highly developed sense of honor. When informed of Mithridates' death at the outset of the drama, she experiences ambivalent emotions, a sense of release and of desolation. When Mithridates returns, however, she informs Xiphares of the allegiance she owes his father and tells him that she will do her best to avoid him in the future. Once Monima has spoken decisively to Xiphares, she seems to have been relieved of an enormous burden. Her forthrightness toward the one she loves gives her the strength to accept a life of subjugation as Mithridates' wife. "My heart was all prepared to face its fate," she adds.[23]

Another show of courage prevails at the end of the drama when Monima, believing Xiphares to have been killed by the Romans, seeks to end her life by hanging. Though unsuccessful in the attempt, she tries again when Mithridates' servant brings her poison. She seizes it with near ecstasy.

> Come now, what ecstasy!
> Give, Arcas, tell the King who sends it me,
> Of all the many gifts his grace inspired,
> I now receive the dearest most desired.
> At last I breathe; and Heaven has set me free . . .
> Now, mistress of myself, for once I may
> Decide my fate according to my say.[24]

Monima does not die, as the events indicate. Instead, her pain has caused her to develop a sense of independence. Her life has become her own for her to do as she pleases. Giddiness follows this realization of freedom. Xiphares' love has given her a sense of belonging and security. Unlike Junie who flies forth into a life of ultra spirituality, or Berenice who is resigned to her fate, Monima at the end of the drama pledges herself to this world in body and spirit.

II

Mithridates is a perfectly conceived play. It ends at its point of departure. It begins with the rumored death of Mithridates and terminates with his actual demise. The drama, thereby, creates a circular sensation, linking its structural and its philosophical aspects, describing technically and ideationally the idea of eternal death and rebirth, the sacrifice of the old king for the sake of future development.

The symbolism in Mithridates is exciting. The drama is set in a seaport. The sea has been used in other Racinian plays as an instrument for Acomat's escape (*Bajazet*) and as a means for departure (*Berenice*), but never has the water image played such a decisive role in acting upon events and characters.

The vast expanse of blue marks adventure, warfare, excitement of all sorts, potentialities. Since water is one of the four basic elements, it is considered *prima materia*, without which life could not exist. Yet, water has its dangers. Too much of it causes drowning. In this sense then, water is capable of destroying man's equilibrium, symbolically speaking, causing a rejection of life's process.

For Mithridates, water represents the excitement of conquest, the new, the forceful, the intrinsically dynamic qualities of youth. "Princes, the sea is alive with ships," he declares, as one can almost sense his gusto. Just as water churns, so the monarch's entire being seems to react to its ebb and flow almost physically. Such constant and repeated motion, however, abolishes all tendencies toward stability. It is a fitting background to his ideational position as the perennial conqueror.[25] Though cerebrally he maintains a static attitude, emotionally he is in a constant state of flux, like a wave moving from love to hate to conquest and back again. He keeps battling eternally in one form or another. Nothing could be more revealing of Mithridates' inner realm than his own description of water:

> They know this torrent, on the point of bursting,
> If it pulls me, will inundate the rest;
> You'll see them all, riding its raging flood,
> Pour in my wake down into Italy . . .
> Let's march; and to her bosom take this war
> She wages at the two ends of the world:

> Within their walls, I'll strike these haughty victors;
> Let them, in their turn, tremble for their hearths . . .[26]

Though other symbols are also prominent in *Mithridates* (flame, city, armaments, blood, etc.) the entire *mise en scène* could be built upon this water image. Flashed on screens, heard from all parts of the theatre, felt at times in droplets or smelled by means of dank odors, the sensations aroused could vitalize each aspect of the play, the characters of the protagonists and the acerbity of the events. The rhythms too could play a primordial role in marking the atmosphere with fright, anger, calm, and ebullience. The words themselves could be enunciated according to the patterns aroused by the sea, in harsh or relaxed tones, dense or transparent imagery, pure or murky innuendos. All the senses could be activated in this way, ushering in a chaotic world, that of the unconscious.

III

Louis XIV had his own political reasons for declaring that *Mithridates* was his favorite Racinian play. He looked upon this monarch as a courageous conqueror; indeed, he identified with Mithridates. At this particular period, Louis XIV was fighting the Dutch, who were not only Protestants but, to make matters worse, Republicans. These "nefarious" people, it seems, had been publishing libelous articles in newspapers concerning Louis' "dissolute" private life. Though the French suffered many casualties in their war with the Dutch (1672–1678), this armed conflict infused them with a military zest they had never before known. The intensity of the fighting gave the French youth and their monarch a desire for heroics. Taste demanded a military play.

For Racine, therefore, a work in which the political played such an important part served his purpose. Always intent upon maintaining cordial relations with his monarch and those whom he favored, he could not neglect such an important event as the Franco-Dutch war.

Other reasons motivated Racine. Who, better than he, knew the weight of authority, the iniquities blind faith imposes upon one? Who better than he had sought, and succeeded to a certain extent, to liberate himself from such a stranglehold? Who better than he knew the meaning of solitude and rejection? Twice he had been bereft of parental images, when his real parents died and when he was rejected by the Jansenists for choosing a theatrical career.

Racine must have felt most keenly the struggles experienced by both Pharnaces and Xiphares. In *The Theban Brothers*, Racine's projection onto the brothers had been so intense, the tumult so fierce, that he destroyed both of them. In subsequent dramas (*Britannicus, Bajazet*) the good brother is destroyed. Only in *Mithridates* does the son with a positive point of view survive. The fact that Xiphares, the son who does not rebel against his father (authority, the old order, the Jansenists by extension), is spared, indicates, to a certain extent at least, an inner change developing within Racine. Such an evolution may be due to the fact that his former rejection of Jansenist thought (*The Theban Brothers*) had, to a certain extent, subsided. He no longer felt the vitriolic hatred for them that he had once known. They no longer stood for emasculation and negation. Now that he had experienced life on his own and successfully, he did not consider the Jansenists a threat. He could understand and appreciate their teachings. Indeed, Racine would put their doctrine to positive use.

8

Iphigenia

"An Avenging God,
a God detonates the blows . . ."[1]

WITH *Iphigenia*, produced at Versailles on August 18, 1674, Racine reached the peak of success. Never had a play won such admiration from audiences. Indeed, according to Racine's friend Boileau[2] and his son, Louis, *Iphigenia* caused more tears to flow than any other theatrical work.

The most popular author in Paris now, Racine not only surrounded himself with prominent people in the arts and in government, but also benefited from royal favor. Such praise that he now received, however, did not put a damper on the machinations of the ever increasing number of evil wishers throughout the city and the country. They did their utmost to crush whatever praise came his way. Indeed, even before *Iphigenia* was finished, Racine's enemies prevailed upon an academician, Le Clerc, and a mediocre writer, Coras, to compose a tragedy treating the same subject. His rivals' play, fortunately, opened only at the end of May, 1675 and was so poorly received that it defeated its own purpose. Rather than destroy Racine's work, it served to enhance it.[3]

Racine's *Iphigenia*, he tells us in his preface, was based on *Iphigenia in Aulis*[4] by Euripides. To this drama he introduced the character Eriphyle. She was not, however, of his invention since there is historical proof in the work of the Greek traveler and geographer Pausanias to substantiate her existence. Racine felt compelled to include Eriphyle because the *deus ex machina* ending used by Euripides (Iphigenia is saved from sacrifice by Artemis, who carries her off and substitutes a deer for her on the altar) would not have been plausible to seventeenth century audiences. The other alternative would have been to have Iphigenia die. Racine did not want to "sully the stage with the horrible murder of a person as virtuous and as gentle" as she, he declared.

ſ   ſ   ſ

Iphigenia takes place in Aulis, in Agamemnon's tent.

Act I. Agamemnon is confiding his plight to his servant Arcas. His fleet is becalmed and he has been told by the Seer, Calchas, that he must sacrifice his daughter Iphigenia if the winds are to blow again, enabling the Greek ships to sail forth and fight the Trojans. At first Agamemnon complies with Calchas' wishes. He sends for his daughter, promising her Achilles in marriage. Instead, Agamemnon plans to lead her to the altar to be sacrificed by Calchas. Days later, however, Agamemnon alters his decision. He sends Arcas with a message to be delivered to the wedding party (Iphigenia, her mother Clytemnestra, her slave girl Eriphyle) before its arrival in Aulis. The note informs Iphigenia of Achilles' change of heart and asks her to return home. Fate, however, intervenes. Arcas misses the wedding party.

Act II. Eriphyle tells her confidant that she despises Iphigenia and that she came to Aulis to see Achilles, for whom she nourishes a tremendous passion. (It is later learned that Eriphyle is the daughter of Helen and Theseus, that she had been sent at birth to Lesbos where her name, originally Iphigenia, had been changed to Eriphyle. Years later, she was taken prisoner and ravished by Achilles, who plundered and conquered her adopted country. When Iphigenia and her family befriended the foreigner, they were totally unaware of Eriphyle's hatred for them and her passion for Achilles.) When Agamemnon sees his daughter in Aulis, his anguish and shame make it impossible for him to look at her. Ulysses, entering the scene, views the situation lucidly and objectively, and persuades Agamemnon to go through with the sacrifice. Agamemnon acquiesces.

Act III. Arcas, however, cannot bear the weight of such a terrible secret. Yielding to his conscience, he informs Iphigenia, Clytemnestra, and Achilles of what is to transpire. Clytemnestra, consumed with wrath and anguish, beseeches Agamemnon to alter his plan. Appalled by the brutality of such a sacrifice, Achilles refuses to give up his future bride and shouts out his intentions to fight, to overthrow altars and kingdoms, if need be, in order to safeguard his beloved.

Act IV. Now Agamemnon has a change of heart. He decides to send Iphigenia away from Aulis immediately and secretly.

Act V. Eriphyle informs Calchas of Agamemnon's plans. To escape from the vise now becomes impossible. Agamemnon bows to the higher authority that Calchas represents. Iphigenia, docile, willingly succumbs to her father's will, to Fate. She is led to the altar. Eriphyle stands near her, prepared to watch Iphigenia's sacrifice. She is stunned when Calchas calls to *her*, the other Iphigenia, not Agamemnon's daughter. Now, aware that she is the one whose blood the gods have called for, Eriphyle rushes to the altar, takes a knife and plunges it deep into her breast. Minutes later the winds blow. The gods have been placated, the miracle occurs and the ships are free to sail forth.

I

Because the basic ideas around which *Iphigenia* revolves are eternal and universal, they can be restated in every century and culture with varying emphasis: martyrdom and murder, the individual versus the collective, the outer (persona, mask) personality and the inner structure.

Martyrdom (sacrifice), whether it encompasses the ritual slaying of kings or gods, has played a significant role in almost all religions, from the ancient Egyptian Osiris to the Christ. Expressed in psychological terminology, martyrdom indicates the desire (or need) of the unconscious attitude to kill the prevailing conscious orientation, paving the way, thereby, for possible future development.[5]

Calchas, as spokesman for the collective, religious authority, the *status quo*, has ordered Agamemnon to sacrifice his daughter Iphigenia. If he obeys this order, the winds will blow, permitting the Greek ships to sail forth. Symbolically interpreted, the lack of wind indicates a deficiency in dynamism within the Greek society. Energy, therefore, has to be infused into this lethargic Greek corpus in order to make growth (which comes with the departure of the Greek ships) possible. The energy released as a result of the struggle expended in accomplishing the sacrificial act is the very force which makes evolution an actuality.

As King and leader of his people, Agamemnon has been delegated to carry out the "heroic" deed, that of sacrifice. He is looked upon as the "agent provocateur," the force able to renovate society. His mission is arduous, for he must sacrifice the being most precious to him, his daughter. Symbolically speaking, his daughter represents the anima (personification of the female feeling principle within a male's personality), that entity within his unconscious world which must be destroyed if masculine power is to become dynamic. The prospect of exposing himself to the terrifying experience of self-maiming (killing his anima or the Iphigenia-aspect of his personality) makes his blood freeze. As he confides his emotions to his servant Arcas at the outset of the play, he exposes his extreme turmoil:

> I felt my blood run cold through all my limbs.
> I was struck dumb, and no word could I say
> Until a thousand sobs had cleared the way.
> I blame the Gods, and, without hearing more,
> To disobey, upon their altars swore.[6]

Agamemnon is a man faced with a tragic dilemma, a split which exists between the *persona* (mask) he wears and his weak inner being. He is forever trying to live up to the image people have created of him as King. Whenever he becomes aware of this dichotomy between his persona and the man within, which is like a gaping wound, terror ensues. The greater the breach, the more emotional and quixotic is his behavior, the more tragic a figure he becomes. Rage, tears, hate, lust, all come into play.

> No, Heaven, I cannot think thy lofty justice
> Approves this black and wanton sacrifice![7]

Lacking in direction and will, Agamemnon constantly shuttles from one extreme to the other. He grasps at straws in order to muster sufficient force to commit the deed so necessary for the growth and development of the society within which he lives, by extension, within his own psyche. Agamemnon in no way resembles Abraham, Jepthah, Christ or any of the martyrs who burned with zeal, who faced their ordeal with clarity of mind. He does not possess the "true" faith capable of moving mountains.

Agamemnon's lack of fortitude and insight is apparent in several instances in the play. He himself confesses his state when he asks his servant to ". . . save her from my own weakness." His attitude toward Clytemnestra, whom he fears, is similar: "Spare me the curses from a raging mother. . . ."[8] When greeting Iphigenia, he is unable to face her gaze, overpowered by his own sense of "cowardliness." He cannot, therefore, don the hero's personality. He slinks into darkness and solitude to bury his shame.

Agamemnon's relationship with his daughter (insofar as she is considered to be an extension of his personality) is a very close one. As Agamemnon's feminine principle, she seems to proceed intuitively and is fully aware of her father's determination to avoid her eyes: "And scarcely let your glances fall on me,"[9] though she is not cognizant of his reasons for doing so. Her view of the forces at stake are clearer than her father's, whose vision has become dulled with the routine of years. Iphigenia is like a stalk of freshly grown wheat; she stands erect and strong throughout this entire drama.

Ulysses, unlike Agamemnon, is a hero. Master of all situations, he considers Agamemnon's plight in a totally masculine, clearcut, and objective manner. He sees the great forces which are at stake, political and religious ideologies, and is convinced that the personal attitude, though it may be intrinsically creative, is trivial by comparison and, therefore, worth sacrificing for the good of the multitude. "You owe your daughter to Greece,"[10] he says with equanimity. Agamemnon is, in Ulysses' opinion, a public figure, a King, a function. As such, he enters another dimension and becomes a historical and eternal personality. He stands above (or should) the "madding crowd" and must, therefore, become an example to his people. He is obliged to fulfill his duty courageously, virtuously, and bring honor to his land, or else he is not fit to be its ruler. Rejection of the personal world in favor of the collective, the feminine in favor of the masculine, the real in favor of the ideal must be Agamemnon's code of action.

When Agamemnon considers his situation from Ulysses' point of view, his personality undergoes a change: he experiences extreme inflation and identifies with his *persona*. Charmed with the power which resides within his grasp, leader of nations and peoples, his role appears rather attractive to him.

> Under my power's and my grandeur's spell,
> These names of king or kings and head of Greece,
> Still flattered the proud weakness of my heart.[11]

He views himself as the Creator of History, a Leader of Destiny, a Titan capable of all actions. Agamemnon is suffused with power.

> Let us deliberate no longer. Let us brave her violence.
> My self-seeking glory wins the day.[12]

Drenched in self-admiration, he speaks to his daughter from lofty heights, pointing to the nobility of her sacrificial act, the pride she must take in her noble origins, in the great historical role she is now about to fulfill. She will stride the path of queens and rulers, he intimates, she, Agamemnon's daughter.

> We must submit, my child; your hour is come.
> Be worthy of the greatness of your rank.
> In agony I pass on Heaven's decree,
> The falling knife will kill you less than me.

> In dying, show you're worthy of your name;
> Make Gods, who have condemned you, blush with shame;
> Go; let the Greeks, who want your sacrifice,
> From its first gush, my own blood recognize.[13]

Though Agamemnon speaks out boldly to his daughter, still he hides behind a mask, wearing the countenance of the man he would like to be. His words to those who know him are, therefore, hollow, one dimensional, devoid of any solid foundation or moral fiber.

Because of the breach within his own psyche, Agamemnon's self-esteem suddenly deflates and he opts for an opposing attitude. He bemoans the fact that he is a leader of peoples and looks with envy upon the average and commonplace existence of his servant. "Sad destiny of kings," he cries out.[14] How much simpler it would be, he declares, to take orders rather than to give them, to act automatically without thinking. Victimized once again by his own swirling emotions, he turns on the cerebral Ulysses, castigates him boldly for his rigid and "philosophical" concepts. To uphold the sacrificial point of view, Agamemnon lashes out, is not a sign of strength in Ulysses' case, because he is not personally involved, he does not have to kill what is most precious to him, his son.

> But if you were to see Telemachus,
> Your son, with blindfold eyes, approach the altar,
> At that dread spectacle you'd soon be seen
> Changing your lofty language into tears,
> Feeling the deep pain that I feel today . . .[15]

Ulysses, a man of firm metal, of vision, courage, and insight, accustomed to living by his wits and intelligence, sympathizes with Agamemnon's plight.

> My Lord, I too am father, and my heart
> Can sympathise in full with your sad heart.
> And, shuddering at the blow that makes you sigh,
> Far from blaming your tears, I too, would cry.[16]

He sees Agamemnon's situation from a cosmic point of view, impersonally. (Ulysses has no *persona*.) Artfully, he appeals to Agamemnon's vanity, offering him abstractions, power, admiration, and he reiterates the fact that Agamemnon is a man destined for great things.

> Bring the honour that shall spring from it to mind.
> See Hellespont all white beneath our oars,

> The flame through red, perfidious Troy that roars,
> Her people in your chains, proud Priam spurned,
> Helen by your hands to her spouse returned . . .
> And your great triumph, that will then become
> The eternal talk of centuries to come.[17]

When Agamemnon identifies with the kingly role, he seeks any excuse to bolster his decision to accept authority's dictates. Were he not to sacrifice his daughter, he reasons, it would be tantamount to conceding Achilles a moral victory (as Achilles was against Iphigenia's murder). "Must I grant victory to the superb Achilles?"[18] Agamemnon questions. To sacrifice Iphigenia (his feminine principle) seems less difficult to him than to suffer a moral defeat with its ensuing loss of prestige. Agamemnon, therefore, it not yet prepared to expose his personal, vulnerable, and intimate side to the masses, fearing his people will see him for what he really is, a coward and not a King.

Agamemnon deliberates until the end of the play, floating about blindly in that nebulous area between the *persona* and the *ego*. Unable to grasp the principles involved in his struggle, or at least to abide by them, he finally agrees to Iphigenia's sacrifice only because he is caught in a vise. Public opinion forces him to act like a King, a giant, though he is a dwarf at heart. Just as a heroic position is forced upon him, the entire situation is taken out of his hands by the presence of Eriphyle, the other Iphigenia who is called upon to become the sacrificial agent.

✝   ✝   ✝

Clytemnestra is a different type. Instinctual, passionate, she is a being who lives on a personal and unconscious level; totally incapable of seeing any political or philosophical forces at stake in her own personal dilemma or of understanding her husband's fear and trembling. She is the protective mother archetype who will destroy friend and foe, anyone who stands in the way of her daughter's happiness and well-being.

When Clytemnestra discovers Agamemnon's intentions, she cannot abstract herself from her immediate situation; her fury, therefore, knows no bounds.

> I'll teach my treacherous husband that he lied.
> He'll scarce sustain the madness in my mind.[19]

Like a wild animal, a lioness protecting her cubs from imminent danger, Clytemnestra expresses her feelings in bestial and bloodthirsty terms.

Your daughter's butcher, it but now remains
For you to serve her up in banquet to her mother.
Barbarian! This your happy sacrifice,
That with such care and cunning you prepared!
The horror of endorsing this dire order,
You monster, did not paralyse your hand?[20]

Burning with anger, she seeks to strike down her oppressor and in so doing finds herself experiencing the anguish of death itself. She moans, "Must I so often die while yet I breathe?"[21]

Clytemnestra does not look upon her husband as a ruler, nor does she see him as a Creator of History or as a Molder of Destiny, but rather as a monstrous, sanguinary animal. She rebels against him and against what she considers to be his blood-lust, with all the viciousness of a caged animal. She lunges forth with the power expelled from her extreme inner chaos and, like a pythoness, spews forth her poisonous tirades.

O monster, that Megaera bore in her womb!
Monster, that hell has thrown into our arms!
What? Must you still live?[22]

Clytemnestra never alters her attitude. She fights Agamemnon every step of the way, prevails upon Achilles to help her in her course, and undergoes any hardship to protect her daughter, her *raison d'être*, from evil intent.

✶ ✶ ✶

Achilles, associated with the adolescent, the romantic lover at the beginning of the play, grows in both strength and stature.

Capable of intense emotion, his wrath can flow freely, as does Clytemnestra's. When he learns he must give up his bride, Achilles is determined to protect her at all costs and goes a step further, seeking revenge upon all of her would-be murderers.

But my just anger carries me beyond.
It's nothing, shielding you, I rush to avenge,
And at the same time punish this vile game
That dared against my love to use my name.[23]

When Iphigenia refuses to reject her father's decision and is determined to go through with her sacrifice, Achilles reacts almost viciously, promising his beloved a blood bath. He fails to understand her reasons for compliance and, with uncontrollable wrath, threatens to overturn altars, kill priests, flagellate all those representatives of the law, whether lay or spiritual; even Agamemnon will be struck down if he stands in his way.

> If heaven hungers for corpses and for blood,
> I'll see its altar drenched in a great flood.
> The blindness of my love allows me all.
> The priest shall be the very first to fall.
> The pyre, struck down by me and scattered wide,
> In pieces, shall their butcher-blood stream ride;
> And if, mid all the horrors that shall fly,
> Your father too shall stricken fall and die . . .[24]

Achilles is unlike any other character in the play. Sincere, honorable, naive in certain respects, he sees events collectively, in terms of cosmic forces, but always in connection with himself and his desires. There is a balance between the collective and the personal, the unconscious and the conscious, within his young personality. Possessor of both physical and moral strength, events and societies become subservient to his will. Like David, Siegfried, Roland, he seethes with hatred for those who would make him suffer. Achilles will carve out his destiny along with Iphigenia. He, the hero, is above gods and can dictate to them.

> The Gods are sovereign masters of our days;
> But glory, Sire, within our own hands stay.
> Why plague ourselves with their supreme decrees?
> Like them, to be immortal let us dream;
> And understand by fate, let him, who dares,
> Achieve a destiny as great as theirs.[25]

Achilles represents the force of the future, the builder of societies, the heroic youth who challenges all: authority, religion, the *status quo*.

✦ ✦ ✦

Iphigenia is described throughout the play in terms of goodness, gentleness, beauty, and "light." Floating high over other mortals who are struggling through their existences, she seems to live in a rarefied atmosphere, far above the ground. Iphigenia can be looked upon in two ways: as a projection of Agamemnon's psyche (his feminine principle) or as an entity unto herself. In either case, she accepts her fate, strangely enough, with eagerness. Indeed, when she learns of the sacrifice she must endure, she is not shocked. "I did not pale." When identified with her father she defends his project and counters Achilles' protests, "Remember, whatever he may have done, remember, he is my father."[26] Only briefly and almost as an afterthought does Iphigenia change her stand, when Clytemnestra and Achilles persuade her to do so (III,vii). Quickly, however, she reverts to her earlier decision of sacrifice.

Considered as an entity unto herself, Iphigenia looks upon her sacrifice in a personal, not in a collective manner, in terms of her own grandeur, not of her country's welfare. Pride swells her countenance and she sees herself playing out a heroine's role in history. Moreover, she reasons, there are advantages to her demise, death can also end her worldly torments.

Such a masochistic attitude as she has now expressed appeals to her by its very uniqueness. She becomes literally mesmerized by the idea of death as an initiation into another realm of existence. Standing alone and erect, as she watches her transformation in her mind's eye, she no longer sees herself merely as her father's daughter, but, through her sacrifice, as a Virgin Princess, the one adored in most all religions as He or She who must die. As Christ walked the road to Calvary before his Father's eyes, so Iphigenia will offer herself up for immolation before Agamemnon's gaze. Iphigenia is only a partial human being as the Virgin Princess; she remains undeveloped, stunted, never having reached womanhood.

Eriphyle is Iphigenia's counterpart. Indeed, Iphigenia calls Eriphyle (whose real name is also Iphigenia) her sister. Eriphyle represents Iphigenia's unconscious, unchanneled and destructive side, her *shadow*.[27] As Iphigenia's shadow, her personality is made up of characteristics which have never been recognized by Iphigenia's ego. She is even described in terms of blindness, darkness, "without light, my sad eyes search for clarity."[28]

Eriphyle, orphaned, enslaved, a stranger in a foreign land, rejected by her lover, lives within her own dark and ambiguous world. A prey to her emotions, like Clytemnestra, she cannot reach beyond her immediate realm into the light of consciousness. Unlike Clytemnestra, who seeks to protect her offspring. Eriphyle tries to destroy everything about her, Iphigenia in particular.

Eriphyle is jealous of Iphigenia's family, her beauty, her gentleness, her security, the love and admiration everyone heaps upon her. She feels intense hatred for this Princess (or ego personality) who stands between her and Achilles. Subtly she joys when Iphigenia suffers, sadism marks her personality and, therefore, she accepts Iphigenia's gentle affection "only to arm herself against her."[29] Never having been exposed to kindness, she does not know how to react to it, how to handle the emotions as they come into being. Unable to attract Achilles because of her harshness, she is driven to a frenzy of despair. Eriphyle thunders forth like a dazed animal, slashing at anyone and everyone who prevents her from reaching Achilles, relating to him in the most vicious act when her rapport with the conquering hero is threatened. Since she seeks to destroy Iphigenia, it is she who plays out the treacherous role and reveals to Calchas Agamemnon's intention to send his daughter away from Aulis. Insidious in her demeanor, she is equally horrendous in her outlook.

Eriphyle, the outcast, is a stranger wherever she goes. She is identityless since she does not know from whence she came and feels no rapport with others. Knowledge of her background, it has been told her, could come only with her destruction.

> I know not whom I am: as height of horror,
> My ignorance is sealed by an oracle;
> And, when I wish to trace who gave me breath,
> It warns, I cannot know this without death.[30]

Iphigenia would have remained the Virgin Princess had she not been forced to cope with her shadow personality. Such a confrontation occurs when she discovers Eriphyle's love for Achilles. During this instance, she comes to grips with her opposing aspect and rage floods her system.

> Yes, you love him, traitress.
> And all these ragings that you paint me,
> These arms, all bathed in blood, you ever see,
> These ashes, torches, Lesbos' murdered toll,
> Are strokes with which love prints him in your soul;[31]

Eriphyle, Iphigenia's shadow, is destroyed. The struggle waged in accomplishing this act affords the impetus necessary to bring both sides of Iphigenia's personality (conscious and shadow aspects) together. Formerly opposing forces coalesce and bring harmony and balance to the psyche. Iphigenia, therefore, emerges from Racine's drama as a woman capable of assuming the role of Achilles' Queen. Both will brave the new world.

If Eriphyle is considered as an extension of Agamemnon's psyche (another facet of his anima), her death represents the destruction of its carnal and unavowed aspects, the integration and transformation of these entities into dynamic forces, because after her death the winds begin to blow.

II

Racine's poetry, a manifestation of his volatile personality, is studded with colors, sounds, rhythms, images, intangible elements which can act trenchantly upon the spectators' nerves. (See Introduction for a discussion of these symbols in terms of the theatrical performance.)

One of the most important images in *Iphigenia* is that of water. Though this image played an incisive role in *Mithridates*, where it mirrored the character of the King and also served as a vehicle to enhance the plot, it becomes the *sine qua non* of *Iphigenia*.

The image of water as a motionless expanse in the beginning of the drama represents a state of inertia, an incapacity to evolve or change. If the water continues to remain in such a condition of stasis, the Greek ships will be unable to sail and the battle will not be fought. So water now assumes the enormous dimensions it has in the Great Flood stories which figure in most world religions; in the Exodus, when the Red Sea parts, permitting the Hebrews to leave Egypt; in Creation legends such as the birth of Venus; in the miracle when Christ walks on the water, etc. In each of these myths water plays an intrinsic and positive role.

Water is a source of life and growth. If it lacks motility, it is like a human being who cannot breathe. It must, as of necessity, die. In the beginning of *Iphigenia* water is personified. Agamemnon, describing the men using their oars, is angered by the sea's irresponsive attitude. Though his men beat the sea with their oars, he declares, yet it remains immobile: "and fatigued in vain an immobile sea."[32] The sea remains placid, indifferent to human feelings, independent and brazen in its outlook.

Ulysses describes the Hellespont as white beneath the many oars thrusting down upon it with force and energy, the sea as the crowning glory of Greece's mighty fleet, the pride of a nation.

> See Hellespont all white beneath our oars,
> The flame through red, perfidious Troy that roars . . .
> See the dressed sterns of all your vessels gay
> When they sail back with you to Aulis' bay . . .[33]

Water becomes a hateful and destructive force for Eriphyle. It is this body which forced her onto Achilles' ship, which brought her prisoner to a foreign land; fearful, weeping, lonely, she rages against the cruelty of the seas.

Clytemnestra is terrorized by water. "Sea," she personifies, "you will not open up new abysses."[34] She cannot look into her own depths, or brush past facades which will take her beneath surfaces. Blinded by her own instinctual nature, she fears the depths, the chaos, the unknown, and the darkness which lurks around it.

The water image which represents a condition of stasis in the beginning of the drama, as well as various aspects of the protagonists' personalities, reflects, certainly, the unconscious state of the Greeks at this time. Rooted in their own lethargy, they have become decadent and lacking in insight. Such stagnation has to be halted for a new life force to emerge, for the psyche's potential to come to the fore.

When the wind, representing spirit and creativity, does finally blow at the end of the drama, after Eriphyle's *blood* sacrifice, a tremendous dynamism is infused into the Greek people, because the water's depths, representing the unconscious, have been stirred. A new attitude has come into being. Such an alteration of point of view could not, however, have emerged had blood not flowed.

Whenever a strong change occurs in a conscious attitude it ensues after a cruel act has been perpetrated. Change, symbolically speaking, means the death of one way of facing life, or of one ideational content, and the birth of a new one. Eriphyle's blood, therefore, has to drench the earth, thunder has to shake the altar, the wind has to blow strongly and uproot whatever traditional structures stand in the way. The sea has to storm and bellow. Indeed, so strong are its waves and tides that the shore groans from the violence, turning white with shock.

> Seizes the sacred knife and stabs herself.
> Her blood has hardly flowed, reddening the earth,
> When Heaven's thunder bursts upon the altar;
> The winds in happy shudders tease the air
> And the sea responds with all her mighty moaning,
> While groans the farther shore flecked white with foam;
> And of itself the pyre's flame sudden flares.
> The sky flashes with lightning and gapes open . . .[35]

The image of blood is used throughout *Iphigenia* by nearly all of the protagonists with varying nuances of meaning. Though this image is present in all Racine's dramas, never has it been used with such force and such intent: as an actual blood sacrifice in the traditional manner, that is, both symbolically and actually.

Agamemnon, for example, talks of the blood which must flow, of Iphigenia's sacrifice. He is so shaken by the realization of the ordeal he must experience that he feels congealed, immobile, unable to act. Ulysses, aware of the situation, understanding the meaning of the blood bath which must occur if a true sacrifice is to be enacted, accepts whatever violent act must ensue. "Blood is needed perhaps and of the most precious type."[36] As for the youthful Achilles, he is at the outset oblivious to the true meaning of blood. Let blood flow, he remarks, anywhere and everywhere. He speaks as does the conqueror. Later, when apprised of the situation, his anger bursts forth and he vows to spill blood; unmercifully, if his beloved sacrifices herself. Iphigenia, however, intent upon playing the role of martyr, speaks of blood with an almost lascivious delight. Eriphyle, on the other hand, accuses Achilles of having "sucked" the blood of lions and bears and of having earned his cruelty, violence, and evil nature from these beasts.[37] When Clytemnestra talks of the blood which Agamemnon seeks to shed, she calls it "a horrible feast," a thirst, a cruelty.[38]

Only at the end of the drama does the word blood, used abstractly until then, since it has merely hovered over Iphigenia and her family as a threat rather than as a reality, take on realistic import. Blood becomes a living force, something with which a person must contend. As Eriphyle's blood flows forth, man's earthly realm changes violently and immediately as in an apocalyptic vision.

To intensify the emotions associated with the blood image, Racine adds a series of brilliant pictorial descriptions: flame, torch, fire, light, clarity, burning, blinding. The effulgence becomes that much greater when juxtaposed with other tonalities: blackness, smoke, obscurity, night, tomb, cinders. These images are used by Racine as a decor, as a rhythmical orchestration setting off the stark pain associated with blood, acting as the core of its dynamism, enacting the same role as the eye of a tornado.

Chains, irons, bands, constricting images are added to the blood and other searing pictures, to show further the force of conflict, the play of emotions within each of the protagonists. The theme of enslavement, of imprisonment, infuses the entire situation with a claustrophobic atmosphere, Greek and Jansenist fatality, the irrevocability of destiny.

The absolute path which must be taken and from which there is no turning back (in the form of sacrifice) is made all the more excruciating by the inclusion of all types of auditive sounding nouns, adjectives, verbs: the voice which strikes the ear, the air which breathes with noise and vibrates, the wind which calls, cries, silences, all that permeates the atmosphere, the chill, the gore, the storm, the trembling, the shouts. Percussion sounds vibrate and deafen those victims who approach them, who come within their grasp, who are compelled to follow destiny's dictates. These beat out the path, the tonalities of the walk and the rhythm of the gait, the stifling sounds of the breathing as the end nears, finally the shocking finale, the sacrifice not of the lamb, but of the tiger. Indeed, a veritable symphonic score could be written to accompany the rhythmical and sonorous patterns inherent in this drama.

III

A myth is a creative expression of an original religious experience and as such can be viewed in varying lights. The fact that Racine chose to dramatize the *Iphigenia* myth rather than another Greek legend indicates the depth of his projection upon it.

Analogies can be drawn between Racine and Agamemnon. Both were asked to sacrifice something very precious, Agamemnon his daughter (his anima in the form of Iphigenia and Eriphyle), and Racine his dramatic career—the former by the Greeks, the latter by the Jansenists. Unable to acquiesce to such a severe order, Racine did away with his spiritual leaders (Calchas). Such a rejection, tantamount to a destruction of the father image, was all the more traumatic for Racine in view of the fact that he had been fatherless since the age of three. Racine might have floundered in a sea of despair had not other forces intervened to fill the vacuum created by the missing image, his instincts. Racine's sensual world, crushed and constrained during the course of his existence by Jansenist teachings, had now gushed forth unhampered, all stops removed. The Eriphyle side of his personality was running wild, as witnessed by the passionate creatures inhabiting all his dramatic works. Once the bulk of his plays had been written and his passions had (to a degree) spent themselves, his conscious personality (Iphigenia) learned to cope with his instinctual world (Eriphyle), giving it the attention it so needed. Then the void set in. It was at this point that Racine longed to renew contact with the sustaining spiritual force in the form of his Jansenist fathers (Calchas). The price? His career. *Iphigenia* is, to a certain degree, a symbolic recounting of Racine's inner struggle.

Racine's sacrifice, as revealed by *Iphigenia*, was not complete. He had been capable of killing only part of the anima figure (Eriphyle); the other aspect (Iphigenia) was "too virtuous" and "too gentle," he had indicated in his introduction to the play, to destroy. What he meant, in reality, was that he was not yet prepared to eliminate the most beautiful aspect of his existence, his spiritual child—his plays.

9

Phaedra

PHAEDRA opened on January 1, 1667 at the Hôtel de Bourgogne. Two days later, Pradon's *Phaedra* opened at the Hôtel de Guénégaud. Racine experienced failure; his rival, success. Such a situation could not have been due solely to chance. It was certainly the result of a concerted, ruthless, and persevering attack on the part of Racine's enemies, a desire to destroy him as a playwright.

Racine's foes were in phalanx-like positions now. The Duchesse de Bouillon, one of Mazarin's nieces and La Fontaine's protectress, led the frontal attack. She tried and succeeded in dividing public opinion. According to Louis Racine, she and her brother

> reserved the first boxes for the first six performances of both plays, and consequently the boxes were either filled or empty, as they wished.[2]

The question arises as to why the Duchesse de Bouillon was so forthright in her hatred of Racine. Only suppositions can be offered. Certain critics maintain that Racine's *Phaedra* was in part based on the Duchesse de Bouillon's illicit affair with her young nephew, the Chevalier Philippe de Vendôme. In this case, her vindictiveness would be a natural consequence.

A handsome, fine warrior, a passionate hunter, a member of the Societé du Temple and *ipso facto* a debauched individual, the Chevalier Philippe de Vendôme may have been the "incestuous" object of La Duchesse de Bouillon's desire. This passionate relationship had begun, it is said, in 1669 or 1670, when she was fifteen years old. When the murderess La Voisin came up for trial during the sordid "Affaire des

Poisons," the Duchesse de Bouillon was accused of having tried to poison her husband in order to be able to marry her nephew. On January 29, 1680 she appeared in the Chambre Ardente with all the other criminals. Though she was acquitted, she was exiled to Nérac near the Pyrénées.[3] Only later was a reconciliation affected with her husband.[4]

The Duchesse de Bouillon had literary ambitions herself and invited men and women of letters to her Salon: Mme Deshoulières, Benserade, Segrais, Boyer, Pradon, all of whom were envious of Racine's reputation and were more than willing to annihilate him in whatever way they could. It was, therefore, not by accident that Pradon's play was preceded by an *épître* to the Duchesse de Bouillon.

Other reasons have also been forwarded for the Duchesse de Bouillon's overt acts against Racine. She was a rebellious character in her own right, who detested court life and the hypocrisy of social codes. She was, therefore, naturally hostile to Racine, whom she considered a social climber who had always done his best to attract all those in high positions to his orbit in order to interest them in furthering his work. His success at court had even won him the favor of the King, of Madame de Montespan, and of many other notables.[5]

Racine was not passive in this situation. He did his utmost to prevent Pradon's play from opening. When he failed in his endeavor, he suffered the consequences but did not turn the other cheek. A rather startling "quarrel of sonnets" resulted from the anger elicited by the dual productions of *Phaedra*. Strangely enough, neither Racine nor Pradon took part in the angry interchange, only their friends who had meant well. Instead of resolving matters, they shed still more fire onto the already brilliantly lit scene.[6] Both Racine and Pradon rejected authorship of the sonnets. To add to the enmity on both sides, it seems that Racine and his friend Boileau had been threatened with bodily harm. As a result, they asked the Grand Condé, the King's brother, to intercede on their behalf.[7] He settled the affair after having talked with both antagonists and their seconds, and asked them to use reason rather than rancor.

By March Racine's *Phaedra* had won the day. Even Saint-Evremond, so hostile to Racine, had conceded his enemy's victory.

✼ ✼ ✼

Racine declared in his preface to *Phaedra* that Euripides' *Hippolytus* had been the source of his inspiration. The Greek play dramatizes the conflict between two rival goddesses, Aphrodite and Artemis. Hippolytus is the hero and Phaedra is merely a secondary character. Racine's version places Phaedra in the center of his tragedy and all else radiates outward.

Racine mentions Seneca's *Phaedra* as differing from his own. He does not, however, refer to Garnier's *Hyppolytus* (1573) or to La Pinelière's play (1635) of the same name, both of which were inspired by Seneca's work. Racine's attention may have been attracted to the Phaedra legend by Quinault's *Bellérophon* (1671) and Thomas Corneille's *Ariane* (1672), plays in which love becomes the instrument of fate. This, however, is merely supposition. On the other hand there is no question that ancient literature worked most forcefully on Racine's imagination and temperament: works such as Ovid's *Heroides,* a series of dramatic monologues in the form of love letters written between mythological lovers which included Paris and Helen, Phaedra and Hippolytus. The subtlety of his thought, his extreme insight, might have captivated Racine's own fervent feelings. Analogies can also be drawn between Phaedra's love and Virgil's description of Dido's passion for Aeneas. Whatever the inspiration, Racine's tragedy bore his own personal stamp.

Racine includes two very interesting statements in his preface to *Phaedra,* First, he defends her personality. She fulfills, he asserts, Aristotle's requirements for the tragic character in that she inspires pity and terror.

> Phaedra is neither altogether guilty nor altogether innocent. She is committed by her destiny, and by the anger of the gods, to an illegitimate passion which she is the first to abominate. She tries her best to vanquish it. She prefers to let herself die rather than reveal it to anyone. And when she is compelled to disclose it, she speaks of it with an agitation which clearly indicates that her crime is rather a punishment of the gods than of her own volition.[8]

Secondly, he insists upon the drama's utterly moral nature.

> The least faults are severely punished in it. The mere thought of crime is here regarded with as much horror as crime itself. The weaknesses of love are shown here as true weaknesses. The passions are only portrayed to expose all the chaos of which they are the cause, and vice is here throughout painted in colors which make its hideousness known and hated. Such is the proper aim that any man who works for the public should cherish.[9]

Phaedra takes place in Troezen in the Peloponnesus, about fifty miles south-west of Athens.

Act I. Hippolytus tells his tutor Theramenes that he is going to look for his father Theseus, who has not returned from his latest expedition, and also confesses his love for Aricia, whose family Theseus has had exterminated. He seeks to flee the court so as not to succumb to the temptation of countering his father's will. They leave the stage. Phaedra and her confidant Oenone enter. Phaedra, Theseus' wife, wants to die. Oenone begs her to tell her the reasons for her pain. She loves Hippolytus, Theseus' son by another woman, she confesses. News of Theseus' death is announced. Since he is free now, Oenone encourages Phaedra to tell Hippolytus of her love.

Act II. Hippolytus declares his love to Aricia, the daughter of Theseus' former enemies, who also adores him. Their joy is interrupted. Phaedra, now alone with Hippolytus, declares her love for him. Aware of his shock and shame, she takes his sword and demands he kill her. When he does not budge, she decides to kill herself, but Oenone grabs the sword from her.

Act III. Phaedra tries to win Hippolytus' affections by offering him the crown. News of Theseus' arrival, however, alters the situation. Phaedra despairs. She again thinks of death. In order to change the course of her thoughts and to exculpate her of her guilt, Oenone suggests she accuse Hippolytus of trying to win her. Indignant at first, she then accedes.

Act IV. Oenone, speaking for Phaedra, accuses Hippolytus of having wanted to seduce his mother. Theseus damns his son and asks Neptune to punish him. Hippolytus reveals his love for Aricia to his father but never tells him what really went on between him and Phaedra. He leaves and asks Aricia to go with him. Theseus tells Phaedra of Hippolytus' love for Aricia. Phaedra is stunned and succumbs to anger and jealousy, then extreme remorse.

Act V. Hippolytus leaves with Aricia. Theseus learns that Phaedra is about to die, that Oenone has thrown herself into the sea. Just as Theseus begs Neptune not to carry out his curse, he learns of Hippolytus' death: a monster thrust up from the sea seized him; as he fought him off and killed him, his horses got frightened and dragged him to his death. Phaedra now appears, confesses the truth and dies on stage from the poison she has taken. Theseus now knows extreme sorrow.

I

To characterize Phaedra's outlook most concisely, one might quote from St. Matthew (5:27–28): "I say to you that everyone who looks at a woman lustfully has already committed adultery with her in his heart." So feels Phaedra.

Phaedra's anguish is first experienced by her in her own mind. Her sense of morality is so highly developed that, even before the drama begins, before she has *acted*, prior to her committing symbolic incest with her step-son Hippolytus, she is guilty. In her desire to exculpate herself, she clings to the notion that as long as the crime lies buried within her, as long as her love for Hippolytus remains an abstract notion, no one will be aware of it and she will, therefore, be considered innocent by others. Her undoing takes place in three different steps when she reveals her feelings, leading audiences and readers alike down into her "labyrinth" or inner world. Once the secret has been revealed, it comes out into the open and has to be dealt with as a *reality*.

Because Phaedra feels her guilt so strongly at the beginning of the play, she is pictured as being at death's door, as suffering from some secret ill, a prey to mental derangement: unable to sleep, longing to see the day (Sun), "Eternal chaos broods within her mind." Emotions are slowly consuming her. Such havoc manifests itself physically. Phaedra herself describes her state as weak, her "eyes" as dazzled and blinded by the light (day), which she despises and for which she also longs.[10]

Strangely enough, Phaedra exhibits ambivalent attitudes toward day and night (I,iii): enticed and fleeing chthonic powers,[11] attracted and repelled by brilliance. She hates blackness and yet is forever searching for "the shadow of the forest." This love-hate for these two powers describes symbolically her emotional state, the fear of revealing her gnawing secret which seems to constrict her very life flow as does a growing throat cancer, and her desire to confess her pain by cutting out the swelling impeding her life. Both acts elicit excruciating pain.

If we glance at Phaedra's heritage we realize why both night and day are basic to her psychology. Phaedra is the granddaughter of Helios, the Sun. Her mother, Pasiphae, had fallen in love with a white bull presented to her husband, Minos, King of Crete, by Poseidon.[12] The offspring of this union was the monster, the Minotaur for whom the labyrinth had been constructed. It must be noted in connection with this legend that the Creto-Mycenean culture was a patriarchate in its earliest days. It was transformed, as this myth intimates, into a matriarchate, where the Great Mother archetype prevailed. She was adored as a Nature Goddess, frequently inhabiting caves and forests. The bull, the symbol of fertility, was looked upon as both a youthful god (son-lover) and as the Nature Goddess' victim.[13] The Minotaur was her vehicle in the Phaedra myth. It was the Great Mother who sent the "Aphrodite mania," which consisted of sexuality and hysteria to her enemies. These obsessions, frequently repressed or dormant, as they are in the beginning of *Phaedra*, surge forth with all the power Aphrodite (Venus) seeks to pour forth. Phaedra, considered from this view, becomes a "psychic fragmentation" of the Great Mother. She is not a suprapersonal power as is Venus, but rather a depersonalized being, a suffering Queen, a victim herself of the Great Mother archetype. What makes Phaedra so fascinating is the reevaluation of the feminine principle which she in part depicts.

Phaedra as both the daughter of Pasiphae and the granddaughter of Helios possesses divergent characteristics, instinctuality and lucidity. She inherited enormous insight and the judging principle from her grandfather. It was Helios, let us recall, who shed his light in the skies, dispersing the cloud which hid Venus and Mars as they were lovemaking. Indeed, it was this very action which had led Venus in retaliation to curse all Helios' descendants, which would include Phaedra. From her mother, a mortal woman, Phaedra was prone to all the material and lustful forms of life. Her struggle then revolves, broadly speaking, around the solar and earthly principles cohabiting within her.

The "monstrous" incestuous love she bears for Hippolytus is visible to her. She is, however, unable to cope with it, to understand its meaning, its negative, shadowy aspects. The emotions elicited by this passion play havoc with her judgment. She tries to destroy this uncontrollable love by rejecting it, seeking darkness and, thereby, clothing daylight—the sun. She exiles Hippolytus from her court and forces her thoughts into other paths. It is to no avail. In fact, her torment grows more potent. It intrudes upon her sleep. As the day withdraws and her grandfather (Helios) sinks beneath the horizon, she approaches her chthonic realm; sleep slinks off.

Phaedra's ambivalent attitude toward darkness reaches into all domains. Her constant longing and fear of these shadowy realms stems from the fact that Hippolytus represents the "darkness of forests." Somber regions are his habitat. Phaedra speaks:

> How sweet to sit amid the shaded woods!
> When might I follow through the noble dust
> A chariot driven breakneck in the track?[14]

Phaedra wanders aimlessly in her blind turmoil. Without realizing it, she has fallen into a trap. By trying to control her secret, by imposing her imperious will upon her mouth, by annihilating the word, the thought, the light of consciousness, she merely fosters the growth of her passion which, like a fungus, thrives in dark, damp realms. To relegate a mania to the depths of one's unconscious is as destructive as

starving an animal. Animals grow vicious and uncontrollable when
unfed, as do fixations. A positive orientation can be adopted by feeding
the beast within a being, by releasing a mania from its imprisonment
through understanding.

Oenone, Phaedra's servant, prods her mistress into revealing the
source of her pain. Phaedra's first step in her undoing or her salvation
(depending upon one's attitude) is now taken. She confesses her love
for Hippolytus, blames Venus for her "fatal anger,"[15] and discloses in
so doing the godly source of her passion and its uncontrollable nature.
"My pain (evil) goes back further,"[16] she states. Indeed, its origin stems
from elemental times, before her birth. While detailing her pain to
Oenone, Phaedra withdraws slightly from the realm of utter darkness
and in so doing becomes victimized by her own emerging secret, ready
to ooze forth like pus from a boil.

> I saw, I blushed, I paled at sight of him;
> A strange disquiet seized my stricken soul;
> My eyes could see no more, I could not speak;
> I felt my body burn and freeze in turn;
> I recognized the fearful sting of Venus,
> The destined torments of the blood she hunts.[17]

What Phaedra is actually experiencing on a symbolic level is the
dichotomy between the dictates of her conscience (as originating from
her solar principle, her judging faculty) and her instincts (her mortal
and earthly side). She describes in detail the manner in which she went
about trying to annihilate the bruising and burning love sent to her by
Venus. First she lit fires to the goddess, erected altars, and paid homage
to her in every way. Sacrifice means to "render sacred." Phaedra is
either unwilling or unaware of the price demanded by Venus: blood.
Phaedra's constant battle against the subjugation of sensuality is, therefore, unproductive. The conflict excoriates her all the more fiercely
because of her extremely developed moralistic sense. She is weakened
by the intensity of her struggle.

Venus, who has demanded Phaedra's blood, is now slowly going
to receive it. Phaedra's entire existence, centered around Hippolytus,
has turned into a prolonged flagellation.

> At once my wound, still open, gushed afresh,
> It's no mere passion tingling in my veins;
> It's Venus tense extended on her prey![18]

Her speech is constellated with such images, centering around the Sun
symbol, as fire, sun, blood, day, illumination, brilliance, eye, torch.

Each represents to a greater or slighter degree the suffering that can arise through self-knowledge brought on by illumination. Slowly, Phaedra becomes the Sun's victim because she is unwilling or still unable to accept and assimilate the insights provided by her vision.

Other images are used by Racine with expertise to indicate Phaedra's extreme desire for enlightenment and the cleanliness and purification which ensue. She finds the garments and accoutrements she wears[19] extremely difficult to bear. These, considered symbolically, represent the mask she has donned to hide her pain, the evil which gnaws at her vitals.

> And heavy are these veils, these baubles vain.
> And whose unwelcome hand, with all these knots,
> Has on my brow with care arranged my hair?
> Oh, all of you pursue and persecute me![20]

The lines just spoken by Phaedra concerning her excess of accoutrements have other significances. They refer back to the role played by Helios in revealing Venus' escapade with Mars. The lovers had been hidden in a net, so the story goes, a veil-like cloth. When the Sun shown his countenance upon them, disclosing their lustful antics, he rid them of their coverings. Like her grandfather, Phaedra seeks to rid herself of her dismal veil, to reveal the guilt she feels so strongly, and in so doing redeem herself. The ordeal is difficult and requires the experience of death.

The drama's entire frame of reference changes with the announcement of Theseus' demise (I,iv). It is no longer a question of deceiving Theseus, of committing incest, but rather of admitting the "shameful" love an older woman bears a virgin boy. Phaedra's second theme, a counterpart of the Faustian myth, blends in with ease. Phaedra is now ready to extract her second confession from herself. Like her mother Pasiphae, who fell in love with the white bull,[21] so Phaedra longs to unite with Hippolytus.

Hippolytus, the virgin hunter who roams the woods, whose strength is unparalleled, whose youth is extraordinary in its freshness, represents the young male fully attuned to nature, experiencing a *participation mystique* with earthly forces, reveling in the paradise of the uroboric state.

Phaedra, so distant from this realm of pristine cleanliness, desires union with it. As a son lover, however, she would be acting contrary to nature. According to traditional concepts, the mother usually represents past and worn concepts. These must be superseded by youthful attitudes as represented by the son if culture is to pursue its course.

Youth and age, therefore, cannot fuse any more in Phaedra's case than in Mithridates'. Two worlds or two generations must follow one another and not be crushed by the other; otherwise, imbalance results. So long as Phaedra's love remains unfulfilled, she is a passive female. Once her secret has been divulged, her arrows are unleashed and she turns into an active force ready to dominate, crush, and mutilate Hippolytus.

Oenone has been considered by many as the drama's evil force. It is she who advises Phaedra to reveal her love; to Oenone first, then to Hippolytus. It is she too who commits the act of treachery at the end of the drama. In reality, Oenone is the instigator of the action. She plays the same role the Serpent did in the Adam and Eve myth. Without her there would be no drama, no action. Phaedra would have remained immersed in her secret world from beginning to end; in like manner, neither Adam nor Eve would have been provoked. Oenone is Evil in that she is the *agent provocateur*, a dynamic force who injects motility into what is a static situation. There is no question but that Oenone is motivated by fine sentiments. She gave up her family and friends to care for Phaedra ever since her childhood. Indeed, she has always lived in Phaedra's shadow, helping her as best she could.

When Phaedra first confesses to Oenone, she begins her speech in a semicomposed manner. Slowly, however, she lapses into the irrational, losing her identity almost completely. "Now I have forgotten what I came to say."[22] She suffers from aphasia as did Nero when confronting his effulgent emotion. This momentary speechlessness indicates an unconscious desire to prevent herself from disclosing her secret; also, the emergence of a will emanating from within, a suprapersonal force intent upon burying what lies beneath. Oenone represents that other will which prods and urges Phaedra to confess her torments.

During Phaedra's second confession to Hippolytus, she once again lapses into an irrational state, diving even more steeply into the abyss. Speaking in semi-clothed, ambiguous terms, she loses all notion of distance and in so doing creates a climate of non-time. She takes on the stature of a visionary, a Delphic oracle, and declares that Theseus, having visited the "marshes of the dead," will never return.

> I seem to see my husband still before me.
> I see, I speak, my heart . . . Where am I straying?
> My lord, my raving love breaks out despite me.[23]

Concepts of space-time identity have vanished. Phaedra now looks upon Hippolytus, not as he really is, but as she had once gazed upon the young and brave Theseus: "Engaging, young, bewitching every heart."[24] Father and son have become *one* in her mind, each a mirror image of the other. Phaedra now begins reliving the entire Minotaur legend, but not as an onlooker. She too has changed. Just as Hippolytus is transformed into Theseus, so she identifies with Ariadne. A complete transference of identities occurs, which indicates psychologically a rejection of herself, her role in life, her existential domain and an unconscious longing for death.

As Ariadne she feels a great affinity with the labyrinth. In effect, Phaedra has always been jealous of her sister's experience with Theseus and since she has been unable to live the story herself (either with Theseus or his son Hippolytus) she becomes for the son an actual labyrinth in which he symbolically wanders and is destroyed.

Accompanying Phaedra's revelation to Hippolytus, her belief in her own transformation into the Virgin Princess Ariadne, there is a concomitant withdrawal into her own labyrinthian domain. A total eclipse of reality, of the world she cannot face, takes place.

> I, Prince, alone, my vital help alone
> Would have taught you the Labyrinth's twists and turns.
> How many cares your dear head would have cost me.
> A thread would not have satisfied your lover.
> Companion in the risk you had to brave,
> I would myself have run ahead of you;
> And Phaedra, down with you in the Labyrinth,
> Would have returned with you or with you perished.[25]

Since Phaedra is so closely associated with the labyrinth, we might do well to examine this symbol more closely. The labyrinth, designed by Daedalus to house the Minotaur in Crete, was so complex a structure that anyone inside could not possibly find his way out. It had a double aspect, it was both repugnant and fascinating. It represented a test, an exciting journey, an initiation into another dimension of existence, for the hero who passed through its portals and came out alive, as had Theseus. The labyrinth also stands for the unconscious realm. It is a dark area indicating loss of vision and, by association, the irrational and chaotic. This state, or this "fall" of the spirit (consciousness) into the primeval abyss (unconscious), is only temporary for the one who is ready, psychologically speaking, to experience the labyrinthian test, as was Theseus. He emerged from its intricate halls into the light and back to the spiritual world. Such, however, was not the outcome for the undeveloped Hippolytus.

Phaedra's symbology now becomes complex. As she relives her

sister's experience on another level, she sees herself in her frenzy as
Ariadne leading Hippolytus, the Minotaur's killer, out of the maze,
out of chaos into the world of illumination. Such a reversal of the
actual events is indeed fascinating in view of the fact that Phaedra
herself stands for darkness, for the labyrinth and for chaos.

The Minotaur which Theseus had really killed, but which, in
Phaedra's imagination, Hippolytus has done away with, was a monster
whose lower half was that of a man and whose upper half was that of
a bull. The inversion of the Platonic notion (that the upper half of man
is the godly side and the lower, the beast) indicates the reversal of
Phaedra's own concepts. The top half has become carnivorous and destructive, indicating that man has been using his spiritual forces in an
unregenerate and harmful manner. The Minotaur-vision indicates an
animalization of the head or a regression of this function to an anthropoid state. Such an implication has both political and psychological
equivalents.

When a myth treats of monsters or tributes, of victorious heroes
who destroy evil beings, it usually indicates that the land from which
this legend arises is suffering a type of political tyranny. Such was the
case in Crete at the time the Minotaur was destroyed.

The psychological implications are equally interesting. Man is the
victim of his monstrous, instinctual aspects and must render these in
tribute or sacrifice to his finer or higher half (ideas and feelings). To
kill the monster as Theseus had done was to vanquish instinct, which
had become a tyrannical, destructive, and oppressive force.

By reliving the Ariadne-Theseus story, Phaedra is actually indicating her longing to have Hippolytus enact the same drama for her; that
is, to kill her instinct as she projects it onto the bull. As Phaedra's vision
becomes more and more clouded, she becomes ever more trapped in
her own maze and pursues her frenzied dialogue.

> Well then, now Phaedra, in her naked frenzy.
> I am in love. Do not think, though I love you,
> I approve my love or deem it innocent;
> Nor that a craven self-indulgence has
> Nourished the poison of my insane passion.
> Unhappy target of the spite of Heaven,
> I loathe myself much more than you abhor me.[26]

Suddenly, Phaedra is recalled to the light of consciousness. Her
shame, her guilt know no bounds and she begs Hippolytus to take his
sword and cut her open.

> Come, here your hand must strike.
> Impatient now to expiate its crime . . .[27]

Hippolytus is unwilling to commit such a deed; Phaedra grabs his sword and seeks to do away with herself.

When Phaedra recovers from her affective onslaught, she feels the extreme impact of her heinous confession. "I've uttered words no human ear should hear."[28] Urgently, she seeks to grovel, to return to labyrinthine darkness, below the earth. Dejection, abjection, guilt sets in ever more starkly. In an even more weakened state after her revelations, Phaedra once again listens to Oenone's counsel.

Oenone suggests that Phaedra reign over Troezen, Theseus' land, now that he is dead. Though at first she rejects such reasoning as shocking, she finally succumbs.

> I, reign! Impose my will upon the people,
> When my weak reason reigns no more o'er me!
> When I have lost dominion o'er my passion!
> When I can barely breathe beneath my shame![29]

She offers Hippolytus the crown, to lure him her way, hoping to dazzle him with power. Again Phaedra's vision becomes distorted. She visualizes Hippolytus at this point as the father of her son (the one she had by Theseus), making him her husband. She very nearly salivates at the thought.

The shock of reality intrudes with Theseus' unexpected return, which paves the way for Phaedra's final act and her undoing. Fearful of Theseus' revenge, she impulsively blames Oenone for her situation, as Adam used Eve as his scapegoat.

> Your tears prevailed upon my true remorse.
> I would have died this morning, winning pity;
> I took your counsel and dishonoured die.[30]

Despite the fact that Phaedra disclaims responsibility for her confessions, her shame is so intense that the very center of her being seems to be shattered. Death, she is convinced, is the only exit left to her. "Let me die. May death my shame forgive!" she states.[31]

Had Phaedra not confessed her love no one would have known of her crime and she would never have been the ignominious person she becomes in the eyes of the world. By the same token, she would never have experienced either sacrifice or redemption through death. Had her guilt not come out into the open it would never have been a *reality*. Her sacrifice, therefore, would not have been *authentic* and for this

reason unacceptable to Venus in the beginning of the drama. Just as
Oedipus suffered and repented when facing the realization of his acts,
so will Phaedra. Oenone's presence is positive, from Phaedra's point
of view. It permits her to fulfill her destiny.

Phaedra, who has been dying ever since the beginning of the
drama, does not yet succumb. A deceit must transpire first. Oenone
persuades Phaedra to tell Theseus that Hippolytus wanted to seduce
her. Feelings of revulsion emerge as she says, "I dare, to brand and
blacken innocence."[32] Another force comes to her aid in making her
decision to march down the steps of Evil—jealousy. She has learned of
Hippolytus' love for Aricia and can no longer bear the humiliation of
rejection. Her pride utterly destroyed, the Terrible Mother aspect of
her personality swells forth in its most blatant form. Like a viper she
spews forth her poison which will destroy the unsuspecting Hippolytus.
With kaleidoscopic emotion, she sounds out her rancor, recapitulates
the gradations of her passion, now blazing with renewed fury. Oenone
leaves to arouse Theseus' anger.

As a ray of lucidity returns, Phaedra sees herself in all of her
bestiality and she is shattered by the vision: "What am I doing? How
my reason wanders!"[33] Remorse surges forth. She can no longer look
at herself. The eye, first mentioned at the outset of the drama, sees her
plain at this juncture, that Platonic eye, that of God who discerns the
blackest notions within man's unconscious, his most evil thoughts
mentioned by St. Matthew. This eye, this guilt, is in fact Phaedra's own
highly-developed conscience. Just as her grandfather Helios had illuminated what should have remained hidden (Venus and Mars), so
her inner meanderings have also been brought to light.

> Of this most sacred Sun from whom I've sprung?
> My forebear is father, master of the gods;
> The sky, the whole world's full of my forefathers.
> Where may I hide? Flee to infernal night.
> How? There my father holds the urn of doom;
> Fate placed it, so they say, in his stern hands.[34]

Phaedra, like Lady Macbeth, seeks to wash away her sins. Her unconscious emerges once again and floods her conscious realm, paving
the way for another vision. She sees her entire family before her,
Minos, most specifically, who has become judge in the underworld,
whose function it has become to observe the "pale" humans passing
before him. Phaedra has now regressed to a child-like stage. She is
ashamed as she stands guilt-ridden before him, fearing his condemnation; "his shadow" will shudder when he hears her story. What

Phaedra is actually seeing at this time as projected onto her father is her own judging aspect, her sense of righteousness, that spirit of authority which lives so strongly within her, as does the Sun.

Phaedra, psychologically speaking, is now living partially in the underworld; that is, she has become capable of facing her own "shadow" (her heretofore unacceptable and inferior characteristics). The fact that she associates her father with this sense of authority indicates that the matriarchal society, of which she is a representative, has succumbed to the patriarchate. No longer is she ruled by her instincts, but rather by the stern father image.

> Minos in Hades judges all the shades.
> Ah, how his stricken ghost will start and shudder,
> When he beholds his daughter come before him,
> Compelled her trembling tespasses to tell,
> And crimes perhaps unheard of even in Hell!
> What will you say, my father, at this horror?[35]

Phaedra is prepared for the final, the ultimate sacrifice which Venus is intent upon receiving. The acceptance of her death, her destiny, paves the way for her travels on earth as an aspect of the negative mother. She rejects any further attempts on Oenone's part to distract her from her goal. "I will not hear you more. Get out, you demon," she declares.[36]

Oenone's role in the drama, as the instigator of the action, has now been completed. Her suicide (or exit from the action), therefore, is a dramatic necessity and comes as no surprise. Through her intervention, Phaedra succeeds in coming to grips with the higher conscience within her, forcing herself thereby to unite the split facets of her personality (as represented by the earth and sun principles), through sacrifice of herself.

When Phaedra finally confesses the truth to Theseus, she gives dignity to her negative ("shadow") aspects, thereby ending their virulence. With her death she enters the underworld, "the earthly womb," as it was looked upon by the ancients, preparing the way for her eventual transformation and redemption.[37]

✦ ✦ ✦

Hippolytus is the carrier of consciousness in this drama. It is through his presence that Phaedra will experience her transformation.

Hippolytus is the typical son-lover (Pentheus, Narcissus, Acteon) figure and he experiences the same fate as his forebears. There is one

difference between them, however; Hippolytus lives on a higher psychological level. He is devoted to Artemis, to the goddess of chastity
and of the hunt, but at the same time is capable of loving a person outside himself. His love for Aricia, the spiritual type of woman rather
than the lascivious, indicates that he is experiencing a *higher* consciousness, an all-encompassing masculinity rather than merely the
"lower" phallic worship. This higher concept of the masculine role in
life implies an affinity with the "solar" masculine world. Phaedra, on
the contrary, only lusts for the phallus.

From the very outset of the drama we learn that Hippolytus seeks
to emulate his father.[38] Frightened by his own indolence, his shadow-
like existence in the heart of the forest, he seeks to become a hero. This
does not imply for one moment that he condones his father's "youthful errors," his inconstancy. On the contrary, these are qualities Hippolytus despises. He looks upon his father's "noble exploits,"[39] his
heroic and courageous side, as worthy of emulation. Hippolytus is very
much aware of the fact that he has not broken forth from the adolescent realm.

> Since no such monsters crushed by me till now
> Have given me the right to err like him![40]

Hippolytus is still the dutiful son at the outset of the play. He refuses to act against his father's will, particularly since he is away from
home. Theseus' destruction of Aricia's family, his order that she remain childless so that her entire race may be annihilated, still prevails.
Unwittingly, it is Theseus who creates conflict within Hippolytus. The
dynamism resulting from the antithetical attitudes (his desire for Aricia and the spirit of authority which reigns within him, preventing him
from giving vent to his feelings) paves the way for his own evolution.

Once Hippolytus falls in love with Aricia, he detects a change
within his being. He cannot articulate or assess the depth or meaning
of this transformation. He is, in effect, emerging from the uroboric
state of total identification with Artemis, the goddess of the chase
whose habitat is the forest. The forest, usually associated with the
domain of the Great Mother, is obscure, overrun with luxurious foliage
and for the most part inaccessible to the Sun (male). Hippolytus' affinity with Artemis (that stage of unconsciousness which is the child's
undifferentiated world) is now receding slowly.

Theramenes expresses the changes he has noted in Hippolytus'
conduct. He no longer seems to be the enemy of woman, he has become
aware of the meaning of independence, he is seen less frequently in
the woods.

> Admit the change in you; for some time now
> You are less often seen, proud and untamed,
> Driving a chariot furious on the shore,
> Or expert in the art that Neptune fashioned,
> Breaking a champing, rearing charger in.
> Less often without shouts the woods re-echo;
> Charged with a hidden fire, your eyes grow heavy,
> Why, there is no mistake, you burn with love;
> You sicken with an ill you would conceal.[41]

Hippolytus has now reached the stage in which he will struggle to liberate himself from what is commonly termed "world parents." It was Theseus who had forced open Hippolytus' eyes. "Theseus opens your eyes, wishing to close them,"[42] says Theramenes.

With the shame a sensitive adolescent alone knows, Hippolytus expresses his "despair" and his embarrassment at first becoming aware of the opposite sex. Naiveté and candor mark his words to Aricia, particularly when describing himself as "rash" and as "proud." In an almost parallel scene in which Phaedra portrays her passion to Oenone and the forces she has been using to try to quell it, Hippolytus informs Aricia of the fight he has waged to subdue his feelings. "I flee your presence; find you in your absence."[43] It is to no avail. Aricia's image follows him always (as Hippolytus' has been impregnated into Phaedra's mind), even to "the forest," Artemis' sanctuary.

> Your face pursues me in the deepest woods;
> The light of day, the shadows of the night
> Thrust in my eyes the loveliness I flee . . .
> My chariot, javelins, bow, all weary me;
> No more do I remember Neptune's lessons;
> My moans alone reecho through the woods,
> My steeds stand dull and know my voice no more.[44]

Though Hippolytus is the object of Phaedra's desire, he is also a reflection of her. He holds the same relationship to Phaedra as the Moon to the Sun. This affinity is not only brought forth by the imagery (he worships Artemis the moon goddess, and Phaedra her grandfather Helios), but in his forbidden love for Aricia.

The fact that Aricia has invaded the forest indicates, symbolically, her dominion over Hippolytus on both conscious and unconscious levels (sleeping and waking). Such a situation is comparable to Hippolytus' intrusion upon Phaedra's world. His newly emergent feelings, born with his love for Aricia, have caused such a change in his outlook upon life that he no longer understands himself. "I seek myself and find myself no more."[45] This transformation, as we have already seen, indicates in part, a departure of adolescence and an oncoming of maturity. By the same token it reveals the burgeoning of Hippolytus' ego.

No longer ruled by undifferentiated attitudes (forest, unconscious, darkness), by the passivity of youth, Hippolytus sees the world about him for the first time and understands his function within it. He knows selfconsciousness now. Such illumination has been gained through his love for Aricia. Concomitant with this new stage of development is the termination of his feelings of "wholeness" and of "participation mystique" with mother nature. Childhood joys, those offered by the nondifferentiated realm of "paradise," are over.

When Phaedra, in whom Venus (the Great Mother) acts out her love quest, takes Hippolytus' sword to kill herself, she has usurped what is common sharing to every hero, his instrument of power. Hippolytus, who does not take the shining blade from her hand, is, symbolically, divesting himself of a certain courage and forthrightness, an ill omen which implies his future demise. Had the sword been used adroitly by Hippolytus, it would have led to the extermination of the Terrible Mother as this force lived out its existence in Phaedra. He could not. His struggle for autonomy was doomed to failure.

Upon Theseus' return, Hippolytus wants to be his father's son and earn heroism.

> While I, obscure son of a famous father,
> Lag far behind even my mother's steps.
> Allow my courage to engage itself.[46]

When Theseus accuses him of harboring adulterous intentions and of being a monster of impurity, Hippolytus' reactions are heroic. Rather than reveal the horrendous situation which would have caused his father great pain, he declares his innocence but says no more. "View kindly the respect that seals my lips."[47]

Another burgeoning aspect of his personality also comes forth at this juncture, his dignity. No longer acting as an adolescent, he admits his love for Aricia and the purity of his intentions. In a moment of extreme despair, he utters words reminiscent to a certain degree of Christ's, "What friend will pity me when you forsake me."[48]

It was Neptune, in answer to Theseus' supplications, who sent the monster from the sea to destroy Hippolytus. A companion of the Great Mother, this entity with horns, scales, who looked like a bull, a dragon, a horse roared forth from under the waters, foamed and lashed about on land, making his way toward Hippolytus. Infused with fight, the young hero hurled his javelin toward this creature, wounded him; and, as the animal writhed with pain, it exhaled flame, driving Hippolytus' horses insane. They ran wild, dragging Theseus' son to his death.

> Meanwhile, surged from the sea a mountainous wave,
> With wild sea horses lashed to furious spray;
> The flood approached us, broke and vomited
> A monster raging through the quivering spume.
> His forehead wide was bristling sharp with horns;
> And all his body nailed with tawny scales;
> Indomitable bull or dragon bold,
> With fleshy haunches tortuous fold on fold.
> His long-drawn bellows set the seashore trembling.
> The sky with horror viewed his monstrous rumbling,
> The earth was all a-quiver, air infected,
> The waves that spewed him forth drew back deflected . . .
> Alone Hippolytus, a hero's son,
> Halted steeds and seized his javelins,
> Aimed at the monster and with expert throw
> Wounded him deeply, tearing wide his flank.
> Leaping with rage and pain the monster now
> Falls bellowing at the startled horse's feet,
> Rolls on his back, thrust forth his flaming jaw,
> Engulfing them in fire and blood and smoke.
> Sheer panic seizes them, and deaf to all,
> Nor rein nor voice restrains them any more.
> Their master, powerless, tries to hold them back—
> The bit runs red with dark and bloody foam.
> Some even say they saw, amid the affright,
> A god who pricked with spurs their dusty flanks.
> Fear hurls them hurtling on across the rocks;
> The axle creaks and snaps. The bold Hippolytus
> Sees all his shattered chariot fly in pieces;
> He falls himself entangled in the reins . . .
> Dragged by the very steeds his hands have fed.
> He calls to them; his voice now frightens them;
> They gallop on, with him—one gaping wound.
> The plain reverberates with our mournful cries.[49]

The monster sent by Poseidon symbolizes cosmic forces or "nonformal" potentialities.[50] It is part of a primal power. It erupts like a volcano, without forewarning, and exteriorizes itself in the most hid-

eous ways. Some psychologists feel that Phaedra's "monster," inhabiting the profoundest realm of her unconscious, represents an
imbalance in her psychic functions, an overly affective state. As such,
the monster is at opposite poles to the hero. In Hippolytus' case (the
hero), he tries to fight the monster, attempting thereby to liberate his
conscious attitude from the hold his unconscious has upon it. When
he wounds the monster at first, the battle goes in his favor. In the end,
however, he can no longer resist the onslaught of affectivity. It drenches
his higher consciousness, that part of him he has fought so valiantly
to attain.

The horses which finally drag Hippolytus to his death represent
the world of instinct. These animals, sacred to Poseidon, cannot fight
the god who is fulfilling Venus' will and punishing the hero who has
"dared" scorn Phaedra, considered as a fragment of Venus, or a vehicle bearing her will. Hippolytus, fighting for autonomy, is scourged
for his rebellious attitude.

Associated with Hippolytus throughout the play is the water symbol, the fluid area from which the sea monster emerges. In this context
water represents a dynamic aspect of the female personality, the stuff
from which creation emerges and into which it dissolves. When submerged in water, there is a symbolic return to the pre-formal state, implying first death then rebirth. Aphrodite, the "foam-born," as she
was frequently called, arose from the sea and therefore associated it
with fertility. As she arises in Hippolytus' world, however, she is an
agent of destruction, as she also is for Ophelia. It was she who nourished the monster who emerges from her depths to kill the young
hero.

✦   ✦   ✦

Theseus is by reputation the real hero type. The son of Poseidon,
according to some legends, his mother having been impregnated by the
Sea King and King Aegeus on the same night, he braved the world when
a youth. The Theseus depicted by Racine, however, has few of the
characteristics of the great hero who killed the Minotaur, who slew
the monster at Epidaurus, the wild sow near Attica, the man who
founded Athens. As the play begins, Theseus is thought to be dead.
Psychologically, he was just that. Theseus had lost his vision and it is
returned to him only at the end of the play.

Theseus is viewed in different ways by the other protagonists.
Hippolytus seeks to emulate his valor and his rational ways. He looks
down upon what he considers his father's base side, his "inconstance,"

his instinctual outlets which place him under the sway of the Great Mother.

As far as Phaedra is concerned, Theseus the man is non-existent. She sees her husband only in Hippolytus as a young man, forceful, god-like, the heroic killer of the Minotaur. When he returns, she looks upon him as a symbol of moral authority, of the *status quo*, as the one to whom she must confess her sins if she is to atone for them.

It must be recalled that Theseus, when a youth, had been raised in a patriarchate. He had, in one of his escapades, if not killed at least battled the Terrible Mother in the form of Medea, who had tried to do away with him. With age, however, Theseus' masculine principle, implicit in his highly developed sense of wisdom and judgment, has succumbed to less lofty objects of desire. He has become mainly pre-occupied with the sensual sphere, lusting only after sexual adventures. The hybris which frequently accompanies the attainment of valor did not escape Theseus. He has fallen victim to it, as have many heroes, thus paving the way for Venus' eventual victory. When, at the outset of the play, he is thought to be dead, he is in effect in the underworld. Looked upon psychologically, his stay in the realm of the shadows indicates a regression into an unconscious or primal state. In Hades he is surrounded by phantoms emerging from his unconscious, archetypes representing his fears and anguishes, all of those entities he never faced when experiencing those tension-filled youthful years. When he emerges from the underworld or from his unconscious state to the light of consciousness and returns to his kingdom, he is unable to adjust to the situation confronting him at home. He has lost the ability to communicate with the outside world, to relate past and present, unconscious to conscious contents. His acuity has been dulled.

When he sees Hippolytus, therefore, he is taken aback. He cannot equate the purity he reads on his son's face with the blackness of the crime of which he is accused. Before permitting his rational powers to view the situation analytically, he reacts affectively. His anger burgeons forth and he rejects his son. In this instance Theseus is indeed Poseidon's rightful son, stirring the seas of his unconscious, cleaving the rock of authority. Utterly possessed by his daemon, he cast his curse, "Chased by an avenging God, escape you cannot."[51]

As Phaedra's husband, Theseus had permitted himself the luxury of bathing in inactivity and pleasure. The tensions which had marked his youthful struggles had been released. He had become the decadent hero par excellence, the aged hero who had lost his judging faculties and who was no longer capable or worthy of holding the title of King. The suffering he bears at the end of the drama with the death of his son, which he himself has caused, indicates the extent of his own blindness and the crushing weight of the sacrifice imposed upon him.

II

Phaedra is Racine's most perfect tragedy so far, from both a technical and an analytical point of view.

Structurally speaking, *Phaedra* begins very nearly as had *Mithridates*, with the rumored news of the King's death. A double illusion is created this way for both the spectator and the characters involved.[52] The characters' instincts, formerly enclosed in a Pandora box-like structure, are now set free to act in accordance with the personalities from which they emerge. When Theseus returns, very much alive, a clamp is set on the emotions which had just begun to flow forth freely. Unlike Mithridates, who is effaced from life's scene, Theseus survives the ordeal. In *Mithridates*, both Xiphares and Monima are united, paving the way for a future life of happiness. In *Phaedra* all die, except for Theseus and Aricia, indicating that whatever attitudes Phaedra, Hippolytus, Oenone represented could lead only to sterility and had, therefore, to pass from view.

Racine increases both the suspense of his drama and its accompanying anguish by means of certain technical devices: Phaedra's three confessions of love and the symbolism associated with each of the characters in question.

Phaedra's confessions, first to Oenone, then to Hippolytus, and finally to Theseus, like three stages in her inner development, increase the danger of her situation. The conflict waged within her being becomes that much more horrendous, her pain increasingly excoriating. It is as though Phaedra were tearing her own being asunder, flaying flesh, dismembering herself with each confession.

The imagery and symbolism used by Racine not only carry the play forward but involve the audience likewise. Symbols such as day, night, sun, forest, water, labyrinth create an entire hidden world of essence and in so doing add to the drama's depth and frenzy. Viewed from this realm, the characters are like strange magnetic spheres hovering about in a world beyond man's control and understanding, reminiscent of planets in their unalterable courses in the heavens.[53]

The several themes interwoven in *Phaedra* blend and rise forth in solo-like formation, diminishing as they finally return to their rightful places within the musical framework of the opus. The predominant theme is that of death, it is the alpha and omega of the play. Death, in *Phaedra*, does not indicate an end to life, but rather a transformation of the psychological attitude carried by the character. Death implies the end of previously held notions and the eventual birth of a new frame of reference. Transformation is not a simple process, as witnessed by Osiris, who had to undergo dismemberment; and Christ, the crucifixion. Phaedra will earn her redemption through death. The subordinate themes, Hippolytus' maturation and bid for autonomy, Theseus' blindness and his ensuing remorse, fill out the pattern.

III

Phaedra marks a change of emphasis in Racine's theatre on several counts. As far as kingship is concerned, it introduces a king who inspires pity and compassion, unequal to the task set before him.

With Mithridates, for example, Racine had created a ruler who had gained vision at the end of his life, who no longer preached revenge to his son, but rather wisdom in the conduct of political affairs and joy in his earthly union with Monima. Agamemnon in *Iphigenia* struggles to force the governing principle to reign within him first, rather than his personal desires. Though he wrestles with the problem, matters are taken out of his hands when Eriphyle is substituted for his daughter. His suffering has permitted him, nevertheless, to understand his higher mission, the collective role a king must play in performing governmental duties. In *Phaedra*, however, Theseus is a king who rests on his laurels and because of his inactivity has not grown with age. His development has been stunted and his ego has turned into a flabby mass from desuetude. Theseus inspires pity for his lack of insight, for all the negative characteristics which had been buried within him as a youth, but which had risen forth with age. In Theseus' case, his decadence is all the more painful when set in opposition, as Racine has done so brilliantly, to his strength as a young man.

Another important development, in the concept of sacrifice, is introduced in *Phaedra*. This theme had also been dealt with in a masterful manner in *Iphigenia*. Agamemnon's daughter, a virgin-like creature, willingly sacrifices herself when she becomes aware of the forces at stake. She does not resemble the innocuous creatures heretofore depicted by Racine, Antigone (*The Theban Brothers*), Junie (*Britannicus*), or the blinded Berenice. Rather, she is a composite of certain already-existent types, possessing the insight of Monima, the strength and wisdom of Andromache, the pride of Hermione. She is both strong and tender, lucid and incisive. She has the qualities of a real queen, able and ready to sacrifice her personal existence for the welfare of the collective.

With Phaedra, we are exposed to another aspect of the Christian myth wherein sin, sacrifice, and redemption are enacted. In the beginning, Phaedra's crime lived in her mind alone. There it was held captive but tortured her to such an extent that she lost all her strength, could not sleep, and was forever pursued by remorse. She was guilty, as St. Matthew's pronouncement had stated: "I say to you that everyone who looks at a woman lustfully has already committed adultery with her in his heart." (5:27–28)[54] When her thoughts are given expression, the reality of her plight becomes unbearable. The pathos, suffering, and guilt that she now reveals are antipodal to the stoic conception of honor, virtue, courage, and heroism (*Britannicus*). The action of *Phaedra* then consists in exteriorizing and thereby concretizing her shadow aspects, those negative, shameful, autocratic, and evil traits. The fact that Racine was preoccupied with a being's painful and weak traits was the result of his immersion in the Christian interpretation of negative characteristics.

> One of the essential features of the Christian myth and the teaching of Jesus is the attitude taken toward weakness and suffering. A real transvaluation of ordinary values is brought about. Strength, power, fullness, and success, the usual conscious values, are denied. Instead, weakness, suffering, poverty, and failure are given special dignity. This point is developed throughout Jesus' teachings and is given its supreme representation in the crucifixion itself, where God is degradingly scourged and dies the shameful death of a criminal on the cross. This is what was beyond the comprehension of the Romans, for whom honor, strength, and manly virtue were the supreme value.[55]

Theseus, as the King, is a symbol of the *Self* and, as such, reveals it as being very much in need of compassion. Phaedra, the Queen, a fragment of the Great Mother archetype, has been totally degraded. Hippolytus, the representative of youth, has been annihilated.

If we are to look upon *Phaedra*, to a certain extent only, as a projection of Racine's own psychological framework, we can readily understand why he abandoned the theatre after this work. Certainly, the difficulties with which he had to contend during its production must have worked upon him and disgusted him. More important, however, was the fact that the creation of this work revealed an ability on Racine's part to look at himself fully and openly. His so-called weak or evil traits, his lust, his desire for money and fame, his need to fulfill himself as an artist, his existential joy, no longer tore at him. He had reached a state in life whereby he accepted himself as he was. The need to explore, the anger, all of his aggressive characteristics which had formerly been expressed in his works, had now been liberated. He no longer felt the need, therefore, to channel them in further plays.

Racine became reconciled with the Jansenists and their way became his. When marriage was suggested, he complied. His life would now be spent not in the creation of plays, but of progeny.

PART III—BEYOND THE CLASSIC

How beautiful it is to live! and how immense
is God's glory!
(PAUL CLAUDEL, *L'Annonce faite à Marie.*)

10

Esther

> "Prostrate I fall
> at the Eternal's feet . . ."[1]

*A*FTER the production of *Phaedra* (1677), Racine abandoned the theatre. He became officially reconciled with his Jansenist masters, whose counsel he now followed. He married the pious Catherine de Romanet, had seven children, was named advisor to Louis XIV and, along with Boileau, became official court historiographer. After Racine repudiated the theatre and assumed a bourgeois life, his personality altered. His tempestuous emotions calmed, his life became orderly, and he achieved a sense of harmony and balance. Moreover, the divine now assumed a primary role in his life; God became his frame of reference and everything seemed to emerge from this source. It would appear then that Racine had undergone an intense inner illumination. No longer was his faith imposed upon him from the outside by his Jansenist masters, as it had been when a youth studying at Port-Royal; it glowed within him like a cool blue flame.

When Madame de Maintenon, the wife of Louis XIV, asked Jean Racine to write a play after twelve years had elapsed, he greeted her request with feelings of anxiety and "agitation."[2] Indeed, he was so upset that he consulted his good friend, the essayist and poet Boileau. Despite the fact that Boileau dissuaded him from accepting Madame de Maintenon's offer, Racine acquiesced, compelled perhaps by some personal reason.

Racine had good cause to be anguished at the thought of returning to playwriting. The theatre, the pivotal force around which much of his life had centered, had been the cause of his break with Port-Royal and Jansenism. It had also been the reason for his extraordinary creativity and success as a dramatist and for the concomitant traumas and turmoil.

Unwittingly, then, Madame de Maintenon was asking Racine to return to a life replete with dangers for one so sensitive. To revert to the "sacrilegious" world of the theatre was like stepping into a seething cauldron of temptation. Risks, however, confronted him either way. To refuse to comply with Madame de Maintenon's request would certainly succeed in offending her and thereby jeopardize his lucrative, important, and influential post at court. Furthermore, he was also exposing himself to the wrath of Louis XIV. Racine, a frequent visitor to the King's domain at Marly, where only the most intimate were invited, could not underestimate the meaningful nature of his rapport with the monarch.[3] Yet, were he to accept Madame de Maintenon's offer, he might be compromising not only his religious principles but his own reputation as an artist. After all, she had imposed limitations upon his creative spirit when she asked him to write an "instructive" as well as an "entertaining" work that the girls of Saint-Cyr could put on themselves, "some moral and historical poem from which love would be entirely banished."[4] Madame de Maintenon had founded Saint-Cyr, a school for young ladies of impoverished noble families, and was intent upon providing suitable entertainment for them.

François Hébert, the Curé of Versailles, was convinced that Racine accepted the assignment to further his own ambitions. Other writers and scholars commenting on this same point felt that self-interest was not the only force which provided him with a reason for writing *Esther*. It has been suggested that there was in Racine a genuine feeling of gratitude for Madame de Maintenon, a real desire to "edify" the concepts of the young ladies at Saint-Cyr,[5] as well as a deeply religious feeling that needed expression.[6] It is the opinion of the present writer that the long years away from the theatre and the exercise of his creative dramatic genius must have taken some toll from Racine. The "request" that was in the nature of a command, in addition to his by now urgent inner need, must have presented an irresistible temptation.

Racine probably began writing *Esther* at the end of 1687 or early 1688, first in prose, as was his habit, then in verse.[7] According to his son, Louis, Madame de Maintenon (3, 1688) indicated that she was his mentor and that he consulted her every step of the way.

> My *Esther* is now finished and I went over the entire work following your suggestions and I myself made some changes which increase the play's pace. . . As for me, Madame, I shall not consider *Esther* truly finished until I shall have received your definitive opinion and criticism concerning it.[8]

Racine had always been an avid reader of the Scriptures. His approach to the Bible, as indicated in his drama *Esther*, was not merely passive. The annotations he made of certain Psalms, of the Book of Job, his reflections on some passage of the Scriptures, all of which are scant, demonstrate his active interest in Biblical study. At the library of Toulouse, there still exists an original edition of Racine's *Esther* with marginal notations made by one of his daughters indicating the sections of the Scriptures which had inspired certain lines of his plays: Lamentations, Jeremiah, Proverbs, Deuteronomy, etc. Furthermore, Racine's knowledge of Jewish history included the study of sections, or entire works, of Josephus and Philo, and a translation of parts of the latter's *De Vita Contemplativa*, as well as some texts concerning the Essenes. Man's rapport with the Divine Principle also fascinated Racine, as witnessed by his preoccupations with subjects such as sacrifice, martyrdom, and guilt, so prominently displayed in his dramas (*Andromache, Bajazet, Berenice, Esther*, etc.) and in his translations of *The Church of Smyrna's Letter Relating to the Martyrdom of Saint Polycarps*, and of Eusebius on *Saint Denys*.

In view of Racine's upbringing and the dominant role Jansenism played in his life, it is to be expected that he would approach the story of Esther from a Christian point of view. In this connection one might refer to Esther's prayer (I,iv), in which she mentions the coming of Jesus Christ: "The Saint you promise and whose coming we await?"[9] Yet, the tenor of the work does in certain respects denote an "essential trait of Judaism" in that Racine has underscored the fact that the protagonists do not merely await God's miracle, but rather participate actively in bringing it about.[10]

The immediate source for Racine's play was of course the Biblical Book of Esther. He did, nevertheless, draw heavily from the *Additions to the Book of Esther*,[11] which furnished him with details concerning the characters of Ahasuerus and Esther as well as the famous prayer which Esther utters just before she undertakes her mission. Racine, was not, however, familiar with the Megillah tract in the Talmud.[12] In fact, his knowledge of Jewish custom and ritual was very scant indeed. In his preface to *Esther* he wrote:

> It is also said that the Jews even today celebrate with great ceremonies of thanks giving the day when their ancestors were delivered by Esther from the cruelty of Haman.[13]

It would seem that Racine had never witnessed a synagogue service celebrating the feast of Esther. This may not be entirely due to his disinterestedness in such matters, but rather to the difficulty involved in finding a synagogue in his area. None was to be found at Saint-Cyr and Racine would have had to go to Provence or "travel to Metz or to Bordeaux" in order to find one.[14]

Racine not only drew on the Scriptures for inspiration for his play, but on his own national heritage, so constellated with religious literature: the many liturgical dramas, for example, of medieval France, such as *Le Jeu d'Adam*, the Miracle plays centering around Our Lady, the Mysteries and Passions depicting Christ's ordeal—all remarkable examples of religious primitivism shot through with intense spiritual fervor. Though few of these dramatic works possessed valuable literary qualities, they remain outstanding because of their rigorousness of spirit, their hand-hewn quality, characteristics basic to the sculptures chiseled onto the great cathedrals of France.[15]

The religious dramas which flourished during the Renaissance were more sophisticated, more artful, and denoted a greater interest in theatrical techniques and less preoccupation with the divine. Few works were fired with the fervor that makes for a drama's living quality; rather, they were intellectual exercises, theatrical renditions of philosophical, historical, and literary readings. Notable among these exceptions were *Saul Mad* (1572) by Jean de La Taille, *The Jewesses* (1580) by Robert Garnier, and *Abraham Sacrificing* (1550) by Théodore de Bèze.

The story of Esther itself had been the topic for plays before Racine: *The Play of Queen Esther* (1512), *Hamanus*, written in Latin by Thomas Kirchmaier (1574), *Aman*, by André de Rivaudeau (1566), *Esther*, by Pierre Mathieu (1578), Montchrétien's *Aman* (1602), the anonymous *Haman's Perfidy, King Ahasuerus' Favorite* (1617), Jaspien Marfrière's (pseudonym for Ville-Toustain) *The Beautiful Esther* (1620), Du Ryer's *Esther* (1643). We are not certain, however, how many of these plays Racine had actually read.

᚛ ᚛ ᚛

Madame de Maintenon, Louis XIV, the Prince de Condé, Bossuet, and other notables were present at the opening of *Esther* on January 26, 1689. The production took place in the large vestibule of the dormitory of Saint-Cyr. The sets, created by Bérain, decorator for court productions, were in fine taste, as was the music composed especially for the choruses by J.-B. Moreau, the king's music master. The Persian-inspired costumes embroidered with pearls and diamonds[16] were much lauded. Racine and Boileau stood in the wings throughout the per-

formance, giving the young ladies last minute instructions and probably lessons in courage as well.[17]

It seems that Louis XIV was so delighted with the performance
that he attended all subsequent ones that year. The Marquis de Dangeau commented on the play's success in his *Memoirs*; and Mme de
Sévigné, in a letter to her daughter (February 21, 1689), expressed her
positive reactions to Racine's endeavors:

> We listened . . . to this tragedy with so much attention, that it was
> noticed. . . . I cannot tell you how very pleased we were by this play;
> it is not an easy work to perform, and one which will never be imitated;
> there is such perfect and complete rapport between the music, the
> verse, the songs, and the characters that one longs for nothing else . . .
> everything about it is simple, everything is innocent, everything is sub-
> lime and touching.

Madame de La Fayette, less enthusiastic, was convinced that *Esther's* popularity was due to what she called the "allegorical" nature of
this drama. Esther, she claimed was modeled after Madame de Maintenon, Ahasuerus after Louis XIV, Vashti after Madame de Montespan,
Haman after M. de Louvois.

✦ ✦ ✦

Racine's three-act *Esther* includes choruses which intervene every
now and then, reciting and chanting their parts.

Act I. In Esther's apartment. She is telling her friend Elise how
Ahasuerus, King of Persia, had chosen her to be his bride. He had
rejected the former Queen, Vashti, when she refused to show herself
at a feast after he had requested her to do so. Unbeknown to Ahasuerus,
however, Esther is a Jewess and an orphan who has been brought up
by her Uncle Mordecai. Ever since childhood he has told her that
hers will be a difficult and special destiny. Now that Esther has become
Queen, Mordecai still advises her in secret and guides her actions. It
is he who earlier warned Esther to reveal to the King the regicide
planned by two of his functionaries. Now, he informs her of Ahasuerus' decree, instigated by his minister Haman, to have all Jews killed
in ten days. Mordecai asks Esther to intercede before the King on their
behalf. Such a request, however, presents danger: to appear before
the King without having been summoned is punishable by death.
Esther is torn between her fear of the King and her desire to save her
people. The prayer she utters, however, infuses her with sufficient
strength to fulfill her mission.

Act II takes place in Ahasuerus' throne room. Haman confides to Hydaspes, an officer, his hatred for the Jews and for Mordecai in particular because he has refused to prostrate himself before him. The King is agitated, Hydaspes informs him, as a result of a terrible nightmare. To soothe him, he has had the Annals of his reign brought and read to him. Both leave, and Ahasuerus enters accompanied by Asaph, another officer. Ahasuerus wonders why he has never rewarded the man who saved his life and of which the Annals had reminded him: Mordecai. When Haman enters, the King asks him how he would recompense a subject to whom he was deeply grateful. Haman, certain that he is that person, lists the rewards which are in order; a lavish procession, the donning of royal robes, the riding of one of the King's horses. Ahasuerus orders Haman to accord these honors to Mordecai. Esther enters, trembling. She seeks to complete her mission, but faints instead. After being revived, the King reassures her of his love and offers her half his kingdom as proof of his great affection. Esther invites both Ahasuerus and Haman to a banquet.

Act III is enacted in Esther's apartments. Haman's wife, Zeresh, who senses the danger her husband is running by remaining at Court, suggests that he escape. Haman, however, is reassured when he enters the banquet hall and thoughts of flight vanish. Esther reveals her origin, speaks of her people and their history, and denounces Haman's treachery. Ahasuerus, aghast, realizes that Haman has manipulated him like a "toy." As Haman begs for mercy at Esther's feet, Ahasuerus, misunderstanding his intentions, has the impression that such a position denotes an affront toward Esther. He has his guards remove Haman and put him to death. The Jews are saved. Mordecai becomes the King's minister.

I

King Ahasuerus,[18] we learn from the very outset of the drama, is a dual figure, as are a number of characters in Racine's works: Agamemnon, Pyrrhus, Titus. . . . In outward appearance, Ahasuerus embodies all the qualities intrinsic to a monarch: sound judgment, self-control, wisdom. As an Oriental potentate, he stands far above his subjects. His wealth, his vast kingdom, his might, the remoteness that he maintains (one may not enter his presence, unless bidden, on pain of death), inclines those surrounding him to cower. His distance is further emphasized when he wears his crown of "gold" (implying an affinity with the Sun God and with Christian saints). The supernatural and magical power frequently associated with the collective figure of the King are here implied.

Yet, beneath this might and glitter, there stands another kind of individual, a man who is prey to a play of opposites within his own being. Not a sick King in the sense of Amfortas (*Parsifal*) nor an aged one (King Lear), but rather one in the prime of his life who has not yet awakened to the realities of the world, to his own situation as well as to that of his people. It is for this reason, his inability to develop a higher consciousness, that he "thoughtlessly" accepts the advice of his minister Haman. Because of this lack of awareness on his part, he is frequently caught off balance, confronted with his own ignorance concerning all that is transpiring within his kingdom (externally) as well as inside the palace walls (internally). Because he resents such a lacuna on his part and feels frustrated by his limitations, he is given to frantic outbursts of rage. Even Haman declares

> You know how, terrifying in his tantrums,
> He often snaps the springs of all our plans.[19]

Ahasuerus is as "unconscious" of his situation as Lot was when lying with his daughters, as Judah with Tamar.[20]

Ahasuerus' vision (external and internal) has been dulled in part by the obesity of his ego.[21] An inkling of the divergencies which exist between his lion-like *persona*, the formidable image it projects, and the weakly structured "lamb-like" inner being, is first offered by Esther in her description of the King's rejection of Queen Vashti. Ahasuerus, she claims, had acted rashly by sending Vashti away after she had refused to obey his command and show herself to the dignitaries he had invited to Susa. Since Ahasuerus had considered Vashti's affront mortal to his pride, it would seem that his inflated ego and, therefore, his omnipotence were threatened. Ahasuerus' identification with his *persona* at this particular moment was so intense that he lost complete contact with his inner world and the feeling principle buried so deeply within its folds. As soon as some sort of equilibrium had returned, however, he came to regret his actions.

> And how the king, against her hot with rage,
> Drove her both from his throne and from his bed.
> But from his thoughts he could not banish her:
> She long held sway over his wounded soul.[22]

We learn as an aftermath of this episode that, though Ahasuerus is a man who walks in darkness and with unsteady footsteps, when he

relates to the feeling principle within himself he is usually led in the
right direction. A case in point is his choice of Esther for Queen.

> At last, he said, with eyes of tender love:
> "Be Persia's queen"; and from that very moment,
> He placed his royal crown upon my brow.
> More splendidly to show his joy and love,
> He heaped with gifts the grandees of the Court.[23]

Paradoxically, the beginning of Ahasuerus' enlightenment or self-
awareness arises from his unconscious. He has a nightmare which is
related by Hydaspes (II,ii) to Haman.

> His Majesty seems plunged in deepest gloom;
> Last night some dreadful nightmare haunted him.
> While all the world around lay silent sleeping,
> His voice cried out in terrifying tones.
> I rushed to him. His words were all distraught:
> He murmured of some threat, aimed at his life;
> He mentioned enemies, wild ravishers;
> Even the name of Esther passed his lips.
> Shuddering the whole night long, he lay awake.
> Weary, at last, of an elusive slumber.
> To dissipate three mournful images,
> He sent to fetch the famous chronicles,
> Where the deeds of his reign compiled with care,
> Are faithfully recorded every day.[24]

The King is so shaken by this dream that he has the Annals of his reign
brought and read to him, hoping they will soothe him. From these he
learns of Mordecai's valor. His emotions swiftly alter from fright to
guilt. His ignorance of the role Mordecai had played in saving his life
by preventing the regicide, and the fact that such a deed of goodness
and sincerity has gone unrewarded, scandalize him. Indeed, Ahasuerus
is overwhelmed with guilt at his own ineffectiveness.

> Too damnable neglect of such a service!
> Most certain consequence of royal cares!
> A prince, surrounded by tumultuous tasks,
> Is ceaselessly enticed to fresh horizons;
> The future makes him grace, the present grips;
> But, swift as lightning, ah! the past escapes.[25]

The nightmare is the factor that has succeeded in changing Ahasuerus' orientation and attitude. The stimulation, the "libido-current"

aroused within him because of his dream, has given birth to "new psychic contents" which in turn generate insights and revelations designed to act as guideposts in his daily activities.[26] What had previously remained unrevealed, Mordecai's role in preventing the regicide, now becomes the focal point around which Ahasuerus' interests radiate. For the first time the King begins to experience emotional attunement to the situation he is living. The active masculine principle that was related to his awakening feeling floods him with a sense of justice and activates a deep moral force which had almost been deadened by years of desuetude. Right must now be tended to. This re-focusing of attitudes and of activities paves the way for Ahasuerus' eventual illumination.

There are certain questions concerning Ahasuerus' personality which still remain ambiguous. When, for example, he asks Haman how he would recompense a man who had saved his life, it is difficult to ascertain whether he is acting out of naiveté or subtle artifice.

> Drawn near, proud pillar of your master's throne,
> Advising spirit, who so often have
> Alone assuaged the burden of my rule.[27]

One might be led to opt for the first alternative, in view of the fact that Ahasuerus has always considered Haman to be his trusted friend and adviser. There is, therefore, no reason at this early date to assume that any complication has as yet altered the established relationship. If this is indeed the situation, an external event would have to interfere to disturb the *status quo*, breaking up, thereby, the enduring and warm rapport between the just-awakening King and his advisor.

The needed external force now appears. Esther, unsummoned, enters Ahasuerus' "inner court," thus risking death. All elements considered as stable and secure (the law of the land), which have heretofore prevailed, now grow shaky.

Esther, who refers to Ahasuerus as a "sacred monarch," a power among powers, quivers before his might, thereby appealing at the same time to his pride. She does so intuitively, since she is unaware of his egocentricity. She sees him only as a powerful masculine force, the possessor of very nearly godly strength: "On this sacred throne, surrounded by lightning."[28] The King, deeply moved by her anguish, is again guided by his feelings and seeks to allay her anxieties.

> I am myself disturbed; and without trembling
> May not behold her pain and her distress.
> Calm my Queen, calm the fears convulsing you.
> Sovereign mistress of Ahasuerus' heart,

Experience only his impassioned love.
Half of my kingdom is yours for the asking.[29]

The two extremes within Ahasuerus' personality have confronted each other, the overly rigid *persona* and the weak inner man. He describes these antagonistic forces within himself in terms of "enemy stars," implying that a struggle is about to ensue. That such a dichotomy should be inherent in Ahasuerus' personality is not surprising in view of the social and religious customs prevalent in his land.

Socially, the King remains withdrawn and remote from his entourage and certainly from his people. He fosters, or does nothing to discourage, his position by simply obeying the laws of the land. In this case, the interdiction placed upon a person entering the King's "inner court" without having been requested to do so is directed against Esther. Were he to have her put to death, Ahasuerus would symbolize a collective figure emanating from a strictly patriarchal system. The fact that he permits her to live and even goes so far as to express his love for her, as well as offer her half of his kingdom, indicates the disintegration (or integration, depending upon one's point of view) of a patriarchal system.

When a patriarchal religious system is in the process of developing, the dominion of the matriarchal society and its religions (as witnessed in this case by the Babylonian, Assyrian, Phoenician, etc.), which are uroboric in character, must be broken. The "devouring mother" figures, therefore, which are part and parcel of these matriarchal polytheistic religions, considered as man's bitterest enemy, must be crushed and a strongly and purely patriarchal attitude adapted.

Zoroaster[30] had tried, as was suggested in the *Gathas*, to transform the feminine dominated societies with their sybaritic and erotic rituals into highly moral ones based on abstract conceptions. He asked of his votaries a life devoted to discipline, virtue, and morality. Psychologically speaking, however, when emotions are suppressed, they simmer for a time within a personality or culture, then erupt with renewed virulence. Such a state of affairs occurred in Persia. In the latter *Avestas*, the power of the moon goddess and the bull god (Mithra), deities Zoroaster had sought to annihilate, increased with even greater impact. In this connection, the worship of Drvaspa (the "Fashioner" or the Cow) again became popular, with its accompanying sacrifices of horses, oxen, and other cattle.[31] Anahit, goddess of the waters and of the stars, both beautiful and sensual with her golden slippers, her girdled waist which forced up her rounded breasts, was alluring to all men. She not only demanded sacrifices of them, but encouraged both men and women to indulge in sexual rites associated with her role as fertility goddess. When Artaxerxes ordered the Persian Magi to instruct the priests of Babylon, the two religions had become so confused that the rituals and mysteries of Mithra became blended with those of the Great Mother (Ishtar).[32]

These two forces (the masculine associated with good or the positive, and the feminine connected with evil or the negative) cohabited in Ahasuerus' depths. Only through insight into his situation, revealed to him partially through his nightmare and fully through Esther's unprecedented entrance into his "inner court," does he become aware of the conflicting entities within his personality. What had remained undifferentiated within his depths, his inner antagonisms, now came to the fore. The struggle is resolved when he makes his decision not to kill Esther. As a result, his masculine consciousness, which had grown through Esther—that is, through his relationship with the feminine principle—no longer feels threatened. Ahasuerus is able to express his love and admiration for his wife as well as to speak candidly of the role she, a woman, plays in his life, as inspiration, as representative of "innocence and peace,"[33] "light," radiance and joy. Furthermore, Esther can be looked upon as a redemptive power, having saved Ahasuerus from self-destruction, complete submersion within his own unconscious attitude.

↗ ↗ ↗

The women peopling Racine's theatre have, for the most part, always been *magnae matris*. They are evil, Eve-like enchantresses who, similar to their counterparts in the early polytheistic religions (Cybele, Ishtar, Aphrodite), try to reduce men to the state of servant or destroy them completely. These mother goddesses seek to emasculate the masculine principle, using the phallus, creative as it is, to serve them and them alone. Racine was always drawn to these *ewig Weibliche* types, volatile, passionate, inconsistent, and unfaithful beings. Never did he look upon woman as a supremely virtuous being, that is, as a Sophia or a Mary. Esther, in this instance, marks a surprising and fascinating departure from Racine's roster of female creatures.

The name Esther[34] itself, associated with the Babylonian deity Ishtar (Star) and the Hebrew name Hadassah (Myrtle), gives a clue as to the identity and function of this figure in Racine's drama.

Ishtar, the Babylonian goddess of love and war, was tremendously appealing in ancient times and was worshipped in various forms and manners in Phoenicia, Assyria, Canaan, and Egypt. Her votaries sometimes practiced ritual prostitution, acts absolutely condemned by the Hebrews. Some scholars feel that Ishtar may have been the "Queen of Heaven" mentioned by Jeremiah. The fact that Esther is associated with Ishtar in her aspect of love goddess points to her own femininity and indicates the fecundating role she is to play in this drama. Symbolically speaking, Esther, is a *vas hermeticum*, a vehicle through which enlightenment will occur. Though Isthar's war-like side remains invisible in this story, its presence is keenly felt and would unleash destruction should Esther fail to complete her given task.

The star, associated with the name Ishtar, has been from the very beginning of time the symbol of the spirit and of illumination, a light shining brightly in the heavens and piercing the surrounding darkness. The Egyptians drew the star in their hieroglyphics as an image "rising upwards toward the point of origin" and implying, therefore, "to bring up" or "to educate," "to teach."[35] Though the spirit or the educating faculty in the human being is frequently connected with the male principle, in Esther's case, she herself bears this content, indicating that "illumination" will occur through her.

The name Esther is also identified with "myrtle," an evergreen with white or pinkish flowers and dark fragrant berries. In ancient days the myrtle was sacred to Venus and, consequently, linked to the Great Mother cults or matriarchal societies. This is another instance, then, when Esther embodies the female principle, representing a flourishing plant-type, nourished by "mother" earth and under her dominion.

Esther, we conclude, is a combination of both "spirit" (male, star) and "earth" (female, Ishtar, myrtle), a transpersonal and guiding principle occupied with the mysteries involved in saving her people, impregnated with the divine, yet very much a woman personality-wise and in her capacity as wife of a reigning monarch.

In the beginning of Racine's drama, Esther is a passive human being. She is in fact a vehicle, a function through which God's will is carried out via Mordecai. Indeed, she is very much a "daughter of God," a living manifestation of the purity instilled in her by the divine principle. She is warm and gentle, endowed with natural beauty and kindness, for which reason Ahasuerus chose her above all the other young girls to be his wife. Esther is, furthermore, deeply rooted in her origins and her God. In a sense, she is still living in a state of "paradise," accepting, obeying, but never confronting.

> Prostrate I fall at the Eternal's feet,
> And taste the joy of His oblivious peace.[36]

Esther's inertia at the outset of the drama can be compared to that of Sarah when wandering with Abraham. Like her, Esther undergoes a "harem experience"[37] when placed in Ahasuerus' harem before being chosen as his bride. In psychological terms, such an ordeal signifies the danger the female principle undergoes when living in a patriarchal society. It is always in peril of being lost or of regressing to the point where all feminine identity and individuality are obliterated. Both Sarah (who becomes the mother of Isaac) and Esther (who will be transformed into an active and conscious participant in the task of saving her people) are examples of the survival and strength of the female principle in Judaism.

Though Esther does nothing to ameliorate her situation at the outset of Racine's work, she is never "unconscious" of her life experiences, at least not to the same degree that Ahasuerus is. She is certainly cognizant of the fact that she is living a false life in order to preserve the well-being of her people, but does not act to remedy the dual position she is forced to play because of circumstances. Her *persona* belies her thoughts and her life is experienced with "tongue enchained,"[38] in "secret," in a "solitary and hidden manner,"[39] and always "under the vigilant eye of her uncle" Mordecai.

There is little or no conflict between her inner and outer worlds at this point. She has been raised by her uncle to lead a life of "concealment" and, because of this factor, has been able to build up about her a solid protective facade.[40] Her *persona* resembles a perpetually taut muscle, never permitted to be released for fear of yielding to what she might consider weakness on her part, the revelation of her true thoughts. There is no question as to Esther's dissatisfaction with her situation, but such emotions have not yet reached untenable proportions. She remains mistress of her actions and expressions.

> Alas! through all those days of mercy feasts,
> How great became my secret shame and woe!
> "Esther," I said, "Esther is throned in purple,
> Half of the world beneath her sceptre's sway,
> While bramble hides Jerusalem's drear walks!
> Zion, the dreadful den of unclean dragons,
> Beholds her holy Temple's stones still scattered!
> And the high feasts of Israel's God have ceased![41]

Esther then accepts her dual world because she has never really had to confront it. She is docile in all ways, subservient to her uncle's will, grateful for his kindness. Furthermore, her notions concerning her religion are still abstract; that is, they have not as yet turned into concrete or realized entities, true stumbling blocks in her life.

Slowly, Esther will evolve from such a state of passivity. She will tell her friend Elisa that despite her good fortune she feels an inexplicable atmosphere of dread, a sense of pain. She confides to Elisa her desire to divest herself of her vestments, her diadem. These material objects (as we have seen in both *Berenice* and *Phaedra*) are visual counterpart of the psychological (amorphous) mask she has donned. They slowly force her to face the reality of her existence and for this reason they pall on her. She cannot relate, assimilate, or evaluate these status signs. With the realization that she has been forced (through providence) to live out a hypocritical existence, the shedding of these garments (the exterior mask) becomes, symbolically speaking, imperative. Otherwise, she is likely to smother or disintegrate under their very weight.

Still she does not act and, therefore, has not yet discovered her own identity, her individual inner deity. She remains identified with her people and her collective origins. Unable to look upon herself as an individual severed from the collective image, she accepts her role as a passive tool, a recipient, a vessel-like being manipulated by Mordecai, the representative of God. Mordecai, the propeller of her "enlightenment," calls upon her sense of morality, of "shame," of "guilt," and of gratitude to serve Divinity.

> Under my guardian, the wise Mordecai.
> You know how great my debt to this fond aid.
> My parents had been torn from me by death:
> But he, seeing in me his brother's daughter,
> Became for me my father and my mother.
> Stirred, day and night, by the Jews' wretched plight,
> He brought me forth from my obscure abode;[42]

Esther is compelled to immerse herself through prayer in the universal forces, by means of which she begins to penetrate within herself, "seeking myself"[43] to find or to come into contact with her true identity (*Self*). Through prayer Esther knows a rapprochement with Divinity, that inner or "hidden God," the En-Sof,[44] which has become a living entity within her. She speaks now in terms of a "holy alliance"[45] between herself, her family, her people, and the Divine; she refers to Him as "husband" and as "father"; she understands the punishment He has inflicted upon the Hebrews for their adulterous actions. Esther now sees God all about her in natural manifestations, personified in "storms," "wind." He becomes part of a cosmic vision, walking with her and breathing His strength into her.

Driven by some inner force in response perhaps to God's own

Shekhinah,[46] Esther is now prepared to face the ordeal every hero or heroine must suffer in order to cause the breakthrough from a passive to an active state, from adolescence to maturity, unconsciousness to consciousness, from the uroboric attitude to that of individuation. Like Moses, Joshua, David, Job, so Esther faces her ordeal. She will literally flirt with death when confronting her husband, the "lion" Ahasuerus. Rejecting what is fundamentally alien to her, the "criminal feasts"[47] of which she has had to partake as Queen, the false gods which smother her, she declares:

> And how, in secret and alone, I trample
> This very pomp to which I am condemned,
> This royal crown that must adorn my brow
> On solemn days and ceremonial days;
> How ashes I prefer to such vain baubles,
> And relish but the tears Thou seest me shed.
> I waited for the moment marked by Thee,
> To dare espouse the quarrel of thy people;
> This moment now is come. In prompt obedience,
> I go to brave the presence of the King.
> It is for Thee I go: lead Thou my steps
> Upon this lion proud, who knows Thee not . . .[48]

When in Ahasuerus' presence, however, Esther faints. Such a loss of consciousness indicates her feminine approach to matters, a momentary eclipse of her cerebral attitudes (more pronounced than the speechlessness of Nero and of Phaedra). She is unable to face her situation as would a masculine hero (Joshua, David, etc.). She therefore undergoes her hazardous ordeal in terms of her own personality and psychological orientation.

When consciousness returns to Esther, she looks upon her husband not as an individual, but rather as a collective figure, a ruler vested with a sense of justice and wisdom. Indeed, he is so majestic a personage in her conception that he very nearly becomes a mortal counterpart of the Divine Principle. She sees Ahasuerus "on his sacred throne, surrounded by lightning," possessed of the God-like authority and strength to destroy by reducing everything about him to ashes.

> Alas, what brazen heart, without a shudder,
> Can bear the lightning darting from your eyes?
> Thus burns like fire the wrath of the living God.[49]

Despite the fear and awe which have just arisen as a result of her confusion between her vision of King and God, she is inspired to act cerebrally and forcefully. Craft and ruse become the order of the day. She invites Ahasuerus and Haman to a feast she is going to prepare. At this point, Esther is Ishtar-like. She exercises all her seductive attributes. Her intense appeal fascinates Ahasuerus. Excitedly, he murmurs, "Ah! how you enflame my curious desire!"[50]

The King barely understands the transformation in his wife, from the pale, fainting, confused, dazzled young girl who entered his "inner court," to the new calm woman. He is unaware of the fact that Esther has been extracted from her isolated and secret (passive) existence by the spiritual force (Yahweh), through Mordecai and through prayer, which she adores. This change comes to pass only after Esther has experienced the power of the masculine spiritual God residing within her.

Ahasuerus is all the more bewildered by the change effected in Esther's attitude, in that he too is undergoing a transformation. The flux or motility agitating their psyches generates renewed energy that causes Ahasuerus' excitement to increase as Racine prepares for the play's climax, Esther's revelation.

Esther is now emotionally prepared to divest herself of her burdensome *persona*, releasing, as she does so, her heretofore repressed emotions and feelings. Now, the divine force within her blazes forth in all its resplendence, taking on as it does fresh radiance and beauty. She speaks of God to Ahasuerus in the following terms:

> This God, sole sovereign of the earth and heavens,
> Is not, as wrongly painted in your eyes.
> The Eternal is his Name, the world His work;
> He hears the cries of the oppressed poor,
> Judges all men with laws the same for all . . .[51]

Esther has accomplished her mission. The imbalance within her psyche due to the disassociation between her *persona* and her inner world has now been healed. She can, therefore, experience life "wholly" as a feminine figure in complete rapport with her husband, with Mordecai (the spiritual element within her world), and with her people. The repressed, misunderstood, the heretofore barren feminine principle has given way to a fruitful integrated entity capable of growth and able to live in unison with masculine consciousness and spirituality.

The figure of Esther in Racine's panoply of heroines indicates a harmonious association and relatedness with the female principle, no longer considered solely as an agent of destruction (Agrippina, Roxana, Phaedra) but rather as a meaningful and beautiful force in life, a redemptive power as well.

✝ ✝ ✝

Mordecai's name has been associated with the Babylonian war god Marduk[52] and with Mars. According to Professor Salo Baron, we do not "know of any Hebrew names for Mordecai."[53]

Mordecai represents the "mana" personality. He symbolizes spirituality, permanence, the father image, and age-old wisdom. Imbued with God's essence, he is the instigator and the propeller of the action in this drama. He is comparable in certain respects to another Racinian figure, the seer Calchas in *Iphigenia*.

No conflicts exist within Mordecai's personality. He lives in an undifferentiated world known to many mystics at certain periods in their lives. Never once does he waver between the individual he is and the collective force he serves, the temporal and the eternal, man and God. Mordecai is fully attuned to the universe as well as to himself.

Mordecai is more spirit than flesh. He has experienced the "archetypal God image" and lives under the spell of the *numinosum*.[54] His tremendous energy derives from the impact of the divine force that lives within him, which generates all his acts. In some respects, he can be likened to Job.[55] Both men not only feel God's totality, his immanence and transcendence, but also an intense intimacy with Him. This latter aspect imbues them with powerful personalities. Each, however, expresses his own personality in a different manner; Mordecai through Esther, and Job directly toward God.

Mordecai experiences God's essence through action, masculine consciousness which stems from the patriarchal culture of which he is a product. His fervent prayers, the mystical union which he comes to know, do not cause a lack of consciousness on his part, but rather expand consciousness since his communion with the divine brings him not only more deeply into contact with the primordial unity of the cosmos, the *prima materia*, but also relates him to the world through his people and their need. He looks upon the world and his significance in it with the clarity and purpose of a man whose goal determines the course of his life. His vision of God, therefore, is not escapist; rather, it is deeply rooted to this world and to the people in it.

As spirit, Mordecai, if he is to make his will known and if his work is to bear fruit, must blend with matter ("mater," "mother"). Alone he cannot achieve any kind of solidity. He is very much aware of this fact and for this reason works closely with Esther. Even she realizes the part he has played in her life when she declares: "He brought me forth from my obscure abode."[56] Such a statement clearly reveals Mordecai's function. He is, in essence, going to draw Esther forth from the land of "obscurity" (relative unconsciousness and passivity) to the realm of enlightenment (consciousness and activity).

> And on my weak hands basing their deliverance,
> He urged me hope for the imperial throne.
> Trembling, I fell in with his secret plans.
> I came; but hid my country and my race.[57]

When Mordecai appears for the first time, audiences are already prepared to meet this ascetic and dedicated figure (I,iii). His garments (rags and sackcloth) are in effect an exteriorization and concretization of what is essentially veiled, the wounds and gashes perpetrated upon his people and by extension upon his own soul. These he now experiences physically and intensely. Words are frequently incapable of conveying the full impact of a gnawing pain and for this reason the visual sense is called upon to stimulate the onlooker's reactions. In Esther's case, her shock is so great that it gives instantaneous birth to coruscating anguish. The powerful sensations which Mordecai succeeds in generating within her by visual means pave the way for what transpires.

A fascinating change in the relationship between Esther and Mordecai occurs when he broaches the subject of the Hebrew people and the catastrophe that awaits them should Haman's orders be carried out. More than passion marks Mordecai's features now. The "kindly," "gentle" father whom Esther has looked up to since childhood vanishes and in his stead there appears a being imbued with the might of a Moses, a man who carries God's essence. Before her, Mordecai[58] is shorn of all human and personal qualities. He is God's spokesman, force rather than flesh, spirit rather than matter, collective rather than individual. Possessed of the same dynamism as the Biblical Moses, he speaks and his words are effective.

> What? When you see your people perishing,
> Esther, you hold your life of some account!
> God speaks; and yet you fear the wrath of man!
> What am I saying? Is your life your own?
> Is it not due to them from whom you've sprung?
> Is it not due to God, Who gave it you?
> And who knows, when He led you to the throne,
> He did not destine you to save His people?
> Think well on it.[59]

Mordecai, the recipient of God's emanations, lives in a world of actuality, devoid of time and space. He has, therefore, little patience with Esther when she hesitates to fulfill her mission. Though the danger of losing her life is a definite reality, such details are irrelevant for Mordecai, a man whose vision is apocalyptic.

> Most happy if for Him you risk your life!
> And what need has His arm of your support?
> Against Him can earth's mightiest kings prevail?
> They would unite in vain to war on Him:
> He need but show Himself to scatter them:
> He speaks and to their dust they all return.
> The sea flees at His voice, the heavens quake:
> The whole world in His sight is but a void;
> And feeble man, poor brittle toy of death,
> Is in His eyes as though he has not been.[60]

Mordecai, a man possessed by divine fire, reduces Esther's resistance to ashes. Convinced that everything has been preordained, that God has placed Haman's "criminal audacity" in the path of the Hebrews as a test of their fidelity, he knows that an active demonstration of their faith and trust in God must be forthcoming.

> 'Tis He, who, urging me to dare approach you,
> In front of me, dear Esther, led the way;
> And if His voice must strike your ears in vain,
> We shall still see His wonders shining forth.
> Haman He can confound, can break our chains,
> Though the feeblest finger in the universe,
> And you, having refused this holy office,
> Perhaps will perish and your entire race.[61]

Mordecai has experienced divinity creatively. This force, breathing within him, is forever activating his impulses, and this energy expended in conjunction with his lucidity fosters growth and progress around him.

✻ ✻ ✻

Haman is comparable to Eriphyle[62] in *Iphigenia*. He represents the principle of Evil, the destructive side of cosmic manifestation, a force necessary for change and development. A living representation of Satan, of Gehenna, the dark, shadow, chthonic aspect of man. Haman is a negative figure who, although he turns light into darkness, construction into destruction, spirit into matter, eventually serves a positive purpose. Like Cain, he plays an important role in the universal arrangement of things. He has been placed in the world in order to act as an irritant, a stimulant, a *spiritus agens*, prepared to activate that which has or might become unproductive and decayed—certain elements, for example, within Ahasuerus' psyche, the divine force within the Hebrew people, the rapport between masculine and feminine principles. Though Haman's destructive aspect is never fully realized (as was Cain's) the activity which his presence arouses acts as a catalyzer that destroys the *status quo.*

Haman, a descendant of Aga, the Amalekite King who was defeated by Saul,[63] had been brought to Persia as a child. There, he has risen to become the King's Grand Vizier. Wealthy, powerful, he is the recipient of honors which would have pleased any other mortal. He is, however, driven by a feeling of inner emptiness, of rejection, of solitude which makes him unable to experience the joys which accrue to him. He is overly sensitive to the fact that he is not a Persian, that he is, therefore, different from the others, that he is a self-made man and not born to wealth. When he faces the Hebrews, and Mordecai in particular, he sees very nearly a mirror image of himself (the Hebrews were not Persians, their religion and customs varied from those of the majority), with one exception: this minority group has never felt the terror of solitude. The Hebrews are strengthened by their belief in God and because of it feel loved. Haman, on the contrary has never experienced such feelings of "belonging" and, as a result, is driven by jealousy.

The bravura and powerful personality Haman displays before his entourage are merely a facade. Inwardly, he is as shaky as a pillar with a cracked foundation. For this reason, he cannot tolerate disobedience. Mordecai's refusal to bow down to him when they meet in front of the palace gates acts as a threat to Haman's inflated ego, to what he would like to think of as his omnipotence. This danger has to be destroyed.

> The Universe? Every day a man . . . a vile slave,
> With an audacious brow, disdains and affronts me.[64]

Though Mordecai is "a slave" on the surface, Haman is one in actuality. He is "enslaved" to the earth, to the petty aggrandizements which come with material wealth, with status symbols. He is a being totally devoid of any feelings of spirituality; unlike Mordecai, who is God's envoy. The knowledge of Mordecai's feelings of acceptance by God, the intimacy of his rapport with the Divine Principle, the security, that inner joy and peace which comes with faith, increase his strength. In an opposing progression, Haman's hatred of Mordecai grows swiftly. Rejected from what he considers to be his religious realm, his feeling of enstrangement becomes more and more poignant as had Cain's centuries before. Haman's anger against Mordecai and his people becomes so obsessive that it reaches a frenzy.

> He, contumacious, never bowed before me.
> In vain, all reverence on their bended knees
> Him, whom the greatest king has glorified:
> When all the Persians moved by holy awe,
> Dare not uplift their foreheads from the ground,
> He, sitting proudly, his head motionless,
> Holds all these honours as idolatry,
> Returns my gaze with bold, seditious glance,
> And cannot even deign to lower his eyes.[65]

Haman flinches as he compares his position with Mordecai's. "Greatness becomes insipid" because "the sun illuminates this perfidious being."[66] Haman is aware of his limitations, of the fact that he is devoid of spirituality, but he refuses to accept them. So tormented is he by this very point that he tries desperately to unravel the mystery which enshrouds his rival, to understand the courage and strength of that voice that moves within Mordecai, "You think some secret voice dare speak for him?"[67]

Haman is particularly tortured by the vision of Mordecai's "odious face." Even at night he is haunted by that visual impression. "My troubled mind still sees him."[68] It is Mordecai's "eye" in particular that seems to hold intense terror for Haman. It is through the eye, a representative of "light" or the "divine eye," symbolizing "understanding," that all-seeing eye of God which makes it so uncomfortable for those who have something to hide, that the realization of his own inadequacies blazes forth. The eye reflects a type of mirror image of his sick and distorted inner world, making it visible and comprehensible to him.

Suddenly Haman is overcome with an extraordinary feeling of danger. Some process within his own being has been activated, enabling him to project unknown elements within his own psyche upon Mordecai. The projection of his own qualities influences his actions by increasing their viciousness. The intensity of his aroused emotions cuts him off still further from all human feeling or compassion. He calls for the extermination of Mordecai and his people. "Let entire peoples be drowned in blood."[69] He tries to rationalize his hatred, convincing Ahasuerus of the evil intent of the Hebrews, a people so different and opposed to the laws of the land, a threat and danger.

> Their God Himself, the foe of every god.
> "How long is this vile people still to breed,
> Infecting all your realms with a canting greed?
> Aliens in Persia, against our laws aligned,
> Appearing separate from all mankind,
> Their aim to end our peace, our ills to fan,
> And, everywhere accursed, they curse each man.
> Forestall their trucks, their insolent turmoil punish,
> And with their spoils your treasures replenish."[70]

When Haman discovers that Mordecai is to be rewarded by Ahasuerus, his hybris is violated. His features become distorted with rage, a compensation for his own feelings of inadequacy, rejection, and inferiority. His wrath is even aimed at Ahasuerus.

> He knows he owes me all; that, for his greatness,
> I've trampled underfoot fear, shame, remorse . . .[71]

Zeresh, Haman's wife, feels his pain. Her womanly intuition warns her of an ominous fate awaiting her husband. She begs him to leave the country as speedily as possible and to search out other paths in life. Not the stormiest seas, nor the most vicious tempest, she asserts, could possibly be more hazardous than "this deceitful court."[72] Haman, however, pays no heed. He enters the banquet hall in good spirits, unaware of destiny's role.

Haman, who can be looked upon as another manifestation of Satan, certainly lives up to his reputation.[73] In so doing, he serves a useful function as *agent provocateur*. The turmoil he engenders succeeds in transforming the unbalanced relationships and attitudes which prevailed at the beginning of the drama into harmonious ones at the finale. Yet, since the force he represents has been destroyed (psychologically speaking, repressed) and not integrated into the *corpus*, the balance which has come into being because of his demise can be at best only temporary. Evil will reappear in another form at another time.

II

Esther revolves around a quaternity: Ahasuerus, Esther, Haman, Mordecai. Numerically speaking, the number four in itself is revelatory. Considered as a symbol, it stands for "wholeness and totality," an entity uniting a pair of opposites.[74] According to Plato, the number four indicates the "realization of the idea." In the *Zohar* it is associated with the cardinal points. All of these very brief statements concerning the number four connote a preoccupation with balance and harmony.

Yet, despite the fact that four protagonists are present in Racine's *Esther*, the situation is, surprisingly enough, unbalanced. The first discordant note arises from the preponderance of male figures: three men and one woman. Ideally speaking, for the *coniunctio* to take place, there should be two men and two women. Secondly, the elements representing good (Mordecai) and evil (Haman) are pulling in totally opposite directions, rather than working together. It is obvious then that no unity or understanding between these polarities has yet occurred. As for the two other protagonists (Esther and Ahasuerus), they are still floating in a sea of relative unawareness. Ahasuerus is actually "unconscious" of his situation, ignorant of the fact that he has not rewarded Mordecai for his deed of valor, unacquainted with the true political motivations of those who surround him (Haman, in particular), and uninformed as to his wife's identity. As for Esther, though she may be more aware of her reality, she is, because of her passivity, forced into leading a double life (though the reasons for doing so may be valid). Unable to disclose her true identity, she is plunged into a world beclouded by "secrecy." Since she has not asserted her own individuality, nor realized herself in any way, she is forever being directed by her uncle. Outwardly, however, she gives the impression of being the beautiful and contented wife of one of the most important monarchs in ancient times.

The play of opposites intrinsic to this drama (good and evil) and the natural discord which arises from such an unharmonious situation (personality-wise) are further underscored by the spatial relationships each of these protagonists bears to the other. Both Mordecai and Haman live outside the palace; the former enters it only secretly, when he must guide Esther's actions, whereas the latter does so openly, when called upon by the King.

Since the "palace" is the focal point for interaction on the part of both Mordecai and Haman, it must be examined in terms of its symbolic import. The Kabbalists looked upon the palace ("sacred palace" or "inner palace") as a symbol for the occult center, an area which links all, body and mind, beginning and end.[75] In many legends (King Arthur, for example) the King's palace is endowed with concealed chambers or veiled by a facade hiding secret activities taking place within (as in the case of Ahasuerus and also *Bajazet*). Interpreted symbolically, both situations imply the presence of inner wealth, of spiritual truths or *logos,* and of power. Because of the palace's "containing" and "enriching" aspects, the events enacted in the drama will center about it.

III

Haman is actually Mordecai's counterpart. He is evil, matterbound; Mordecai is spiritual and linked to the eternal forces within the cosmos. These two opposing elements, the yin and the yang, need each other in order to foster growth, to make the *coniunctio* forthcoming. Had Haman not been sacrificed after the welding of opposite forces within the personality, his animal attributes, his dependency upon the feminine aspects of life—that is, his clinging to mother earth and all of her manifestations—would have led to a state of regression. Mordecai, on the other hand, with his air-bound spiritual force, prevails in this struggle for survival. He could not have won out, however, without the help of the feminine principle (Esther), which he succeeded in liberating from darkness. This feminine aspect, now apprised of identity and purpose, in full rapport with the masculine consciousness (Ahasuerus), has achieved a healthy balance between formerly antagonistic forces.

That Racine should have been attracted to the story of Esther above all other Biblical ones at this particular time is an indication of the profound import such contents held for him. The characters and the actions answered an inner need within him or expressed some mysterious change which he was experiencing. Analogies can be drawn between the integration experienced by Esther and Ahasuerus in the drama and Racine's own inner realm as manifested by the stability of his everyday existence. Such harmony as he knew at this period had not just sprung forth full-born. Racine, like Esther, had to go through his ordeal, his initiation. In this connection, it must be recalled that as a youth, while Racine had followed Jansenist teachings, he had lived a life of prayer and self-imposed disciplines, suppressing by the same token, and perhaps unwittingly, his emotions. With the imposition of this blockage, the poet's volatile psyche rebelled. The forces he had sought to enchain had not disappeared; rather, they had grown in intensity and burgeoned forth with all their power, like a breaking abscess. Racine rejected Jansenism in favor of the creative life offered him by a theatrical career. Lustful, cruel, horrendous women (Agrippina, Phaedra, Roxana, etc.) emerged from his pen. Death, violence, anguish, guilt, sacrifice stalked the stage in various garbs. When Phaedra, the last of Racine's heroines, was projected onto the proscenium, it seemed as if all the pent-up poisons had spewed forth from his being, that his body and mind had been cleansed and with this catharsis balance had come into being. Women, in the form of his wife, Catherine de Romanet, took on grace and charm. Creativity centered around more stable forms of writing: history, religious works, essays, letters.

Esther marks a sharp departure from Racine's previous works. Unlike his other plays, *Esther* reveals an existential philosophy of "commitment" to this world and not an escape from it into a realm of "essences." Furthermore, Racine's intense private preoccupation with the divine becomes here an open admission, an almost corporeal reality. The *vagina dentata* types portrayed in his earlier dramas are notably absent in this one. In their stead glows Esther, the young and poignantly beautiful girl whose gentleness is touching, whose mission in life is altruistic, whose belief in God is absolute. There is a noticeable psychological development and change in the attitudes and actions of the two main characters during the course of the drama. As they move forward in their destinies, they are transformed, slowly and painfully, from alienated and fragmentary beings whose passivity mirror their sterile lives, to positive and integrated protagonists whose expanded consciousness and divinely inspired existence takes on purpose and stature.

11

Athaliah

> "My strength is God alone,
> whose cause I serve . . ."[1]

No sooner had the news spread that Louis XIV had asked Racine to write a second play for the young ladies of Saint-Cyr than conjectures as to the topic he would choose livened the tongues and pens of those in and out of Court. Mme de Sévigné suggested, in a letter to her daughter (March 7, 1689), that Racine's new work would dramatize episodes from the lives of either Absalom or Jephthah. Racine, however, kept mute on the subject. We know only that he began writing his drama *Athaliah* at the end of 1689 and that he finished it in June of 1690. The King's music master, Jean-Baptiste Moreau, was again called upon to compose the incidental music for this work,[2] including the songs to be sung by the chorus.

Racine had high hopes for this drama. In fact, he was quite confident that it would be greeted even more warmly than *Esther* had been. Fate, however, in the form of devout curates and jealous poets, worked their venom into the hearts of those who counted; namely, Madame de Maintenon and her husband Louis XIV.

Godet des Marais, Bishop of Chartres, François Hébert, Curate of Versailles, to mention but the most influential, condemned *Athaliah* outright, on the grounds that this play was lascivious, that it would corrupt the morals of the young girls of Saint-Cyr, that it was in all ways antithetical to Christianity. Enemies such as the Duchesse de Bouillon and Madame de La Fayette continued to level their darts Racine's way. Pamphlets circulated alluding to Saint-Cyr as a virtual harem; to Madame de Maintenon as a Sultana and Louis XIV as an

Oriental Sultan, to *Athaliah* as an allegory in which Jehoash, the child King, was the Prince of Wales, future James III of England, Mattan was Pastor Burnet, Advisor to William of Orange, Athaliah was William of Orange, and Jehoiada, the High Priest of Judah, was the Archbishop of Canterbury, Sancroft.[3] The song writers Maurepas and Clairambault, jealous of Racine's popularity and the favor he enjoyed with the King, wrote disapproving ditties concerning both Athaliah and its author.

The Jansenists were, for the most part, favorably impressed with *Athaliah*, Antoine Arnauld, though he preferred *Esther* because of the virtue it inspired, voiced his admiration for *Athaliah*. Father Pasquier Quesnel also expressed his unmitigated praise of *Athaliah*.

So successful had Racine's enemies been in suppressing *Athaliah* and in attacking its author that only one document describing this play's first performance is extant. The Marquis de Dangeau noted in his Journal that *Athaliah* was first performed on January 5, 1691 before the King, Madame de Maintenon, the Dauphin, and a few distinguished people. A classroom without a stage and without decor served as the theatre. The young ladies acted without costumes, wearing their severe black school uniforms, adorned every now and then with a pearl or a ribbon. On February 8th, a second so-called "rehearsal" took place at Saint-Cyr. This time Madame de Maintenon and "very few ladies" attended.[4] A third "rehearsal" was given on February 22 for a few "intimates," among them James II and his consort. It was at this time that the final decision not to give an official production of *Athaliah* at Court was made.[5]

Racine was deeply hurt by this turn of events. What motivated the King's decision is still a matter of conjecture. Explanations are plentiful; proof, however, is sparse. Many feel that the Jesuits were angered over Racine's continued relations with the Jansenists; certain curates were truly concerned, seemingly, over the immorality to which the young ladies of Saint-Cyr could be exposed; others were perhaps jealous of Racine's popularity and his intimacy with the King and Madame de Maintenon; members of the government might have looked upon the allegorical nature of the play as a possible means of jeopardizing France's relations with England.

In a moment of despair Racine turned to his good friend Boileau. He confessed his disappointment in the outcome of his project and asked him where he thought he had failed in the writing of his play. Boileau, it would seem, according to Louis Racine, who related this incident in his *Memoirs*, declared that *Athaliah* was the dramatist's masterpiece. "I am well versed in these matters," he said to Racine, "audiences will return to it."[6] Though rancor surely must have been present within Racine's heart when confronted with the campaign waged against him and his work, still, the pain he had endured during his life had strengthened him inwardly. "He had fortunately," according to his son, "become detached from love of wordly glory a long while back, and certainly he knew better than anyone else what vanity really entailed."

Though *Athaliah* was never performed publicly during Racine's lifetime because of the King's orders, still he remained on very good terms with his sovereign. Racine was invited to Louis XIV's intimate gatherings at Marly, granted the privilege of attending the "awakenings" of the King whenever he so desired, and was recompensed for his latest theatrical efforts by being named "Gentleman Ordinary of the King's Chamber."

ᔆ ᔆ ᔆ

Only two plays treating the subject of Athaliah had been performed in France prior to Racine's work: a Latin version of *Athaliah*, which had been given at the Collège de Clermont (1658), and a school tragedy in French (1638), performed at the Collège de Tiron (Perche). Neither of these two plays had ever been published and to our knowledge Racine saw neither of them.

Racine's immediate source for *Athaliah* was, of course, the Bible. More specifically, Kings II (11) and Chronicles II (22 and 23). An inveterate reader of the Bible, Racine could not help but be drenched by its spirit and forcefulness. He certainly fell under the spell of the imagistic enunciations of the Prophets, Isaiah, Jeremiah, Ezekiel, and was highly receptive to the musical qualities intrinsic to the Psalms.

Greek influences are also discernible in *Athaliah*. Certain similarities between Euripides' *Ion,* a drama treating the legend concerning the son of Creusa and Apollo, have been underscored. The scene, for example, in which Creusa interrogates Ion has been likened to the one in which Athaliah questions Jehoash.[7] Resemblances between *Athaliah* and Sophocles' *Electra* (the recognition scene), also between *Athaliah* and *Oedipus Rex* (the secret which is kept from the hero, but revealed to the audience), have been underlined. Certainly, Racine did not repudiate such influences. Indeed, in his preface he mentions the effect Greek drama had upon his writings.

> I have also tried to imitate that continuity of action of the ancients, which ensures that their stage is never left empty; the intervals be-

tween the acts being marked by the heavens and moralizing of the Chorus commenting on all that takes place.[8]

The Jewesses by Garnier, *Rodogune* and *Polyeucte* by Corneille, *The League's Triumph* by Nérée have also been thought of as having exerted a strong influence upon Racine's *Athaliah*. There is no doubt that Racine drank deeply from the mainstream of literature. Nevertheless, he tapped his own springs, and wholly fresh creations gushed forth from them, vigorous in their intensity.

✦ ✦ ✦

The Book of Kings, from which Racine drew his play, relates the history of the Hebrews, beginning with the last days of King David (973) to the release of Jehoiachin from his Babylonian prison 561 B.C.E.[9] The Book of Chronicles or the *Paraleipomena*, the Greek title, equally important as a historical basis for Racine's play, is a history of Judaism from Adam to Cyrus (538 B.C.E.). Supplementary information is given in this work concerning the Kings of Judah and other details.[10]

Racine chose the story of Athaliah, daughter of Ahab and Jezebel and mother of Ahaziah, to dramatize. It must be recalled that Jezebel, renowned for her cruelties, her deceits, and her persecution of the Prophets, had also introduced the worship of Baal to the Kingdom of Israel and had a temple constructed to his worship in Jerusalem. After her husband's death, Jehu became King of Israel. Though she tried to seduce him, he would not stand for her evil ways and had her thrown out of the window, trampled on by horses, and her carcass eaten by dogs. Athaliah, her daughter, married Joram, King of Judah. She continued the worship of Baal and persuaded her husband to follow her in her idolatrous ways. Destiny reserved a severe fate for both: all their children except Ahaziah were killed by the Arabs and Philistines, while Joram died of an excruciating malady. After Ahaziah reigned for one year, he decided to visit Jehu, and was killed by his order. When Athaliah learned of the massacre, she usurped the throne, then had all the progeny (forty-two children) of the House of David exterminated.

> And then Athaliah the mother of Ahaziah saw that her son was dead, she arose and destroyed all the seed royal.[11]

Jehoshebath, Ahaziah's sister and daughter of Joram by another woman, noticed the little Jehoash, still breathing. She took him and brought him to her husband, Jehoiada, the Chief Priest of the Hebrews, who hid him in the Temple where he was brought up in secrecy.

Racine's play begins at this point. It takes place in the Temple in Jerusalem.

Act I. Abner, one of the officers of the Kingdom of Judah, comes to see Jehoiada, High Priest of the Hebrews. He deplores the worship of Baal in his land. Jehoiada, however, is confident of God's power. When alone with his wife, Jehoshebath, he tells her that the moment for action has now arrived. The identity of Jehoash, legitimate king of Judah, whom they have brought up in the Temple under the name of Aliacin, must be revealed. Jehoshebath, however, fears for the young lad's life.

Act II. Zachariah, Jehoiada's son, rushes onto the scene terrorized. Athaliah has entered the Temple and has seen Aliacin. She is shocked by this encounter. Athaliah explains the reasons for her consternation to her faithful Mattan, Grand Priest of Baal. She has had a dream in which the very child she now sees in the Temple has stabbed her. She insists upon discovering the identity of this lad. She questions him and is touched and moved by his simple and straightforward answers. She asks him to come to the palace and live there. She offers him wealth and pleasures. He, however, refuses Athaliah and she is angered.

Act III. Mattan, who has prodded Athaliah to demand the child from Jehoiada, arrives at the Temple. He is certain that Jehoiada will refuse to deliver the child, thereby giving him an excuse to destroy the Temple and annihilate the Jews, leaving him spiritual ruler of Judah. Jehoiada is aware of the critical situation. He has the Temple doors closed. Suddenly, the Divine spirit flows into him. He has a prophetic vision in which he sees clearly the fate of the Hebrews, a disastrous future followed by a glorious renaissance.

Act IV. The great ceremony takes place. Jehoash is told of his true identity and is anointed king. Just as Jehoash promises to remain faithful to Hebraic law and tradition, a young Levite announces the arrival of Athaliah and her army. Jehoiada orders resistance. He invites the chorus to prayer.

Act V. Zachariah relates the details of Jehoash' coronation. Athaliah enters the Temple. She demands both Jehoash and King David's treasure which, it has been said, is hidden in the Temple. Jehoiada feigns compliance. After Athaliah enters, Jehoiada pulls back the curtains, reveals Jehoash sitting on the throne. Moments later, Athaliah finds herself surrounded by an army of Levites. The proclamation of Jehoash as King, we are told, has led to the dispersal of the queen's army and the strangulation of Mattan. Athaliah, powerless, curses Jehoash and is dragged from the Temple and put to death.

I

Athaliah is a *vagina dentata* type: authoritarian, domineering, cruel, amoral, power-hungry. She is a woman who is guided by affects and clearly not by reason. She functions on the most primitive of levels and is one of Racine's most primordial beings. Uncontrolled, opinionated, unable to discern the meaning of "moral judgment,"[12] she seeks to destroy everything in the way of her path to power. The tension and consequently the fire which is generated by her turmoil and her constant battle with events and people are the heart of the drama. Athaliah shares certain characteristics with other Racinian figures such as Hermione and Roxana, yet there is something about her which makes her unique among his heroines. Unlike the others, her bloodthirstiness (more so than Agrippina's) is the outcome of an excruciating pain experienced long before the outset of the drama, the murder of her son Ahaziah. Unable to bear this loss, she went wild with fury, like a maimed animal. Hurt turned to revenge. She had the offsprings of the House of David murdered. A solitary figure now, she tries to fill the void in her heart through an insatiable power lust. The feeling value or love principle (Eros) within her personality, as a consequence, has become so repressed as to be virtually nonexistent. A power-driven female is usually divested of individual "womanly" characteristics and, as a result, is transformed into a collective mythical figure. In Athaliah's case, she becomes a tyrannical Queen.

In no way does Athaliah resemble the warm, tender, mourning mother, bereft of her sons (Andromache, Hecuba); rather, she is the prototype of a raging demoniacal murderess, Medea in a way, but more like Lilith, Adam's first wife according to the Talmud, or Lamia, the night spirit or "evil demon" of Greek religion. The Lilith-Lamia types, along with their sisters, the Sphinx, Gaia, Sheba, and Delilah, are all death-dealing, elemental figures and are classified as Terrible Mother archetypes.

Athaliah's crimes are just as blatant and artful as those of her prototypes, perhaps even more dangerous. In addition to her fiercely vicious acts, her homicidal mania, her offenses take on mythic proportions because they are also of a metaphysical or religious nature. Her actions represent, symbolically, a death struggle between two universal principles, Yahweh's patriarchal, monistic, spiritual religion and Baal's matriarchal, polytheistic, and materialistic view of life. Athaliah in effect continued the worship of Baal which her mother

Jezebel had first introduced into Israel,[13] setting up her own priest-hood with its "shameful mysteries,"[14] defying Yahweh and ever pre-pared to attack Him and His sanctuary, the Temple. Removed from the personal level, Athaliah's fight assumed cosmic proportions; mystery, fright, and the supernatural pulsated within every area of her activities.

As a mythical figure, Athaliah can be looked upon not only as a negative mother archetype, but also as a positive one. Like Lucifer, the "light bringer," she is an irritating and destructive force introduced into a given situation in order to force a step in human development. In this case, she provokes the Hebrews into establishing a patriarchal society and, by the same token, to take stock of themselves. Athaliah is action personified, a catalyzer. The agent of her enormous energy is buried within her unconscious and emerges from this irrational world in the form of a dream. It is the dream which provokes Athaliah to enter the Temple, bringing about, thereby, a head-on collision be-tween the two opposing religious principles as represented by Yahweh and Baal.

The oneiromantic visions thrust up into Athaliah's conscious mind during her dream indicate the urgency of her plight. Because of the dream's importance and because of the light it sheds on the drama, it will be analyzed in detail.

Athaliah's dream can be divided into two parts: past and present. In the first part, she sees her mother Jezebel coming to her in "deep night" and "arrayed in pomp, as on the day she died."[15] She speaks to her daughter and warns her of the terrible fate awaiting her unless she kills "the cruel God of the Jews." Now Jezebel's "shadow seems to lean over her bed"; and when Athaliah extends her hands to kiss her mother, the form she believes she is touching disintegrates and she finds herself holding onto bones and bruised flesh.

> Yet all I found was but a horrid mush
> Of bones and mangled flesh, dragged in the slush,
> Of bloody strips, and limbs all shameless scarred,
> That bit by bit the wrangling dogs devoured.[16]

In the second half of the dream Athaliah sees a child clothed "in shining raiment," and just as she is admiring his sweetness, modesty, and nobility, she feels him plunging a dagger into her breast.

> At sight of him my fainting spirits rose—
> But when, reviving from my fatal fears,
> I praised his sweetness and his modest mien,
> I sudden felt as though the treacherous boy
> Had plunged a murderous knife deep in my breast.[17]

One must recall that, when under the sway of dreams, a feeling of oneness with the universe sweeps over the dreamer, resulting in an elemental attachment to the *pleromatic* world.[18] When living on such a primitive level, one is much more receptive to certain unknown and seemingly "unbelievable" contents which flash into the conscious mind, a *"reality in potentia."*[19] Since the unknown exists in the unconscious either as past, present, or future and reveals itself under certain circumstances in the form of symbols and images, it can be looked upon as "Janus-faced," pointing back "to a pre-conscious, prehistoric world of instincts," while, at the same time it "potentially anticipates the future."[20] What occurred in Athaliah's dream was a resuscitation of her empirical past and a symbolic view of what is to come.

What was the symbolic significance of this dream that its effect should have been so intense and its dominion so extensive? When Athaliah saw Jezebel's shadow leaning over her in her dream she was in effect looking on her own destructive, guilt-ridden nature through projection.[21] Seemingly, Athaliah had identified with her mother to such an extent that she had never been able to grow as an individual; stunted, passive in this respect, she lived a "shadow existence" in her actions and her beliefs.[22] If her life were to pursue its course, certainly Athaliah would tread in her mother's footsteps.

The fact that Jezebel was "arrayed in pomp," the very clothes she wore on the day she died, indicates the sensual and earthly nature of her attitude as opposed to that of the moralistic force she calls the "cruel Jewish God," the bitter adversary of the ithyphallic Baal. The patriarchal and spiritual society Yahweh represented, therefore, must be destroyed if the Athaliah-Jezebel brand is to survive.

Athaliah reaches out to touch her mother, expressing the harmony she feels while within her fold. Instead, she comes into contact with disintegrated, decayed bones and flesh, trampled on by horses and fought over and half-eaten by dogs. Horses usually represent man's instinctual physical nature; in Jezebel's case, and in her daughter's, this aspect of their personalities has taken possession of them, driving them wild and compelling them to act as destructive beasts. Though bones usually represent life and strength, in this instance they are associated with decay, rotted flesh, and blood, the implication here being that in their present condition they have lost all usefulness. In effect, they have become negative elements and must be eaten, digested and absorbed, symbolically speaking, by some outside entity or being in order to be reborn or transformed into something positive. In Athaliah's dream, the dog is the aggressive instrument which can effect the change necessary for renewal. The animal, legendary companion of the dead, has now become the mutilator of the Terrible Mother, eater of corpses and, like the jackal-headed Anubis, is a dismemberer and then a restorer. The negative-destructive attitude, as represented by Jezebel and her shadowy daughter, have met with a violent end.

The second section of the dream does not deal with dismemberment, but with the image of the child, Jehoash. It tries to make Athaliah aware of the extreme danger to her if her present attitude persists and propels her actions. The child, as opposed to the archetypal image of the old man representing the past, stands for the future, the fresh, the birth of a new point of view. Jehoash has extremely appealing characteristics; he is dressed in priestly and dazzling robes, he looks "noble," "modest," and "gentle." Strangely enough, this child is also capable of horrendous acts, according to the dream. He is then a *complexio oppositorum*, for within him cohabit good and evil. We must, therefore, presume that the extremes in Athaliah's dream (as seen in the image of her mother Jezebel and the child Jehoash) are inchoate elements within her own personality. This is made obvious when Athaliah begins to experience emotions she had thought were non-existent within her. She is utterly captivated by Jehoash' sincerity, his nobility; she feels gentleness and even love welling up within her. Caught off balance or unable to adjust to the new emotions she is now experiencing, her facade of harshness crumbles. Unwittingly, therefore, she exposes her Achilles' heel, the feeling principle, that whole area within her personality which she has repressed and which has remained undeveloped. The child (or what he stands for) is, in effect, the killer of Athaliah's chthonic aspects (those characteristics belonging to the Terrible Mother archetype), ready at all times to destroy the hero if he does not bring about her demise first.

Athaliah's dream, one of the pivotal elements of the drama, immersed her into her own transpersonal realm, her collective unconscious. The emotions and images gushing forth concomitantly are so potent as to remain fixed in her mind. Try as she will, through prayer to Baal, begging him for comfort and calm, the vision gnaws and persecutes her. The dream returns three times in all its gore. Indeed, she is engulfed, trapped like a wildcat within her own inner world. Desperate, she declares that a force beyond her control has driven her to the Temple where she seeks "to attack God in his very sanctuary."[23]

Athaliah's nightmare then is the catalyzing agent. It compels her to go to the Temple to destroy Yahweh's earthly realm. As she enters the Temple, a territory foreign to her sensual ways, something frightening and outer-worldly jars her, suddenly intrudes upon the picture.

Athaliah freezes. Rigid. Paralyzed in her utterance. Temporary aphasia. She has seen something that has very nearly catapulted her into another realm.

> But all at once her tongue was frozen dumb
> And all her pride was stricken to the dust.
> Her rolling eyes, in terror, stared at us . . .[24]

What has Athaliah seen at this moment? The young Jehoash. Why is his presence in the Temple so horrendous an experience? Because the boy in her dream has now appeared in flesh and blood. A very nearly parallel scene to that in her vision. The same tender feelings are expressed now in Jehoash's presence.

> What miracle dismays, distresses me?
> That sweetness of his voice, his childish grace,
> Make my antipathy insensibly . . .
> Can it be possible that I am moved by pity?[25]

Startled, bewildered, she begins questioning the meaning of the new emotions which have arisen within her. Can she possibly be responsive to pity? she questions. As a preventative measure, she quickly reverts to her enticing Jezebel-like facade, tries to lure Jehoash to her palace, promising him glory, wealth, all the material possessions. When he rejects the "matter" ("mother" earth, the "matriarchal") offered him and opts for the patriarchal and spiritual Yahweh, Athaliah reacts still more harshly, attempting to suppress her new-born feelings of tenderness. A conflict ensues of which Athaliah is not even aware, tenderness and humanity versus rigidity and bestiality.

Even Mattan notices a drastic change in Athaliah's demeanor. No longer is she the powerful Queen figure, a woman capable of rising beyond her personal existence into the collective, but rather a timid woman, filled with remorse, fear, guilt, hesitation.

> For two days now, I do not know her, friend.
> She is no more that bold, clear-sighted Queen,
> Raised high above the weakness of her sex,
> Who shattered all at once her startled foes,
> And knew full well the price of moments lost.
> A vain remorse entangles her great soul;
> She flounders, hesitates, just like a woman.[26]

Mattan's assessment of Athaliah's character is indeed incisive. He notes well the outward manifestations of inner changes. Indeed, she has become "human." No longer the symbolical mother goddess, the atemporal, archetypal figure, Athaliah now begins to experience weakness, the emotions and pain known to a real mother. The heartless, defiant woman who swore vengeance has now been superseded by another whose anger is "wavering . . . uncertain." Athaliah only now becomes vulnerable.

Mattan, until then subservient to Athaliah, tries to destroy her. As her power diminishes, so his increases. Unsettled, lacking in self-confidence, no longer relying upon her own judgment, she listens to Mattan. Instead of evaluating her situation and achieving a new level of consciousness which would have saved her, she resists the help offered by her unconscious (in the form of a dream) and lets herself be guided by her regressive consort-priest. There remains no possibility of a positive conclusion. Insidiously, and to serve his own ends, Mattan urges Athaliah to demand that Jehoash be delivered to the palace.

When Athaliah enters the Temple, an area she should have fled had she followed the warning offered in her dream, the atmosphere tingles. She strides forward, demands the child and treasure, is nearly blinded by the sight of the "royal child." In a desperate attempt to destroy the prophecy as revealed in her dream, she calls upon soldiers to destroy the child king. It is all in vain.

Unlike Phaedra, who takes her own life after having caused destruction about her, or Roxana, who is assassinated after having disseminated death, Athaliah is killed, but her demise makes possible the advent of the child king—a new spiritually oriented and positive society.

✓ ✓ ✓

Since Mattan, the priest of Baal, is under the dominion of the Great Mother, Athaliah, he can be looked upon as her male consort.

The Canaanites looked upon Baal as the "husband" of the land. He was the fertilizer of "mother earth" and, as a reward, demanded the first fruits which emerged. Taking this ritual literally, the first-born were sacrificed to Baal. When archaeologists began excavating Gezer they found small bones placed in jars which dated form 1100 B.C.E. The Canaanite religion was neither ethical nor moral. It focused on the orgiastic, sensual, luxury-loving aspect of "mother" nature. The fertility and magic rites of Baalim were anathema to the Hebrews. When Jezebel married King Ahab of the Kingdom of Israel (847), it is said that she brought with her four hundred and fifty of Baal's sensual and ecstatic prophets.[27] Athaliah continued this ithyphallic worship.

Mattan, always subservient to Athaliah, wants more than anything to assert himself, to prove his worth. He feels he can do so only
by annihilating Jahweh and his ministers. In his capacity as evildoer,
Mattan is far less colorful and dynamic a figure than was Haman.
Unlike the self-made Haman, whose force lay in his capacity to incite and, through this struggle, to cause clarity, Mattan gives the impression of being a castrated figure whose very efforts lead to blunder
upon blunder.

Mattan first comes upon the stage in response to Athaliah's summoning (II, v). He listens patiently as she relates her dream (as do the
confidants in other Racinian dramas). He even offers suggestions, that
the child be killed and the Temple razed. Though a weakly structured
being, Mattan, however, possesses one important feature; he is extraordinarily perceptive. It is he who guesses the illustrious ancestry
of the "child king"; it is Mattan who is convinced that some "monster"[28] is being nurtured in the Temple. It is he too who senses the
change which has occurred within Athaliah's personality.

Mattan is a solitary figure, an apostate without a family, an un-
believer. Power is the only instinct which can fill the void in his being.
He must, therefore, if he is to survive, destroy all obstacles in his path,
Jehoiada and the Temple.

> When I made bold to stand for the High Priesthood,
> My plots, my broils, my tears, my black despair?
> Beaten by him, I took another course,
> And held fast to the Court with all my soul.
> I captured by degrees the royal ear,
> And soon my voice was made oracular.
> I studied flattering royal hearts and whims,
> And strewed with flowers their paths that edge abysses . . .
> The God I have abandoned troubles me,
> Still planting in my soul some lingering dread;
> And this is what excites and feeds my fury.
> Happy if I, by ravaging his Temple,
> Could thus show up His hate as impotent,
> And plunging in the ruin, sack, and corpses,
> With crime on crime drown all my vain remorse![29]

What Mattan is trying to destroy in effect is not so much Jehoiada and
the Temple, but rather those forces which he projects upon them. He
must obliterate his growing feelings of remorse and guilt which are
concomitant with apostasy, unmanliness, and indecisiveness. To divert

these emotions from their natural course, he supersedes feelings of hate and violence. Such activity (or over-activity) is one of the best ways to prevent reflection. Repose, on the contrary, encourages thought.

When Mattan confronts Jehoiada, his hatred flares. His rational order of consciousness is so upset by the upsurge of his affective world that he thrusts aside logos. His actions will be totally dominated by his world of instincts.[30] What irritates him so when he sees Jehoiada, a being devoid of deceit, of treachery, clear in his outlook, a pillar of strength? Mattan sees his counterpart in him and cannot stand viewing his own weaknesses, which become all the more blatant when placed in apposition to Jehoiada.

Unlike Haman (*Esther*) and Narcissus (*Britannicus*), who are positive evildoers, Mattan has neither positive nor negative traits. First and foremost, he is a function of his Queen whom he serves. Unable to cope with his own inadequacies, he is a being who never comes into his own, is never enlightened. Though he possesses insight, the new feelings which arise from his perceptions do not represent an act of cognition because the new contents are never assimilated or understood in terms of his own life. He is, therefore, like a dead leaf, pushed here and there by someone or by his own instincts.

Mattan inspires neither pity nor fear. He is actually quite extraneous to the drama and is included in it perhaps in contast to Jehoiada, to underline the dualism inherent in the situation and to exemplify a disintegrating matriarchal society.

✼ ✼ ✼

Jehoiada, like Mordecai, is a man who has experienced the *numinosum*, who lives and loves for and with his God. Unlike Mordecai, however, Jehoiada is a fully integrated being in the sense that he has experienced earthly as well as heavenly love. He has a wife, a son, and a daughter. The fact that his family numbers four, the quaternity, symbolizing "wholeness" and "completeness," is another indication of the balance which reigns within the psyche of the head of this family unit. Jehoiada in this respect is unique in Racinian drama. He is endowed with spirit and with flesh. Such relatedness, *hieros gamos*, between the spiritual and the earthly permits him to become a mediator between God and his people, a symbol of God's fruitful union with the earth, a Prophet.

The prophetic vision Jehoiada experiences (III,vii) guides his actions and gives him the strength to carry them out. The scene of the "prophecy" is one of the most remarkably moving sections of all Racinian theatre. The swell and breadth of Divinity not only takes possession of Jehoiada, but overflows these boundaries, impregnating everybody exposed to the scene with supernatural, atemporal feelings. As Jehoiada speaks, his words seem to grow in intensity, to reach a crescendo of emotion and become very nearly unbearable, like a strident note held for minutes on end. Then suddenly the flux ceases, as though the tonal modulations have come to a violent end, at the edge of a precipice. It would be almost impossible to have written such feelings into Jehoiada's verses, to express such poignancy of tone so reminiscent of Isaiah, Jeremiah, and Hosea's outpourings, had not the author himself experienced such an inflow of Divinity at one time or another during his life.

From the very outset of the drama, we note that Jehoiada possesses a highly charged and powerful personality. Indeed, it is one which casts a spell on all those surrounding him. It is also present in his speech, in the images he uses. When, for example, mention is made of the "bloody" Athaliah, who attacks the Hebrew God, Jehoiada counters with an image reflecting Yahweh's power, the drying up of the Red Sea.

> He who can sudden tame the raging waves,
> Can well confound the plots of evil men.[31]

That force of will, which is God's in this instance, is also infused into Jehoiada's being, compelling him to live energetically and dynamically. The miracle of the holy flame is another example Jehoiada gives to indicate divinity's omniscience and immanence: "With fire from Heaven descending on the Altar."[32]

The fact that Jehoiada is a visionary does not blind him to the reality of his people's plight. Rather than being blinded by his vision, overwhelmed and subjugated by it, such anamnesis as he experiences enlarges his vision. Activity, therefore, and not passivity, results. How deeply religious can one be, he questions, if action does not follow?

Once Jehoiada has made his decision—that deceit (hiding the King child) is no longer in order—the battle between Yahweh (Jehoiada and his family, the child Jehoash) must be fought against Baal (Athaliah, Mattan). Like the zealots who fought so valiantly against the Romans at Massada, so Jehoiada will take his stand: righteousness, morality, ethics. Jehoshebath, his wife, is fearful of the outcome. She realizes that the balance of power weighs heavily against them. They have no soldiers, no armaments. The enemy has everything. Not everything, Jehoiada counters, because God is not on their side.

And God on our side count you not at all?
God, Who for innocent orphans deigns to fight
And founds upon the weak His shining might;[33]

Jehoiada is now being propelled by a catalyst within his very being. Intense, he speaks as though in the very center of a whirlwind.
Jehoiada feels degraded when such an apostate as this votary of Baal
comes into his presence. He orders the doors to the Temple shut. The
climactic moment has arrived. To his terror-stricken wife, he offers the
consolation which comes with love and faith in Divinity.

As Jehoiada speaks, his words swell in intensity, reaching a powerful crescendo, until they become very nearly unbearable, like pro-
tracted hammer sounds. Suddenly, the tonal nuances end abruptly and
something seems to possess him. He begins to tremble. An intangible,
amorphous entity encapsulates him. His eyes open wide.

Is it God's spirit taking hold of me?
It is. It warms. It speaks. My eyes are opened,
And the dim centuries revealed to me.
O Levites, let me have harmonious music
To aid the transports of the holy spirit.[34]

The Divine is speaking through him, announcing the eschatological
events.

Under the spell of God's presence, rational order dissolves. The
emotions Jehoiada now experiences are the product of autonomous
contents emanating from an unknown subliminal source within his
own being. His conscious mind succumbs to his intuition, which is dependent upon the unconscious process.[35]

To inject the import of Jehoiada's prophecy, Racine infuses the
entire scene with a counterpoint of speech and choral singing to the
accompaniment of musical instruments. Images and metaphors pierce
the atmosphere like flames, as the prophet reveals the terrifying knowledge of the destruction of the Temple, the scorching of the land, the
anguished cries and lamentations emanating from the Wailing Wall,
the pathetically painful birth of a new Jerusalem as it emerges from
the desert clarity, raising its head once again and paving the way for
renewed light.

Sinners, be consumed: The Lord is awake . . .
Jerusalem, object of my pain.[36]

Jehoiada's vision, like Ezekiel's or Isaiah's, is a primordial experience which affected his entire being and his future course of action.

It gives him strength with God's help, it paves the way for him to follow, it teaches him to inure Jehoash to the hardships ahead.

> Of God's great plans for you and for His People.
> Be brave, my son, and of a shining faith.
> Now is the time to show that zest and zeal
> That deep within your heart my care has planned.[37]

In experiencing divinity within, Jehoiada has come face to face with the *Self*. Such a union between inner and outer man is not merely an unconscious or escapist departure into an artificially constructed paradise; rather, this glimpse of oneness is an act of cognition. For prophecy to be truly valid, it must be a catalyst and be experienced consciously. One of the best-known examples of this type of consciousness was experienced by Moses when he saw "God face to face and by day."[38] What Jehoiada was living through was a *coniunctio* between the collective unconscious as revealed through archetypal imagery, intuitively perceived, and the incisive vision of the conscious personal mind. Such insight into the subliminal workings of the world reveals information concerning past, present, and future activities.[39]

Jehoiada is one of the most powerful father figures in Racine's theatre. He is in reality the final destroyer of the *vagina dentata* type, in the form of Athaliah in this case. It is he also who encourages the maternal, gentle, understanding female figure to reign in conjunction with the family. The importance accorded to such a being in Racine's theatre denotes the place such an *imago Dei* played in his own world. It was the guiding principle which afforded him the equilibrium (his family life) he now enjoyed; the conscious realization of his own worth, his obligations, his piety. Racine's portrayal of the Hebraic Seer-Prophet type also marked the affinity he felt with the Hebrew psyche at this particular time in his life, the preservation and intensification of consciousness within himself because of his understanding of them.[40] No longer a victim of his instincts, he now adhered to a world of moral commandment, not artificially self-described, but rather emerging as a result of his own understanding and acceptance of his shadow personality.

✓ ✓ ✓

Jehoshebath is the prototype of the ideal mother: gentle, kind, pious, submissive, yet endowed with extraordinary heroism. She personifies the positive characteristics of the Great Mother archetype. In this respect, she is almost unique in Racine's theatre. The only character who faintly resembles her is Andromache. Jehoshebath, however, is less outspoken, less intransigent than she, less complex. Indeed, Jehoshebath is unsophisticated. She suffers no moral conflicts. She knows clearly the differences between right and wrong. She is humane and filled with compassion. She reacts in horror at the sight of evil, when Athaliah puts so many children to death, and is always compelled to do what is honorable.

Jehoshebath is the one who saves Jehoash, the King, and in this respect is comparable to the Pharaoh's daughter who saved Moses; to the gardener who rescued King Sargon, who had been set afloat down the Euphrates in a basket by his mother; to Christ, who was nurtured by shepherds according to Saint Luke.

Though Jehoshebath is the fruitful mother, the devoted wife, she is also preoccupied with the spiritual aspects of life. In this respect, then, she has broken the pattern of the Great Mother archetype, the instinctual earth principle which deals only in "matter." Furthermore, Jehoshebath is also the possessor of free will. Like Rebecca and unlike Sarah, she is, to a certain extent, mistress of her own destiny. In addition to this, she can also be looked upon as a redemptive force in that she actively helps save her people by saving Jehoash, by hiding her feelings when it would have been dangerous to reveal them. Jehoshebath then is a woman who is always conscious of her actions, of her role in life.

Jehoshebath is not all-cerebral. She is very feminine, on the contrary, and displays her feelings when she knows it cannot harm. When she does weep, on describing the time she saved Jehoash from his doom, her husband's understanding of these womanly characteristics assures her of the salutary nature of tears: "There's nothing sinful in your tears, dear wife,"[41] he says. Emotions must play a role in life; to cut them out is to inflict lameness upon a personality.[42]

Jehoshebath then represents the female principle integrated into a patriarchal society. Never in danger of losing her femininity, she reacts tenderly, humanely, and with compassion to every situation.

✦ ✦ ✦

The most astounding aspect of _Athaliah_ does not reside merely in the role accorded the Divine, or the strong father image, or the appealing maternal type, but rather in the creation of the child figure.

The child is, symbolically speaking, both the beginning and end, the _renatus in novam infantiam_, because it lives before man comes of age and exists after man no longer does.[43] The child archetype stands for something new, a force in the process of being formed, and, there-fore comes to represent the future, hope, and progress. As he moves toward independence, he struggles for recognition; and because he is a growing force, he comes to represent a future state of consciousness.

When a "sacred" or "divine" child is involved (Moses, Hercules, Sargon, Christ), he frequently symbolizes the mystic center, the phi-losopher's stone which many identify with the God within.[44] These "divine children" share certain characteristics: they have been aban-doned by their parents for one reason or another, they are frequently in danger, they arise miraculously from unknown places and, as a result, are the centers usually of some mystery. The "divine child" must be nurtured as is any ordinary child. Jehoash fulfills all of those require-ments. He was brought up in a Temple by relatives, is of some mys-terious origin, and is called Eliacin when his real name is Jehoash, further increasing his ambiguity.

For Racine, Jehoash is certainly a Christ figure. He is the divine Primordial Man, the "treasure," the *imago Dei*, the most powerful force within Racine's unconscious and his conscious mind. When he created Jehoash, therefore, he made him as perfect as possible, beau-tiful, humble, tender, God's living creation before the sins of man sullied him prior to Adam's fall, *sine macula peccati*.[45] Jehoash's life, consequently, is devoted to God and is nourished by Him.

When Jehoash appears (II,vii), the simplicity of his speech, the righteousness of his thought stuns everyone. It is not until the corona-tion ceremony, however (IV,iii), that his being is infused with a sacred aura, that the entire atmosphere radiates with divine presence. The implications of this ceremony are so vast, the waves of emotion aroused by it are so flamboyant, and the impact of the metaphysical experience so shattering that Racine has the ritual not only enacted on stage, but reported afterward in part by Zachariah (V,i).

The coronation ceremony, looked upon symbolically, is a sacrificial religious ritual. As the divine will made itself manifest in the Temple, speaking through the priest Jehoiada, the young child, Jehoash, was in the process of undergoing an inner transformation, evolving from the realm of the individual to that of the collective, the human to the supra-human, the egocentric to the selfless, boyhood to manhood. Now, Je-hoash must confront the world and its hardships, fulfill the image of the new King, the bearer of goodness.

It might be interesting to examine a certain intrinsic rhythmic pattern at this point. As Athaliah slips down from her role as the archetypal Terrible Mother figure to the individual human level, so at the same time Jehoash ascends from a personal to a suprapersonal being. As the force of Divinity descends into the earthly realm, in this case the Temple, the religious community is imbued with the strength necessary to fight the forces of evil and to display the Ark of the Covenant in all its glory and omnipotence. When danger has reached its peak, Jehoiada tells Jehoash to mount his throne. He then closes the curtains before it. Athaliah enters, demands the child. In one of the most poignantly dramatic moments in the play, Jehoiada draws the curtains and there appears before the Queen the young King in all his dazzling radiance.

> This Temple welcomes him and God preserved him.
> Of David's treasures only he remains.[46]

Suddenly, the inside of the Temple becomes visible, armed Levites rush forth from all corners. Athaliah's soldiers desert her because they too have been overwhelmed by "The voice of the All-Powerful." A new world is now to emerge with Jehoash a leader, ready to devote and sacrifice himself to and for mankind.

> O God, Who seest my pain and my distress,
> O ward off, ward off far from me her curses,
> And never suffer their accomplishment.
> May Jehoash die ere he abandon Thee.[47]

The Hebrews have prayed for the miracle; the miracle of enlightenment has taken place.

II

Divinity is the source and the motivating force behind *Athaliah*, Racine's most powerful and poignant work. Indeed, *Athaliah* could be called a "liturgical" drama. It is set in the holiest of all areas, the Temple where God's will and omniscience is made manifest. A series of events and objects herald forth Divinity's presence: a prophecy, symbols such as the Ark of the Covenant, the presence of the "kingly" child, the coronation ceremony.

Athaliah is also Racine's most perfect play from a structural point of view. As a result of his strict adherence to the unities, the action becomes so concentrated and dense, so imbued with vigor and energy, that the entire work seems to swing forth in a series of mounting crescendoes. The various steps in *Athaliah*, the dream, the prophecy, the coronation ritual, the revelation of the child king, concomitant with the destruction of the forces of evil, are stages in an ever accelerating

drama where lapses or pauses in the action have been completely elim-
inated. *Athaliah* gives readers and audiences alike not one instant to
draw a breath, not one second of relaxation.

Racine's language, so vital and effulgent in all his dramas, so
impregnated with the beauty and sensuality of Greek drama, has now
reached new depths in the *pleroma* of life's process. Divesting itself
of the cluttered raiments of rococo imagery, Racine has reforged on
his own terms, the bone-hard and sinewy language, the biting images
of the Prophets of old. When Racine's characters speak, they talk out
their hearts directly and sincerely to their God as Isaiah had done so
staunchly centuries before when walking forth through the dry and
arid lands of Judah. The images themselves—the Temple, for example
—incised by Racine have been transformed into living and breathing
monuments. The Ark of the Covenant, a vital and viable force, plays
an intrinsic role as it stands "mute" to those bereft of hearing, but
voices its mighty commands to those who have been given the gift of
understanding. The city of Jerusalem is depicted as a being with human traits, infinite compassion, one who weeps over the transgression
of its inhabitants, and walks head high when they stride the path of
righteousness.

✦ ✦ ✦

Since *Athaliah* is a play in which Divinity enjoys a primal role, it
is enacted in the most sacred of areas: the Temple, which King David
had begun to build and which King Solomon completed. For Racine, the
Temple, like the Cathedral, is a sacred area where communion with the
Divine can be experienced. Never before had Racine openly chosen
such a holy locale for a drama. Never had he struck so deeply into the
heart and mind of people and of himself.

For the mystic, the Temple represents the "Center," the core of
the cosmos. Indeed, Philo and Josephus both held that King Solomon's
Temple was a "figurative representation of the cosmos."[48] Included in
the Temple were the seven-branched candelabra symbolizing the seven
heavens and the seven planets, the Ark of the Covenant which contained the two tablets upon which Mosaic law had been inscribed and
which was placed inside the Tabernacle, the holiest of places.[49] Since
God's living word had been imprinted on these scrolls, they came to
represent the spiritual as well as the physical force and energy needed
for perpetual rebirth (eternity), and because of their "containing" quality, they are frequently associated with the womb, the heart, and the

drinking vessel. They are then both energizers and nourishers as well as living entities.

The Temple, therefore, assumes the force of a protagonist living both an exterior and interior existence. On the outside it presents a bold, majestic front; within it is an area replete with secrecy,[50] with mystery, fascination, immense activity and strength.

> As though in the depths of this vast edifice
> God hid an avenger armed to punish her.[51]

It is also a place needful of and offering protection, a holy Temple, "O holy Temple," [52] articulate when necessary and silent if imperative. "The holy arch is mute. . . ."[53] Furthermore, within its walls there resides the "royal child," Jehoash, that "treasure," whose destiny is the determining factor in this drama. When the Temple closes its doors at the end, it envelops the child's enemy, it seals Athaliah's fate, then ejects her from its iron-clad grasp, to be killed by the tidal flow heaving its crushing power against her.

The Temple, Yahweh's sanctuary, stands in the "holy" city of Jerusalem. The city has not only been continually and variously personified by Racine, but was also treated in a similar fashion in the Bible. In Isaiah, for example, Jerusalem is alluded to as a "harlot" (L;21), as a "bridge bringing delight" in the Trito-Isaiah (L.XII, 3–5),[54] as a helpless child in Ezekiel (XVI, 1–4), as a virgin in Jeremiah (31–32).[55] The medieval Christians looked upon the "heavenly" city as "the symbol of the redeemed soul, and the walled city, the symbol of the soul which had come into its own and therewith at the same time, to God."[56] In *Athaliah* Racine looks upon Jerusalem as a ravished woman, "whose hand cut short thy magic years,"[57] and weeping her pain; then able to rise to the calamities which have befallen her and walk head high: "Arise Jerusalem, raise thy haughty head,"[58] unafraid of her neighbors, a leader of people. "The people wish to walk in thy light."[59]

The fact that *Athaliah* takes place in the holy city of Jerusalem, and more specifically in the sacred Temple, indicates a spiritual intimacy on Racine's part with God. He is now able to enter into God's sanctuary totally (his evil aspect projected onto Athaliah and his good elements onto Jehoiada and Jehoshebath) and not merely allude to it. It would seem that an integration of conflicting polarities has occurred within his psyche through projection.

That this "integration" was in the process of taking place can also be attested by the central image in this drama, the child. Archetypal symbol of the *Self*, the child is the fruit or the outcome of a welding

together of formerly opposing polarities (consciousness and unconsciousness, passivity and activity, etc.) within the personality. The
coming together, or the *coniunctio*, of formerly antagonistic entities
paves the way for the creation of a new attitude, a fresh spiritual point
of view which is symbolically represented by the child. Furthermore,
the product which emerges from this union, fostered by the divine, the
child, comes to represent a symbol of unity and totality.[60]

III

The fact that Racine's primal image took the form of a child indicated the harmony and wholeness which had taken possession of his
own self. The disparity between Racine's psychic state when writing
Athaliah and when creating his first play, *The Theban Brothers*, is enormous. *The Theban Brothers* featured two warring royal twins, the
sizygy, two halves of one egg. These brothers not only killed each other,
but were the cause of the death of all the other protagonists in the
work. The series of plays which followed bathed for the most part in
Greek and Roman sunlight, fatality and doom. Phaedra offered no
answer except for man's utter and devastating powerlessness before
the forces of destiny.

After twelve years of silence on Racine's part, a return to Jansenism, a taste of worldly joys in the form of family life, Racine experienced a new understanding of the Scriptures. The Greek and Roman
female types, destructive in the main, still persisted in Racine's group
of females (Athaliah), but to a lesser degree and were countered by
such womanly beings as Esther and Jehoshebath. A deeper realization
of life's forces, as expressed through an assimilation of Jansenist doctrine with its highly moralistic, rigid, stern patriarchal bent, opened up
a whole new world for Racine. He began feeling an affinity, consciously,
with the Hebrews of the Old Testament; and, with such understanding,
new springs and sources of inspiration had been tapped. No longer the
Greek world, but his own heritage, the Judaeo-Christian concepts. This
broadened point of view permitted him to envisage existence not in
terms of death and despair, but rather as a struggle which each being
must undergo in order to bring forth positive and fresh entities, like
the child embedded within each of us which, when allowed to develop,
makes for self-realization.

Racine, it would seem, had become a fulfilled being.

PART IV—A CONSCIENCE AT REST

A Conscience at Rest

"A conscience at rest . . ."[1]

*T*HOUGH Racine's last years were spent actively in the service of Louis XIV, in the capacity of historiographer and Gentleman-in-Ordinary to the Chamber, a great deal of his time was devoted to his home, his family, and his religion.

> The older I become, the more I realize that there is nothing in the world as soothing as a conscience at rest; and to look upon God as a father who will not fail us in any of our needs.[2]

Racine had married, it is to be recalled, Catherine de Romanet, the daughter of a rich Parisian bourgeois, on May 30, 1677. She was a placid, pious, calm and, strangely enough, unlettered woman, a perfect mate for the super-emotional playwright. She offered Racine what he lacked: serenity, stability, patience—qualities his vibrant, tempestuous and passionate nature required. Through her in part, and through God, he thrived and experienced balance and harmony, an equilibrium he had never before known.

Racine's life was made all the happier and fuller with the arrival of his seven children. He watched carefully over their education; and, when he was forced to remain away from his household, he was always there in spirit, writing assiduously to his wife or to his children. Nothing escaped his interest or concern: their studies, their sicknesses, their joys or heartbreaks—minor and major events were the source of Racine's solicitous preoccupations.[3]

Racine also experienced a sense of fulfillment in his children. His eldest son, Jean-Baptiste, always a good student, honorable in character, pleasant in temperament, inherited his father's title as Gentleman-in-Ordinary to the Chamber. Such an acquisition helped him considerably in furthering his career as Attaché to the French Embassy in the Low Countries. Racine's youngest son, Louis, became a poet and author of *Memoirs on the Life and Works of Jean Racine*.

Racine's eldest daughter, Marie-Catherine, for whom his affection was most pronounced, was, it must be admitted, a rather strange and nervous child. She probably inherited much of Racine's extreme sensitivity and passionate personality. As an adolescent, she had wanted to become a postulant at Port-Royal. Since the King, however, had forbidden the reception of novices at Port-Royal, she entered, and much to her chagrin, the Carmelite order. It must be surmised that she was unhappy in this atmosphere. She experienced a fall, after which her health became so bad that Racine had her brought home. It was decided then and there that she should marry and give up all thoughts of entering a religious order. A serious, pious, and gracious young man, Moramber de Riberpré, was introduced to her. Aside from his most endearing personality, he was also able to provide her with material advantages. The couple was married on January 7, 1699 in a Jansenist atmosphere.

Another daughter, Anne, joined the Ursulines at Melun. Racine was deeply moved by the ceremony, which he described in a most poignant manner in a letter dated November 10, 1689, to his son Jean-Baptiste, stationed at the Hague. He wrote that when he saw his daughter, looking like an "angel," take the veil, he could not "cease sobbing," so traumatized was he by the spectacle. The very same year that Anne became an Ursuline nun, his daughter Franchon, twelve years of age, was being prepared by her great aunt Mother Agnès de Sainte-Thècle for her first communion. Racine, it has been said, would have been very happy to see all his daughters take the veil.

Racine was not only a devoted husband and father, but a kind brother as well. When, for example, his sister Marie or her husband was in need, as they had been on several occasions, he was always there to offer and give financial aid, friendship, and understanding as well. In his *Correspondence* with his sister, one can feel the warmth and tenderness of his affection for her. Marie too was grateful for her brother's solicitous attitude. In response to his generosities, she would frequently send him some good country cheese and other nourishing products, looking out for his welfare as best she could under the circumstances. Needless to say, her citified brother and his family were appreciative of her gesture too. Even closer ties were established after the birth of Racine's children, who were frequently sent to wet nurses in the Ferté-Milon. There, Marie watched their growth and took care to further their well-being.

There were times when Racine was forced to stay with the King. When the monarch was not well, for example, Racine was asked to read to him. Louis XIV found Racine's voice so rich and sonorous, his diction so precise, the warmth of his tone so moving, that he enjoyed the hours the playwright spent with him. Plutarch, as read by Racine, became a source of fascination for the King. In 1696, Louis XIV bestowed another honor upon the writer and made him Counselor-Secretary to the King.

As the monarch's historiographer, a post he shared with his friend Boileau, Racine was compelled to travel about the land. In 1678, for example, he accompanied Louis on his campaign to Gand and Ypres; a year later, to Luxembourg. From 1691 to 1693, from time to time, Racine was present at the "famous" siege of Namur. There he was compelled to undergo many hardships and was even within cannon-fire range.

Unfortunately, few works written by Racine as official historiographer are extant. *The History of the Reign of Louis XIV* was, according to Louis Racine, given to the playwright's friend M. de Valincour for safekeeping. When this man's home burned, the manuscript was destroyed. The only historical works remaining are *A Historical Eulogy of the King's Conquest from the Years 1672–1678*, a *Relating of what took place at the Siege of Namur*, and *Notes and Fragments*.

Racine's brief *Summary of the History of Port-Royal*, which he had begun in 1693 and which remained unfinished, has survived. This quite remarkable work paints, in moving tones, the persecution of an extraordinary religious order. It was certainly written with the intention of relating the historical events as they had been experienced by a contemporary with veracity and objectivity. Fervor and warmth, nevertheless, are inherent in every line of the work. The fact that Racine sought to write such a document, and the love which he brought to this undertaking, is an indication of the "devotion" he felt to his childhood home.

His rapprochement with Port-Royal both on a literary plane and on a material and physical one was dangerous indeed. He not only visited Port-Royal, together with his family, particularly at religious festivals, but he helped his aunt Mother Agnès de Sainte-Thècle, who had in the meantime become Abbess of Port-Royal, in whatever way he could and very nearly on a daily basis.[4] In addition to this show of courage, considering the King's negative attitude toward this religious order, Racine voiced enormous concern in both his letters and verbally, to friend and foe, when the Great Arnauld's health began to suffer. His presence at Arnauld's funeral (1694), a highly dangerous act, was another indication of his deep feelings for Port-Royal and all it had meant to him throughout his tumultuous existence.

Racine's affinity with God, who had become the focal point of his existence, was more important to him, seemingly, than his role as courtier at the Court of Louis XIV. Though he always tried to oblige the King in any way he could—indeed, went out of his way to do so because he knew full well that his presence at court could help his family's fortune—his spiritual needs came first. Racine's heart and his soul, his whole life at this time, was immersed in religious readings. It has been postulated that Racine's most urgent desire would have been to see the Petites Ecoles at Port-Royal once again open their doors, permitting them to function as they had when Racine had been a youth, and offer others the benefits of their superb education. Dreams. All in vain.

The year 1698 was a particularly difficult one for Racine. It has been called by many scholars the year of his "disgrace." In a letter to Madame de Maintenon, Racine not only expresses his devotion to her and to the King anew, but his dismay and pain at her having closed her door to him and at his monarch's change of heart on his behalf. This alteration of attitude, he implied, was due to his inferred dealings with Port-Royal.[5] Henceforth, Racine was to appear less frequently at Court.

It was approximately at this period, in April 1698, that Racine was to feel the first signs of what was to become a painful and fatal illness. It began, as he himself described it in a letter to his son at the Hague,[6] with severe pains in his back and erysipelas on his stomach. The symptoms disappeared several weeks later. In fact, Racine felt very much better. By October, however, the pain returned and in a far more virulent form, with accompanying hardness around the liver area. The doctors suggested an operation. The abscess they discovered was too far gone to warrant its extraction. Racine was too weak.

For nearly a year now Racine had been preoccupied with thoughts of death and salvation. Such ideas are present in his *Correspondence* and in statements made by his friends. A definite change of personality was taking place, seemingly. Racine had developed patience and tranquility, great understanding, feelings which brought him a sense of peace and repose. Racine must have felt his condition to be more serious than the doctors had intimated. In this frame of mind he made out his will, a deeply touching document.

Conclusion

"No energy is lost in the world, nor is it merely
the souls of men that are immortal but all
their actions as well. They live on through
their effects." (Goethe's *World View*.)

HOW can we who live in the twentieth century benefit from the works of a man writing three hundred years earlier? What force or power has Racine breathed into his characters and situations that these speak so forcefully to us today?

From a dramatic point of view, the excitement and enjoyment of Racine's works stem from the sheer beauty and poetry of the lines themselves and from the moving and poignant spectacle provided for us by modern directors. From a philosophical and psychological point of view even greater satisfaction can be experienced in terms of the dramas' mythical qualities, the characters and the themes involved.

Racine's dramas plunge audiences into the heart of the myth, into a world in eternal ebullition, a realm which dates back to the very dawn of man and reaches forward to contemporary times. Within this seething domain conjured forth by the dramatist, conglomerations of prowling passions take on corporeal form and live out their existence as Agrippina, Phaedra, Roxana, Iphigenia, Jahoiada. . . . Mixtures and blends of all types with whom we can identify today swirl about in the teeming abyss which forms Racine's heterogeneous panoply.

Racine's gargoyle-like beings who frenzy about on stage are possessed of eternal characteristics. They are generally dominated by their instincts. They long for happiness and fufillment, for some kind of inner harmony, but remain most frequently powerless before the forces of a crushing destiny. Undaunted in their attempts to acquire the object

I desire that after my death my body be carried to Port-Royal des Champs and buried there in the cemetery at the foot of M. Hamon's grave. I humbly pray the Mother Abbess and the nuns to grant me this honour, of which I admit myself most unworthy, both on account of the scandals of my past life and because I have done so little to credit the excellent education that I received at Port-Royal, and the great examples of piety and penitence there placed before me. I have been but a barren enthusiast! But the more I have offended God the more I need the prayers of so holy a Community to draw towards me the Divine Mercy.[7]

Racine was ready to approach his Creator. He died peacefully on Tuesday, April 21st, 1699, of what some people have since and variously diagnosed as hepatic cancer and tuberculosis.

Racine's body was placed at Saint-Sulpice in Paris the first night after his death; then, accompanied by two priests, it was set to rest at Port-Royal des Champs, as he had requested. On December 2, 1711 after Port-Royal had been razed—the very graveyard where he had been buried, desecrated—Racine's body was transferred to the Church of Saint-Etienne du Mont. There, it was again laid to rest.

or objects of their desire, they dilate and smolder with passion each time a confrontation occurs, then wreak havoc on the world about them. Not until Racine's later plays (*Iphigenia, Esther, Athaliah*) are audiences exposed to anything but humanity's negative characteristics: hate, rage, lust, jealousy. Even when spiritual facets are manifested in characters, they are so weak as to be totally ineffective or are counteracted by utterly vicious types so powerful as to annihilate them almost instantly.

The web woven by Racine's creatures, the themes dramatized in the plays, are also pertinent today. Youth is still excoriated in its thrust for independence (Eteocles, Polynices, Nero); the hero is still inflamed as he launches on his conquests (Alexander the Great, Achilles); the ruler is still assailed by conflicts as he attempts to adjust to a collective existence while trying all the while to save his personal world from annihilation (Agamemnon, Mithridates); the martyr is still inflated with fervor with each plunge forward (Iphigenia); the guilt-ridden still cringe as they seek redemption (Phaedra); the spiritually oriented still possess the fortitude and inner fire of the Prophets of old (Mordecai, Jehoiada); the faceless and identityless are still unable to relate to themselves or to others (Pyrrhus). The list is long and the turmoils ever present.

Audiences can profit from Racine's plays if these are experienced in a very special manner. It is not a question here of undergoing *catharsis*, of projecting onto the stage happenings and reliving, thereby, the anguishes of the protagonists involved, ejecting these at the conclusion of the performance and stepping forth from the theatre cleansed and healed.

The procedure is far more difficult and involves extreme honesty with self. When a spectator observes the characters on stage in all their viciousness or beauty, he may come to realize that he is not watching artificially contrived beings, but rather very real people with whom he shares something in common. He acknowledges the fact that he is imbued with similar traits, perhaps not so pronounced, but there, nevertheless, somnolescent within the recesses of his own subliminal world. Such an avowal does not imply that he is a sadist, murderer, or saint. It merely indicates that Racine's creatures are mirror images, vaguely or sharply delineated as the case may be, of those who gaze upon them; that these protagonists are, symbolically speaking, endowed with the same traits, live through similar problems, and are driven by equally chaotic impulses as the spectator. Once such an awareness takes hold of the viewer, he can no longer consider himself all-perfect or all-evil. He begins to accept the idea that, under certain circumstances, he too may have lied or cheated or felt the desire to kill, if not overtly then unconsciously; that he too may have experienced the need to give and to love, depending upon the occasion. Once so-called "insidious" as well as so-called "superior" characteristics have been accepted by the individual, they may be understood and later incorporated into his *whole* personality. Obstacles, however, arise in the process. Negative traits are usually far more difficult to assimilate than are positive ones. If, however, the individual succeeds in incorporating the shadow characteristics into his being, these start to lose their sinister and terrorizing hold upon him. It stands to reason that, once mystery has vanished, so does the fear of the unknown. It can also be affirmed that when the "animal" within man is properly fed and tended to, it can be guided and tamed, and finally put to positive use, paving the way for balance and a productive view for the person or persons involved.

If a spectator refuses to face his own "evil" traits, he is in effect rejecting and seeking to destroy part of himself. He can really never succeed in annihilating what he considers his unpleasant side. What he is actually accomplishing is relegating these unwanted characteristics to a world enclosed in darkness; where they hide, lurk about, and mushroom forth. These negative traits bob up, at times, display their virulence at most crucial moments: during wars, hate campaigns, etc. Grave dangers lie ahead for him who seeks to be all-perfect, for he is unwilling to experience his lot as man on earth. To disregard human attributes which are a composite of good and evil, flesh and spirit, is to increase the size of the break within the psyche. What may result from such disparity? The instinctual world, unfed and unattended, starves, becomes ravenous, and so more and more demanding of the spiritual half. Eventually balance topples and spirituality becomes submerged in darkness. Struggle, pain, and eventual destruction ensue.

What Plato had so dangerously divided within man (when he labeled man's spiritual half his godly portion which must be cultivated, and his instinctual side his animal part which must be destroyed), a view adopted by the Judaeo-Christian ethic, has succeeded in creating intolerable inner conflict within many thinking beings today. It has, as a consequence, also brought about a rift within the social structure itself. The old generation nourished on Plato and Judaeo-Christian notions preaches sagacity, morality, spirituality while refusing to look *down* upon the world crumbling at their feet. The younger generation, on the other hand, flamboyantly embedded in a realm of flesh and escapism, is looking *upward,* searching frantically for some kind of spiritual answer in whatever way they know how.

Two separate and antagonistic worlds exist today. If we seek to pass beyond this divided, disjointed, and directionless existence which permeates the very fabric of our society, a reorientation and reevaluation of what is considered "good" and "evil" must come to pass. Characteristics looked upon as negative by the overly righteous must be integrated into the personality of the individual first, then into the society which he has created; just as more elevated concepts must pass down into the souls of today's angry youth. Only with an acceptance of all man's characteristics—whether they be good or evil—can balance occur. Otherwise, life on earth is a futile journey through waste.

In that Racine's spectacles have the power to arouse, to crush rational and artificial barriers within which man seeks to hide for reasons of protection or inertia, they permit the viewer to see himself partially in reflection, to face certain aspects of himself, and, hopefully, to accept his shadow as part of his whole personality. Stronger, with a more integrated view on life in general, no longer cut or pulled in conflicting directions, he will, hopefully, create an ethic satisfactory to himself and to his time. In so doing, he looks beyond the ossified beliefs which have satisfied former generations and which are, evidently, no longer valid for society today.

Racine's plays are like active organisms forcing themselves onto a body, altering its life flow, its chemistry, its systaltic and metabolic systems. His theatre, therefore, should be taken in small doses, as blood in communion, as the imbibing of a life force, a living *corpus*.

Racine, the Demiurge, the Man of Myths, beckons our way, seeks a confrontation with us as he did with himself———and immediately!

Notes

INTRODUCTION

1. Antonin Artaud, *Oeuvres complètes*, IV, p. 32.
2. *The Complete Plays of Jean Racine* (translated by Samuel Solomon), II, p. 163.
3. *Ibid.*, p. 181.
4. *Ibid.*, p. 183.
5. Jean Racine, *Oeuvres complètes*, I, p. 695.
6. *Complete Plays*, p. 195.
7. *Ibid.*, p. 209.
8. *Ibid.*, p. 229.

PART I [PAGES 11–28]

1. Jean Racine, *Oeuvres complètes*, I, p. 999.
2. Jean Racine's parents were married on September 3, 1638.
3. Racine had made mention of this coat of arms in a letter he wrote to his sister Marie, on January 16, 1697. *Oeuvres complètes*, II, p. 574.
4. *Ibid.*, I, p. 10.
5. Bernard Dorival, *Le Musée national des Granges de Port-Royal*, p. 9.
6. Le Maître de Sacy had published several works of a profane nature under a pseudonym, including translations of *Phaedra* (1647) and of certain works by Terence (1647); his religious writings included translations of the Psalms of David (1666) and of the New Testament.
7. The Duc de Chevreuse and the two Princes de Conti had been educated almost exclusively by Lancelot, who was also the author of *The New Method for Learning the Latin Language* (1644) and *The New Method for Learning the Greek Language* (1655).
8. Jean Racine, *Oeuvres complètes*, I, p. 10.
9. *Ibid.*, I, p. 11.
10. *Ibid.*, II, p. 83.

11. *Ibid.*, I, p. 12.
12. *Ibid.*, II, p. 387.
13. *Ibid.*
14. *Ibid.*, II, p. 379.
15. *Ibid.*, II, p. 380.
16. *Ibid.*, II, p. 402.
17. *Ibid.*, I, p. 17.
18. *Ibid.*, II, p. 410.
19. *Ibid.*, II, p. 433.
20. *Ibid.*, II, p. 438.

PART II—CHAPTER 1 [THE THEBAN BROTHERS, PAGES 31–45]

1. *The Complete Plays of Jean Racine* (translated by Samuel Solomon), I, p. 45.

2. Jean Racine, *Oeuvres complètes*, II, p. 457.

3. René Jasinski, *Vers le vrai Racine*, I, Paris, p.

4. *Pyrame et Thisbé* by Théophile (1617); *La Carthaginoise* by Mont-chrétien; *La Mort d'Alexandre* and *Didon se sacrifiant* by Hardy; *Antigone* by Garnier; *Antigone* by Rotrou; *Horace, Cinna, Oedipe* and more by Corneille.

5. Genesis: I, 1–2 "In the beginning God created the heaven and the earth. And the earth was without form, and void."

6. C.G. Jung, *The Practice of Psychotherapy*, p. 257.

7. *Complete Plays*, p. 44.

8. C.G. Jung, *Symbols of Transformation*, p. 328.

9. J.E. Circlot, *A Dictionary of Symbols*, p. 160.

10. *Complete Plays*, p. 60.

11. *Ibid.*, p. 45.

12. *Ibid.*, p. 54.

13. *Ibid.*, p. 13.

14. Rivkah Schaerf (Kluger), "The Image of the Marriage between God and Israel," *Spring*, 1950, p. 70. "The image of the marriage between God and Israel makes its appearance for the first time in Hosea. Later we come across it in the Books of Isaiah, Jeremiah, and Ezekiel . . ."

15. *Complete Plays*, p. 61.

16. *Ibid.*, p. 46.

17. *Ibid.*, p. 41.

18. *Ibid.*, p. 10.

19. *Ibid.*, p. 16.

20. *Ibid.*, p. 8.

21. Jean Racine, *Oeuvres complètes*, I, p. 117.

22. Gershom Scholem, *Major Trends in Jewish Mysticism*, p. 217.

23. Jean Racine, *Oeuvres complètes*, I, p. 156.

24. *Complete Plays*, p. 32.

25. *Ibid.*, p. 26.

26. *Ibid.*, p. 14.

CHAPTER 2 [ALEXANDER THE GREAT, PAGES 46–63]

1. *The Complete Plays of Jean Racine* (translated by Samuel Solomon),
p. 117.

2. Raymond Picard, *La Carrière de Jean Racine*, p. 112.

3. Jean Racine, *Oeuvres complètes*, I, p. 22.

4. René Jasinski, *Vers le vrai Racine*, p. 159.

5. *Oeuvres complètes*, p. 24.

6. *Ibid.*, p. 20.

7. René Jasinski, *Vers le vrai Racine*, p. 170.

8. *La Carriere de Jean Racine*, p. 23.

9. *Ibid.*, p. 115.

10. *Oeuvres completès*, p. 177.

11. *Ibid.*

12. Albert Trevor, *History of Ancient Civilization*, I, pp. 425–62.

13. Arthur Rimbaud is the perfect example of the burning out of this
kind of hero.

14. Alexander is the chief figure in certain XIIth century French *romans
courtois*, such as *Le Roman d'Alexandre*.

15. *Complete Plays*, p. 111.

16. *Ibid.*, p. 112.

17. *Ibid.*, p. 114.

18. *Ibid.*, p. 117.

19. C.G. Jung, *Psychological Types*, p. 324.

20. *Complete Plays*, p. 117.

21. *Ibid.*, p. 128.

22. Corneille was inspired to write *Cinna* after he had read Seneca's *De
Clementia*.

23. *Complete Plays*, p. 97.

24. *Oeuvres complètes*, p. 187.

25. *Complete Plays*, p. 85.

26. *Oeuvres complètes*, p. 183.

27. *Ibid.*, p. 184.

28. *Complete Plays*, p. 91.

29. *Ibid.*, p. 115.

30. *Ibid.*, p. 107.

31. *Oeuvres complètes*, p. 191.

CHAPTER 3 [ANDROMACHE, PAGES 64–84]

1. *The Complete Plays of Jean Racine* (translated by Samuel Solomon),
I, p. 183.

2. Raymond Picard, *La Carrière de Jean Racine*, pp. 129–137.

3. René Jasinski, *Vers le vrai Racine*, I, p. 206.

4. Certain critics have likened *Andromache* to Corneille's *Pertharite* in
that they both pose the same problem: "that of the virtuous usurper."

Further similarities are unlikely. (Serge Dubrovsky, *Corneille et la dialectique du héros*, p. 329.)

5. Céladon was the hero in Honoré d'Urfé's popular novel, *L'Astrée*.

6. *The Complete Plays of Jean Racine* (translated by Samuel Solomon), I, p. 143.

7. In *Athaliah* we come across an even more realistic mother type, Jehoshebath.

8. *Complete Plays*, p. 209.

9. *Ibid.*, p. 157.

10. *Ibid.*, 180.

11. *Ibid.*, p. 188.

12. C.G. Jung, *Symbols of Transformation*, p. 408.

13. Jean Racine, *Oeuvres complètes*, I, p. 283.

14. C.G. Jung, *Psychological Types*, pp. 448, 451, 539.

15. *Complete Plays*, p. 162.

16. Hybris or inflation. Inflation may be defined as follows: "I use the term inflation to describe the attitude and the state which accompanies the identification of the ego with the Self. It is a state in which something small (the ego) has arrogated to itself the qualities of something larger (the Self) and hence is blown up "beyond the limits of its proper size." (Edward Edinger, "The Psychology of Inflation and Alienation," 1964, unpublished lecture delivered at the Montreal Young Women's Christian Association.)

17. *Complete Plays*, p. 162.

18. When situations affecting a person experiencing a sense of inflation do not fall into the pattern required by the ego-centered individual, anger is frequently the outcome.

19. *Oeuvres complètes*, p. 260.

20. *Complete Plays*, p. 166.

21. *Ibid.*, p. 167.

22. Edward Edinger, "The Psychology of Inflation and Alienation," p. 6.

23. *Oeuvres complètes*, p. 293.

24. *Complete Plays*, p. 202.

25. *Ibid.*, p. 157.

26. *Ibid.*

27. *Ibid.*

28. C.G. Jung, *Aion*, p. 140.

29. C.G. Jung, *Psychological Types*, p. 224.

30. *Complete Plays*, p. 148.

31. *Ibid.*, p. 150.

32. *Oeuvres complètes*, p. 269.

33. *Complete Plays*, p. 211.

34. James Kirsch, *Shakespeare's Royal Self*, p. 286.

35. J.E. Circlot, *A Dictionary of Symbols*, p. 274.

36. *Shakespeare's Royal Self*, p. 286.

37. *A Dictionary of Symbols*, p. 95.

38. *Oeuvres complètes*, p. 247.
39. *Ibid.*, p. 263.
40. *Complete Plays*, p. 174.
41. *Ibid.*, p. 165.
42. *Ibid.*, p. 186.

CHAPTER 4 [BRITANNICUS, PAGES 85–107]

1. Jean Racine, *Oeuvres complètes*, I, p. 395.
2. René Jasinski, *Vers le vrai Racine*, p. 289.
3. A.F.B. Clark, *Jean Racine*, pp. 14–16.
4. *Ibid.*
5. *Vers le vrai Racine*, p. 286.
6. *Oeuvres complètes*, p. 1096.
7. Edmé Boursault, *Artémise et Poliante*, 1670.
8. Saint-Evremond, *Lettre au Comte de Lionne*, 1670.
9. *The Complete Plays of Jean Racine* (translated by Samuel Solomon), I, p. 288.
10. *Ibid.*, p. 290.
11. Agrippina must be looked upon as a symbol similar, in a way, to Goethe's collective "Mothers" in Part II of *Faust*.
12. *Complete Plays*, p. 299.
13. *Ibid.*, p. 301.
14. C.G. Jung, *Psychological Types*, pp. 470–79.
15. *Complete Plays*, p. 303.
16. *Ibid.*, p. 302.
17. Erich Neumann, *The Great Mother*, pp. 29–36.
18. *Complete Plays*, p. 305.
19. *Ibid.*, p. 306.
20. *Ibid.*, p. 333.
21. *Ibid.*, p. 346.
22. *Ibid.*, p. 349.
23. *Ibid.*
24. *Ibid.*, p. 350.
25. *Ibid.*, p. 363.
26. *Ibid.*, p. 367.
27. Erich Neumann, *The Origins and History of Consciousness*, pp. 391–92.
28. The Christian ascetics, influenced by Stoicism, rejected man's instinctual aspect and suffered delusions of the flesh as a result.
29. *Oeuvres complètes*, p. 418.
30. *Complete Plays*, p. 330.
31. *Ibid.*, p. 331.
32. *Ibid.*, p. 351.
33. *Ibid.*, p. 353.
34. *Oeuvres complètes*, p. 406.
35. *Complete Plays*, p. 315.

36. *Ibid.*, p. 317.
37. *Ibid.*
38. *Ibid.*
39. *Ibid.*, p. 327.
40. *Oeuvres complètes*, p. 428.
41. *Complete Plays*, p. 313.
42. *Oeuvres complètes*, p. 393.
43. *Complete Plays*, p. 302.
44. *Ibid.*, p. 310.
45. *Ibid.*, p. 326.
46. *Ibid.*, p. 359.
47. C.G. Jung, *Civilization in Transition*, p. 377.
48. *Complete Plays*, p. 324.
49. C.G. Jung, *Civilization in Transition*, p. 211.
50. *Complete Plays*, p. 317.

CHAPTER 5 [BERENICE, PAGES 108–124]

1. Jean Racine, *Oeuvres complètes*, I, p. 517.
2. Racine had dedicated *Andromache* to Henriette d'Angleterre.
3. A similar situation would again arise for Racine in his later plays *Iphigenia* and *Phaedra*.
4. *The Complete Plays of Jean Racine* (translated by Samuel Solomon), I, p. 376.
5. *Ibid.*, p. 376.
6. *Ibid.*, p. 377.
7. Alexander is not a truly Racinian hero. He is an intellectual creation on Racine's part, a blend of Cornelian characteristics and those à la mode at his time. Written mostly to appeal to his audiences and win their admiration.
8. C.G. Jung, *Symbols of Transformation*, pp. 429–435.
9. Salo W. Baron, *A Social and Religious History of the Jews*, II, p. 93.
10. Emma Hawkridge, *The Wisdom Tree*, pp. 108–16.
11. *Ibid.*
12. C.G. Jung, *Symbols of Transformation*, pp. 414, 408, 424.
13. *Complete Plays*, p. 400.
14. *Ibid.*
15. C.G. Jung, *Two Essays on Analytical Psychology*, p. 143.
16. *Ibid.*, pp. 161–71.
17. *Complete Plays*, p. 401.
18. *Ibid.*, p. 402.
19. *Ibid.*
20. *Ibid.*
21. *Ibid.*, p. 403.
22. *Oeuvres complètes*, p. 429.
23. *Complete Plays*, p. 412.

24. *Ibid.*, p. 411.
25. *Ibid.*, p. 425.
26. *Ibid.*, p. 429.
27. *Ibid.*, p. 431.
28. *Oeuvres complètes*, p. 517.
29. *Complete Plays*, p. 389.
30. *Ibid.*, p. 395.
31. *Oeuvres complètes*, p. 487.
32. *Ibid.*, p. 487.
33. *Complete Plays*, p. 405.
34. *Ibid.*, p. 407.
35. *Ibid.*, p. 419.
36. *Ibid.*, p. 422.
37. *Ibid.*, p. 443.
38. *Oeuvres complètes*, p. 477.
39. *Ibid.*, p. 494.
40. *Ibid.*, p. 501.
41. *Complete Plays*, p. 383.

CHAPTER 6 [BAJAZET, PAGES 125–136]

1. Jean Racine, *Oeuvres complètes*, I, p. 547.
2. It is not certain whether La Champmeslé or Mlle Ennebault played the part of Roxana.
3. Letters from Mme de Sévigné to her daughter, Mme de Grignan: January 13, 15, and March 16, 1672.
4. Gustave Larroumet, *Racine*, p. 82.
5. René Jasinski, *Vers le vrai Racine*, p. 93.
6. *The Complete Plays of Jean Racine* (translated by Samuel Solomon), II, p. 3.
7. *Ibid.*, p. 5.
8. He most resembles Racine's Divinity, the dispenser of grace or punishment or both.
9. He is not to be confused with the Wise Old Man of the Kabbala, a symbol for the occult principle or the archetypal figure emanating from the collective unconscious.
10. *Complete Plays*, p. 12.
11. *Oeuvres complètes*, p. 547.
12. *Complete Plays*, p. 31.
13. *Oeuvres complètes*, p. 553.
14. *Complete Plays*, p. 27.
15. *Oeuvres complètes*, p. 548.
16. *Complete Plays*, p. 46.
17. *Ibid.*, p. 20.
18. *Ibid.*, p. 57.
19. *Ibid.*, p. 58.

20. *Oeuvres complètes*, p. 548.

21. *Complete Plays*, p. 54.

22. *Oeuvres complètes*, p. 543.

23. *Ibid.*, p. 545.

24. *Berenice* is an exception.

25. *Oeuvres complètes*, p. 544.

26. *Complete Plays*, p. 23.

27. *Oeuvres complètes*, p. 591.

28. *Complete Plays*, p. 35.

29. *Ibid.*, p. 43.

30. *Oeuvres complètes*, p. 566.

31. *Complete Plays*, p. 26.

32. *Ibid., p. 29.*

33. *Ibid.*, p. 38.

34. *Ibid.*, p. 45.

35. *Ibid.*, p. 17.

CHAPTER 7 [MITHRIDATES, PAGES 137–150]

1. Jean Racine, *Oeuvres complètes*, I, p. 631.

2. La Calprénède wrote *La Mort de Mithridate* (1635).

3. *Mithridates* was produced shortly after Racine had become a member of the French Academy.

4. Raymond Picard, *La Carrière de Jean Racine*, p. 174.

5. *Ibid.*, p. 176.

6. *The Complete Plays of Jean Racine* (translated by Samuel Solomon), II, p. 103.

7. *Ibid.*, p. 104.

8. *Ibid.*, p. 110.

9. *Ibid.*, p. 118.

10. *Ibid.*, p. 117.

11. Jean Racine, *Oeuvres complètes*, I, p. 137.

12. *Complete Plays*, p. 138.

13. *Ibid.*, p. 146.

14. *Ibid.*, p. 149.

15. *L'Avare* by Molière treats a similar situation.

16. *Complete Plays*, p. 100.

17. Like Benoît in *The Executioners* by Fernando Arrabal.

18. *Complete Plays*, p. 95.

19. *Ibid.*

20. *Ibid.*, p. 100.

21. Xiphares' mother is mentioned merely as being the "horrendous" betrayer of Mithridates. Throughout the drama Xiphares seems to want to expiate his mother's crime by offering his services to his father.

22. *Complete Plays*, p. 91.

23. *Ibid.*, p. 126.

24. *Ibid.*, p. 143.

25. *Ibid.*, p. 99.
26. *Ibid.*, p. 116.

CHAPTER 8 [IPHIGENIA, PAGES 151–165]

1. Jean Racine, *Oeuvres complètes*, I, p. 731.
2. Epitre VII.
3. Raymond Picard, *La Carrière de Jean Racine*, p. 221.
4. Rotrou's *Iphigenia* (1642) also inspired Racine.
5. Death looked upon in such a manner, as a temporary cessation of consciousness, becomes an initiatory process, a means of entering a new psychological dimension or orientation. Whenever an initiation takes place, however, the initiant, symbolically speaking, is frequently faced with grave danger and justifiably so; for there is always the possibility of the conscious ego's being dissolved by the overwhelming power of the unconscious. When, on the other hand, total or severe alienation exists between the conscious and unconscious outlook, such an initiatory journey becomes absolutely imperative if development within the personality is to be achieved.
6. *The Complete Plays of Jean Racine* (translated by Samuel Solomon), II, p. 163.
7. *Ibid.*, p. 165.
8. *Ibid.*
9. *Ibid.*, p. 180.
10. *Oeuvres complètes*, p. 683.
11. *Complete Plays*, p. 163.
12. *Oeuvres complètes*, p. 722.
13. *Complete Plays*, p. 208.
14. *Oeuvres complètes*, p. 686.
15. *Complete Plays*, p. 172.
16. *Ibid.*, p. 174.
17. *Ibid.*
18. *Oeuvres complètes*, p. 723.
19. *Complete Plays*, p. 198.
20. *Ibid.*, p. 208.
21. *Ibid.*, p. 226.
22. *Ibid.*
23. *Ibid.*, p. 198.
24. *Ibid.*, p. 222.
25. *Ibid.*, p. 169.
26. *Oeuvres complètes*, p. 708.
27. The shadow is an area within the psyche which is made up of characteristics considered inferior by the person in question.
28. *Oeuvres complètes*, p. 698.
29. *Ibid.*, p. 690.
30. *Complete Plays*, p. 176.
31. *Ibid.*, p. 186.
32. *Oeuvres complètes*, p. 676.

33. *Complete Plays*, p. 174.

34. *Oeuvres complètes*, p. 731.

35. *Complete Plays*, p. 230.

36. *Oeuvres complètes*, p. 680.

37. Actually, it was true, since Chiron who brought up Achilles had fed him lion flesh, and the marrow of wild boar and bears.

38. *Oeuvres complètes*, p. 716.

CHAPTER 9 [PHAEDRA, PAGES 166–189]

1. Jean Racine, *Oeuvres complètes*, I, p. 790.

2. *Ibid.*, p. 38.

3. René Jasinski, *Vers un vrai Racine*, II, pp. 400–10.

4. *Ibid.*, Philippe Mancini, the Duc de Nevers, one of the Duchesse de Bouillon's brothers, also a pseudo-literateur and intimate of her salon, sided with his sister in her attacks on Racine. He had written some poetry, epistles mostly, and had also enjoyed the reputation of a witty and elegant man. Tongues wagged concerning his relationship with his sister; both were accused of committing incest. Such intimations angered them, as was to be expected, and were never proved.

5. Raymond Picard, *La Carrière de Jean Racine*, p. 234.

6. *Ibid.*, p. 241.

7. René Jasinski, *Vers un vrai Racine*, II, p. 442.

8. *The Complete Plays of Jean Racine* (translated by Samuel Solomon), II, p. 233.

9. *Ibid.*, p. 235.

10. *Ibid.*, p. 244.

11. *Oeuvres complètes*, p. 754.

12. Europa and the bull.

13. Erich Neumann, *The Origins and History of Consciousness*, p. 77.

14. *Complete Plays*, p. 245.

15. *Oeuvres complètes*, p. 757.

16. *Ibid.*, p. 251.

17. *Complete Plays*, p. 250.

18. *Ibid.*, p. 251.

19. There is a similar image in *Berenice*, but not as pronounced.

20. *Complete Plays*, p. 245.

21. Her passion for the bull was aroused in her by Poseidon, who punished Minos for not having sacrificed the animal to him.

22. *Complete Plays*, p. 262.

23. *Ibid.*, p. 263.

24. *Ibid.*, p. 264.

25. *Ibid.*

26. *Ibid.*, p. 265.

27. *Ibid.*, p. 266.

28. *Ibid.*, p. 268.

29. *Ibid.*, p. 269.

30. *Ibid.*, p. 272.

31. *Ibid.*, p. 272.

32. *Ibid.*, p. 273.

33. *Ibid.*, p. 288.

34. *Ibid.*, p. 288.

35. *Ibid.*, p. 288.

36. *Ibid.*, p. 290.

37. Erich Neumann, *The Origins and History of Consciousness*, p. 77.

38. *Ibid.*, p. 92.

39. *Oeuvres complètes*, p. 751.

40. *Complete Plays*, p. 242.

41. *Ibid.*, p. 243.

42. *Ibid.*, p. 243.

43. *Ibid.*, 260.

44. *Ibid.*, p. 260.

45. *Ibid.*

46. *Ibid.*, p. 276.

47. *Ibid.*, p. 281.

48. *Oeuvres complètes*, p. 787.

49. *Complete Plays*, p. 298.

50. J.E. Circlot, *A Dictionary of Symbols*, p. 203.

51. *Complete Plays*, p. 284.

52. This effect is similar to the one Genet achieved in his play *The Maids*.

53. The symbols (labyrinth, light, day, etc.) are discussed in the heading of explication of personalities.

54. Edward Edinger, "Christ as Paradigm of the Individuating Ego," *Spring*, 1966, p. 7.

55. *Ibid.*, p. 19.

PART III—CHAPTER 10 [ESTHER, PAGES 193–217]

1. *The Complete Plays of Jean Racine* (translated by Samuel Solomon), II, p. 319.

2. Jean Racine, *Oeuvres complètes*, I, p. 70.

3. Raymond Picard, *La carriere de Jean Racine*, p. 414.

4. *Oeuvres complètes*, p. 70.

5. *La carrière de Jean Racine*, p. 413.

6. Jahoudah Segall, *Pourquoi Racine a-t-il renoncé au théâtre?* p. 105.

7. *Oeuvres complètes*, p. 70.

8. *Ibid.*, p. 495.

9. *Ibid.*, p. 825.

10. Ch. Lehrmann, *L'élément Juif dans la littérature française*, p. 101.

11. *The Additions to the Book of Esther* includes one hundred and seven verses not in the original Hebrew text. These *Additions* were written two centuries after the canonical text (early part of the 1st century) and originated

among the Egyptian Hellenistic Jews. They "belong to the mass of floating legendary material centering around Esther." R.H. Charles, *The Apocrypha and Pseudoepigrapha of the Old Testament in English*, I, pp. 665–69.

12. J. Lichtenstein, *Racine poète biblique*, p. 66.

13. *Complete Plays*, p. 309.

14. *Racine poète biblique*, p. 81.

15. Georges Mongrédien, *Athalie*, p. 26.

16. *Ibid.*, Madame de Maintenon had spent the large sum of fourteen thousand pounds for the costumes.

17. F.B. Clark, *Jean Racine*, p. 260.

18. Ahasuerus is commonly thought of as Xerxes I (485–465 B.C.E.).

19. Robert H. Pfeiffer, *Introduction to the Old Testament*, p. 732.

20. H. Yechezkel Kluger, "Ruth," *Spring*, 1957, p. 81.

21. Albert Trevor, *A History of Ancient Civilization*, p. 112. Certainly Racine's Ahasuerus in no way possesses the wisdom or the fortitude which names such as Cyrus, Darius, or Xerxes conjure up in our imaginations, rulers capable of conquering and organizing so many races within their own empire: Babylonia, Egypt, Phoenicia, the Ionian Greek cities.

22. *Complete Plays*, p. 317.

23. *Ibid.*, p. 318.

24. *Ibid.*, p. 331.

25. *Ibid.*, p. 337.

26. Erich Neumann, *Origins of Consciousness*, p. 373.

27. *Complete Plays*, p. 339.

28. *Oeuvres complètes*, p. 839. The word *foudre* can also be translated as "thunder" or "thunderbolt."

29. *Complete Plays*, p. 342.

30. Zoroaster, it is believed by some, lived 1000 B.C.E.; others date his era between 660 and 638 B.C.E.

31. Emma Hawkridge, *The Wisdom Tree*, pp. 105–118.

32. Ishtar (Babylonian); Astarte (Canaanite); Ashtoreth (Israelite). Ishtar is also associated with Baal and is both virgin and mother goddess; Venus and the Moon.

33. *Oeuvres complètes*, p. 839.

34. J. Lichtenstein, *Racine poète biblique*, p. 72.

35. J.E. Circlot, *A Dictionary of Symbols*, p. 295.

36. *Complete Plays*, p. 319.

37. Rivkah Schaerf Kluger, "Women in the Old Testament," Lecture at the Analytical Psychology Club of New York, March 20, 1958.

38. *Oeuvres complètes*, p. 819.

39. *Ibid.*, p. 818.

40. An analogy can be drawn between Esther's psychology and that of the Marranos.

41. *Complete Plays*, p. 318.

42. *Ibid.*, p. 317.

43. *Oeuvres complètes*, p. 820.

44. Gershom G. Scholem, *Major Trends in Jewish Mysticism*, pp. 213–15.

45. *Oeuvres complètes*, p. 824.

46. *Major Trends*, p. 229.

47. *Oeuvres complètes*, p. 825.

48. *Complete Plays*, p. 325.

49. *Ibid.*, p. 342.

50. *Oeuvres complètes*, p. 840.

51. *Complete Plays*, p. 359.

52. Marduk is terrified by nothing, not even Tiamat, the sea dragon which he kills. From both its parts, he creates the heaven and the earth. Mordecai is also the possessor of extreme courage and determination.

53. Salo W. Baron, *A Social and Religious History of the Jews*, I, p. 119.

54. C.G. Jung, *Psychology and Religion: West and East*, pp. 7–8.

55. *Ibid.*, p. 359–469.

56. *Complete Plays*, p. 317.

57. *Ibid.*

58. A similar confusion in Esther's vision occurs after her faint, when she looks at Ahasuerus. What Esther has projected onto Ahasuerus she now projects onto God—or Self.

59. *Complete Plays*, p. 323.

60. *Ibid.*, p. 323.

61. *Ibid.*, p. 324. The last line reads "Perhaps will perish with your father's house." The change "and your entire race" is mine. It is a more literal translation.

62. Roland Barthes, *On Racine*, p. 126.

63. Robert H. Pfeiffer, *Introduction to the Old Testament*, p. 733.

64. *Oeuvres complètes*, p. 830.

65. *Complete Plays*, p. 332.

66. *Oeuvres complètes*, p. 832.

67. *Ibid.*

68. *Ibid.*, p. 831.

69. *Ibid.*, p. 832.

70. *Complete Plays*, p. 335.

71. *Ibid.*, p. 351.

72. *Oeuvres complètes*, p. 847.

73. Rivkah Scharf Kluger, *Satan in the Old Testament*, p. 25.

74. C.G. Jung, *The Practice of Psychotherapy*, pp. 207, 316.

75. J.E. Circlot, *A Dictionary of Symbols*, p. 236.

CHAPTER 11 [ATHALIAH, PAGES 218–239]

1. *The Complete Plays of Jean Racine* (translated by Samuel Solomon), II, p. 439.

2. Gossec (1786), Boieldieu (1810), and Mendelssohn (1843, 1845) also composed music for *Athaliah*.

3. M. Charlier, "Athalie et la Révolution d'Angleterre," *Mercure de France*, July 1, 1931, (1163, I).

4. Georges Mongrédien, *Athalie*, p. 60.

5. Racine died before *Athaliah* was ever performed at Court (1702). Only on March 3, 1716 did the first public performance of *Athaliah* take place and that was at the Comédie-Française.

6. Jean Racine, *Oeuvres complètes*, I, p. 77.

7. *Athalie*, p. 36.

8. *Complete Plays*, p. 377.

9. Pfeiffer, R.H., *Introduction to the Old Testament*, p. 374.

10. *Ibid.*, p. 782.

11. Kings, II, 11.

12. C.G. Jung, *Aion*, p. 9.

13. Moses and Elijah denounced the false God Baal. Baal is a representative of the female matriarchal society as witnessed by Samson's imprisonment in the Temple of Dagon, a corn god of the Canaanites and father of Baal. Such an episode is an example of man's (the hero's) servitude to the Great Mother. Another example occurs when Hercules is forced by Omphale to wear woman's clothes. Cf. Erich Neumann, *The Origins and History of Consciousness*, p. 160.

14. *Oeuvres complètes*, p. 877.

15. *Complete Plays*, p. 400.

16. *Ibid.*, p. 400.

17. *Ibid.*, p. 401.

18. Erich Neumann, *The Origins and History of Consciousness*, p. 277.

19. C.G. Jung, *The Archetypes and the Collective Unconscious*, p. 279.

20. *Ibid.*

21. C.G. Jung, *Aion*, p. 266.

22. *The Archetypes and the Collective Unconscious*, p. 89.

23. *Oeuvres complètes*, p. 878.

24. *Complete Plays*, p. 397.

25. *Ibid.*, p. 407.

26. *Ibid.*, p. 418.

27. Emma Hawkridge, *The Wisdom Tree*, p. 143.

28. *Oeuvres complètes*, pp. 895–96.

29. *Complete Plays*, p. 420.

30. *Aion*, p. 279.

31. *Complete Plays*, p. 383.

32. *Ibid.*, p. 385.

33. *Ibid.*, p. 388.

34. *Ibid.*, p. 428.

35. *Aion*, p. 282.

36. *Complete Plays*, p. 436.

37. *Ibid.*, p. 436.

38. C.G. Jung, *Symbols of Transformation*, p. 324.

39. C.G. Jung, *Psychological Types*, pp. 507–08.

40. Erich Neumann, *The Origins and History of Consciousness*, p. 380.
41. *Complete Plays*, p. 390.
42. *Ibid.*, p. 391.
43. *The Archetypes and the Collective Unconscious*, p. 178.
44. *Ibid.*, p. 166.
45. *Aion*, p. 236.
46. *Complete Plays*, p. 455.
47. *Ibid.*, p. 458.
48. J.E. Circlot, *A Dictionary of Symbols*, p. 315.
49. The Ark of the Covenant is a "wooden chest . . . which Moses was commanded by God to construct to contain the two Tablets of the Law. It was lined with gold within and without, and surrounded with a golden mold. . . . This Ark was carried by the Levites throughout Israel's wanderings in the wilderness; then not mobile, it was placed in the Holy of Holies inside the Tabernacle, where it was beheld only by the High Priest on the Day of Atonement." *The Encyclopedia of Jewish Religion*, edited by R.J. Zwi Werblowsky and G. Wigoder.
50. *Complete Plays*, p. 425.
51. *Oeuvres complètes*, p. 878.
52. *Ibid.*, p. 918.
53. *Ibid.*, p. 878.
54. Rivkah Kluger, "The Image of the Marriage between God and Israel," 1950, *Spring*, pp. 305.
55. *Ibid.*, p. 77.
56. Rivkah Kluger, *Satan in the Old Testament*, p. 161.
57. *Oeuvres complètes*, p. 917.
58. *Ibid.*, p. 918.
59. *Ibid.*
60. *Aion*, p. 31.
61. *Complete Plays*, p. 959.

PART IV [PAGES 243–247]

1. Jean Racine, *Oeuvres complètes*, II, p. 620.
2. *Ibid.*
3. Pierre Moreau, *Racine, l'homme et l'oeuvre*, p. 66.
4. Raymond Picard, *La Carrière de Jean Racine*, pp. 450–59.
5. *Oeuvres complètes*, p. 597.
6. *Ibid.*, p. 606.
7. Mary Duclaux, *The Life of Racine*, p. 231.

Bibliography

Baron, Salo, *A Social and Religious History of the Jews*, I & II, New York, Columbia University Press, 1952.

Barthes, Roland, *On Racine* (trans. Richard Howard), New York, Hill and Wang, 1964.

Beauchène, Paul, *La Maison de Racine et la rue Visconti*, Paris, Picard, 1933.

Bénichou, Paul, *Morales du grand siècle*, Paris, Gallimard, 1948.

Bellessort, Andre, *Le Mystère de Racine*, Paris, Correspondant, tome 253, 1913.

Bremond, Henri (Abbé), *Racine et Valéry*, Paris, Grasset, 1930.

Butor, Michel, *Répertoire*, Paris, Les Editions de Minuit, 1960.

Circlot, J.E., *A Dictionary of Symbols* (trans. Jack Sage), New York, Philosophical Library, 1962.

Clark, A.F.S., *Jean Racine*, Cambridge, Harvard University Press, 1939.

Claudel, Paul, *Conversation sur Jean Racine*, Paris, Gallimard, 1956.

Crouzet, Paul, *Tout Racine ici, à Port-Royal*, Paris, Didier, 1940.

Deltour, Félix, *Les Ennemis de Racine au XVII siècle*, Paris, Didier, 1859.

Descotes, Maurice, *Les Grands rôles du théâtre*, Paris, Presses Universitaires, 1957.

Doubrovsky, Serge, *Corneille et la dialectique du héros*, Paris, Gallimard, 1963.

Duclaux, Mary, *The Life of Racine*, New York, Harper and Bros., 1925.

Edinger, Edward, "An Outline of Analytical Psychology" (mimeographed).

———— "Symbols: The Meaning of Life," *Spring*, 1962.

———— "Christ as a Paradigm of the Individuating Ego," *Spring,* 1966.

———— "Metaphysics and the Unconscious," *Spring*, 1969.

Giraudoux, Jean, *Racine*, Paris, Grasset, 1930.

Goldmann, Lucien, *Racine*, Paris, L'Arche, 1956.

———— *Le Dieu caché*, Paris, Gallimard, 1955.

Hawkridge, Emma, *The Wisdom Tree*, Boston, Houghton Mifflin and Co., 1945.

Hubert, Judd, *Essai d'exégèse racinienne*, Paris, Librairie Nizet, 1956.

Jasinski, René, *Vers le vrai Racine*, Paris, Armand Collin, 1958.

C.G. Jung, *Psychology and Alchemy*, New York, Pantheon, 1953.

———— *Symbols of Transformation*, New York, Pantheon Books, 1956.

———— *Psychology and Religion: West and East*, New York, Pantheon, 1959.

———— *The Archetypes and the Collective Unconscious*, New York, Pantheon, 1959.

———— *Aion*, Princeton University Press, 1959.

———— *Alchemical Studies*, Princeton University Press, 1967.

———— *Psychological Types*, New York, Pantheon, 1964.

Kirsch, James, *Shakespeare's Royal Self*, New York, Putnam's Sons, 1966.

Kluger, Rivkah S., *Satan in the Old Testament*, Evanston, Northwestern University Press, 1967.

———— "The Image of the Marriage between God and Israel as it occurs in the Prophets of the Old Testament, Especially Ezekiel XVI," *Spring,* 1950.

Kluger, Yechezkel, "Ruth," *Spring,* 1957.

Larroumet, Gustave, *Racine*, Paris, Hachette, 1898.

Lemaître, Jules, *Jean Racine*, Paris, Calmann-Lévy, 1933.

Lichtenstein, J. *Racine poète biblique*, Paris, Librairie Lipschut, 1933.

Mauriac, François, *La Vie de Jean Racine*, Paris, Plon, 1928.

Mongrédien, Georges, *Athalie*, Paris, Edgar Malfère, 1929.

Moreau, Pierre, *Racine*, Paris, Hatier, 1943.

———— *Racine, L'homme et l'oéuvre*, Paris, Boivin, 1943.

Mourges, Odette de, *Racine or the Triumph of Relevance*, Cambridge University Press, 1967.

Neumann, Erich, *The Origins and History of Consciousness*, New York, Pantheon, 1954.
——— *The Great Mother*, New York, Pantheon, 1955.
——— *Art and the Creative Unconscious*, New York, Pantheon, 1959.

Pfeiffer, Robert, *Introduction to the Old Testament*, New York, Harper and Row, 1948.
Picard, Raymond, *La Carrière de Jean Racine*, Paris, Gallimard, 1961.

Racine, Jean, *Oeuvres complètes*, Paris, Gallimard, 1950.
——— *The Complete Plays of Jean Racine* (trans. by Samuel Solomon), New York, Random House, 1967.

Segall, Jehouda, *Pourquoi Racine a-t-il renoncé au théâtre*, Zurich, Leemann freres, 1919.
Spitzer, Leo, *Linguistics and Literature*, Princeton University Press, 1948.

Trevor, Albert, *History of Ancient Civilization*, New York, Harcourt, Brace and Co., 1936.
Truc, Gonzague, *Jean Racine*, Paris, Garnier frères, 1926.

Weinberg, Bernard, *The Art of Jean Racine*, University of Chicago Press, 1963.

Index

Abeille, l' Abbé Gaspard, 26

Abner [*Athaliah*], 222–239 passim

Abraham, 205

Achilles [*Iphigenia*], 5, 74, 151–165 passim (especially 158ff.), 249

Acomat [*Bajazet*], 126–136 passim, 148

Acteon, 179

Adam and Eve, 57–58, 174, 177, 203, 221, 223, 235

Aeschylus, 126

Agamemnon [*Iphigenia*], 2, 3, 5, 6, 7, 151–165 passim, 187, 198, 249

Agave, 130, 134

Agrippina [*Britannicus*], 2, 3, 89–106 passim, 140, 208, 116, 223, 248, 257 n. 11.

Ahasuerus [Esther], 197–216 passim, 264 n. 21

Alexander [*Alexander the Great*], 3, 50–60 passim, 258 n. 7

Alexander the Great [*Alexandre*, 1665], 46–63, 81, 84, 90, 124, 249; first performances of, 46–48 passim; contemporary opinions of, 48–49, 49–50; genesis of, 46–50 passim, 62–63; historical basis for, 50; plot of, 50–51; structure of, 61; themes of, 51–52, 61–62, 63; characters in, analysis of, 51–52, 53–60 passim, 249, 258 n. 7; symbolism and imagery in, 51–62 passim, 81, 84, 90; biographical significance of, 48–49, 62, 84; Jansenists and, 48–49; hero, theory of applied to, 52–53, 54, 59; doubles in, 51, 52, 56–60 passim; Racine's artistic development and, 61–63

Alienation, 73, 261 n. 5

Also Sprach Zarathustra, viii

Amasie, 24

Amphortas, 199

Amurat [*Bajazet*], 126–127 passim, 144

Anahit, 202

Andilly, d'. See Arnauld d'Andilly

Andromache [*Andromache*], 2, 50–83 passim, 187, 223, 234

Andromache [*Andromaque*, 1667], 64–84, 138; first performances of, 64–65; contemporary opinions of, 64–66; genesis of, 65; plot of, 66–67; focal point of, 67, 84, 138, 255–256 n. 4; characters in, analysis of, 67–84 passim, 102, 112, 114, 143, 187, 198; symbolism and imagery in, 67–83 passim; and "rules" of tragedy, 65–66; time and space in, 82–83; love in, 67, 84; and Racine's emotional development, 84

Anima, 153, 154, 161, 165

Antigone [*The Theban Brothers*], 2, 3, 32, 36, 38, 39, 40, 58, 147, 187

Antiochus [*Berenice*], 109, 111–124 passim (especially 122)

Anubis, 226

Aphrodite, 167, 170, 171, 172, 184, 203; see Venus

Arcas [*Iphigenia*], 152–165 passim

Archetypes. See Symbolism and Imagery; see also entries on plays, on characters in plays, and on specific symbols, images, and archetypes

Aricia [*Phaedra*], 168–87 passim

Aristophanes, 85

Aristotle, 25, 50, 66, 168

Ark of the Covenant, 236, 237, 267 n. 49

Arnauld family, 15